PRAIRIE-STYLE GARDENS

PRAIRIE-STYLE GARDENS

CAPTURING THE ESSENCE
OF THE AMERICAN PRAIRIE
WHEREVER YOU LIVE

LYNN M. STEINER

TIMBER PRESS
PORTLAND · LONDON

Published in 2010 by Timber Press, Inc.

The Haseltine Building
133 S.W. Second Avenue, Suite 450
Portland, Oregon 97204-3527
www.timberpress.com

2 The Quadrant
135 Salusbury Road
London NW6 6RJ
www.timberpress.co.uk

Printed in China
Designed by Susan Applegate

Library of Congress Cataloging-in-Publication Data

Steiner, Lynn M., 1958–
    Prairie-style gardens: capturing the essence
of the American prairie wherever you live/Lynn
M. Steiner.
        p. cm.
    Includes bibliographical references and index.
    ISBN 978-1-60469-003-3
    1. Prairie gardening—United States. 2. Native
plants—United States. 3. Grasses—United
States. 4. Perennials—United States. I. Title.
    SB434.3.S74 2010
    635.9—dc22   2010005069

Catalog records for this book are available from the
Library of Congress and the British Library.

Previous two pages: This showy summer
prairie garden, including bluejacket, stiff
tickseed, and prairie phlox, brings a North
American slant to the English cottage garden.

Opposite: A bouquet of prairie plants
including goldenrods, asters, big
bluestem, and gray dogwood.

To my husband,
Ted,
for patiently listening to my ideas,
visiting prairies and gardens with me,
proofreading a subject that
"really wasn't his thing,"
and offering support
and encouragement
through it all.

CONTENTS

A landscape of prairie plants is a
thing of beauty as well as a gift to the
environment and future generations.

ACKNOWLEDGMENTS

Many people, in many ways, contributed to this book, and all deserve my heartfelt thanks.

For their help in locating the landscapes to use in the book, I'd like to thank Eric Olsen of Outback Nursery; Diane Hilscher of Hilscher Design and Ecology; Mike Evenocheck of Prairie Restorations, Inc.; and Marty Rice, Diane Holmes, and Cindy Hermsen of Wild Ones.

For allowing me to visit and photograph their beautiful gardens, homes, and places of business, I would like to thank Chris and Dave Abresch; Pat and Bob Angleson; Gary Britton; Paul and Susan Damon; Deb Ferrington; Phil Friedlund and Lisa Isenberg; Norm and Daryl Grier; Diane Hilscher; Eileen Hunter and Stuart Krahn; Jan and Dick Koel; Rick and Barb Kraft; Dick and Marsha Krueger; Landscape Alternatives, Inc.; Jeremy Mayberg and Amy-Ann Greenspan; Mequon Unitarian Church; Amy Myers; Ginny Nelson; Robert and Marlene Olsen; Barbara and Don Pederson; Veronika Phillips; Prairie Restorations, Inc.; Connie Ramthun; Sue Reindollar; Kadi Renowden; Lon and Susannah Roesselet; Fred and Marcy Schramm; Connie and Ken Taillon; Andy and Carolyn Van Sickle; Bonnie Vastag; Amy Welsh; and Barb Wolter.

I would also like to acknowledge and thank Merel R. Black of the Freckmann Herbarium at the University of Wisconsin-Stevens Point for generously providing two photos.

I am grateful I was able to enjoy, study, and photograph native plants in certain scientific and natural areas in Wisconsin and Minnesota, as well as in these public gardens: Minnesota Landscape Arboretum, University of Wisconsin Arboretum, Missouri Botanical Garden, Shaw Nature Reserve, and Belwin Nature Center.

And more thanks to Prairie Restorations, Inc., for working so hard to restore and recreate my little patch of prairie, despite the persistence of reed canary grass, artemisia, and almost every other exotic imaginable.

North American prairies are home to many beautiful plants, including blazing stars (*Liatris* species).

INTRODUCTION

North America was once home to a wide variety of native prairie communities. The importance of these prairie communities, ecologically as well as aesthetically, was immeasurable—to indigenous peoples as well as the animals and plants found there. Unfortunately, human activity related to agriculture and urban development has led to the destruction or fragmentation of almost all our original prairies. The continuing invasion of non-native plants as well as devastating insects and diseases has also dramatically altered these grassland ecosystems. Add to this the suppression of the regular fires essential to their existence, and it's amazing we have any natural prairies left at all.

The extinction of these unique North American plant communities is a great loss to humankind as well as to the animals that rely on them for food and shelter. If we allow our remaining remnants to be lost, there will be nothing left of our natural plant heritage to pass along to future generations.

It is this disturbing knowledge and my love of the Midwest and its native plant

A remnant of the tallgrass prairie and savanna that once covered my property.

communities that inspired me to start my own prairie restoration several years ago. It is a modest attempt, just under an acre on my front hillside—really more of a large garden than a restoration. Despite the slow process and the frustrations encountered with the invasive nonnative plants that continue to try to take hold, it has been one of the most rewarding gardening experiences of my life.

I get great joy from my prairie in all seasons. I walk the paths daily in spring, looking for signs of the impending show. I am rewarded by witnessing the opening of the pasque flowers and prairie violets that provide splashes of color against the sandy soil—just a few of the many wonders of nature that I would miss most springs if it wasn't in my own yard. In early summer my prairie buzzes with bees and other pollinating insects looking for the blooms of large beardtongue, lupines, golden alexanders, and harebell, which open above the small tufts of grasses.

In midsummer the prairie really starts to come into its own: black-eyed Susans blend with wild bergamot, prairie phlox, blazing stars, hoary verbena, and butterfly milkweed to create a mosaic of color, and monarchs flutter from flower to flower. In fall the grasses take center stage, as their subtly colored but heavily textured seed heads sway in the wind. Goldenrods and asters add to the show, and birds are regular visitors, looking for seeds and shelter. In winter, when the garden is stripped to its barest bones, my enjoyment comes from the persistent seed heads that break the expanse of snow crisscrossed with the patterns made by the little feet of birds

and small mammals running across the prairie.

As rewarding an endeavor as it is, prairie restoration, or even large-scale prairie gardening for that matter, is not a realistic goal for most homeowners. Luckily, many prairie plants are very adaptable to a wide array of landscape situations, enabling almost everyone to enjoy these great North American plants in their gardens and landscapes.

One of my goals with this book is to introduce you to some of the magnificent prairie communities that once covered much of central North America and foster an appreciation of these vanishing plant habitats. Only by understanding what was once here can we fully appreciate the urgent need for preservation, restoration, and re-creation. It is my hope that once you learn more about these grassland plants and plant communities, you will be encouraged to take steps to try to foster a landscape that reflects our natural plant heritage. By using prairie plants in landscapes and gardens, landowners can help perpetuate what little we have left of these magnificent ecosystems.

The purpose of this book is twofold. First, to provide adequate information for those of you who want to create a prairie garden that is practical for your site and your level of interest. And second, for those of you who are not interested in creating or able to create an entire garden devoted to prairie plants, to help you identify prairie plants suitable for traditional landscape use and how to effectively and acceptably incorporate them into your landscape. The end result should be a

Many prairie plants are well suited to landscape and garden use, even in the most urban of settings.

garden or landscape that reflects a sense of our natural prairies as well as a setting where you can tend native plants and enjoy their seasonal changes and the wildlife they attract.

The plant community descriptions in chapter 1 are the stepping-off point. Once you learn about the plants that grew naturally in the different types of prairies and how they evolved and adapted, you'll have a better understanding of how these ecosystems work and how the plants can be used effectively in gardens and landscapes.

Chapter 2 is for people who want a garden featuring prairie plants. You will learn how to develop a realistic plan to help you create a prairie garden that satisfies your goals. Topics include analyzing your site, preparing the soil, choosing

Prairie plants are not only for Midwestern gardens. Many, such as black-eyed Susan and purple coneflower, are wonderful additions to traditional landscapes and gardens in temperate climates around the world.

appropriate plants for your site and level of interest, planting, and attracting birds, butterflies, and other wildlife.

Chapter 3 provides help for people who would like to use more native plants in their landscape but don't have the space or inclination to create an entire garden of prairie plants. You'll learn how to use prairie plants in ways that are aesthetically pleasing as well as acceptable to neighbors and city officials. You'll learn how to blend prairie plants with traditional landscape plants, what plants do best in small spaces and formal landscapes, and what plants to use for special situations, such as boulevard or parking strips, shady spots, and rain gardens.

Chapter 4 covers the practical aspects of maintaining prairie plants and gardens, including weed control, grooming, record-keeping, and dealing with pests and diseases.

The book is really all about the plants, and the comprehensive Plant Profiles section provides you with all you need to help you choose appropriate forbs (non-woody plants that are not grasslike, sometimes referred to as wildflowers) and grasses to include in your prairie garden or landscape. Each profile includes a detailed description, native habitats, site requirements, hardiness zones, appropriate landscape uses, wildlife attraction, maintenance, and companion plants; other prairie species and available cultivars are often included as well. As much as I would like to tell you about all the plants that once inhabited our prairies, that isn't a practical approach in a book this size. I

whittled down the Plant Profiles to plants that tend to do better in traditional landscape settings, avoiding those that are too aggressive, hard to grow, or difficult to locate in the nursery trade.

Space limitations prevented me from including detailed propagation information for each species. There are many good references available on native plant propagation, especially for wildflowers. If you are interested in this fascinating aspect of native plants, I encourage you to read *Armitage's Native Plants for North American Gardens* (Armitage 2006) or *Native Plants of the Northeast* (Leopold 2005). William Cullina (2000, 2002, 2008) also thoroughly covers propagation in his books.

For inspiration on how to pull it all together, throughout the book you'll find photographs illustrating how your fellow gardeners have created native plant gardens and landscapes. Above all, I encourage you to learn from nature itself: be sure to take lots of walks in our many parks and natural areas for inspiration.

On a final note, gardeners who live outside the area once covered by tallgrass prairies shouldn't feel that they can't use prairie plants in their gardens and landscapes. Many species found in prairies are native to other plant communities found outside the Midwest, such as woodland openings, meadows, and barrens as well as mountain and desert habitats. And even if these plants aren't native to your area, they are still often better choices environmentally than exotic plants that come from outside North America.

CHAPTER 1

Inspiration from the Natural World

Grasslands, which include steppes, meadows, heaths, and pampas, are found on every continent except Antarctica, but the prairie is unique to North America. This Great Plains ecosystem characterized by long, hot summers and cold, dry winters is home to a unique plant community bereft of trees and dominated by magnificent grasses, with a smattering of colorful forbs. It truly has a distinct sense of place found nowhere else in the world.

To the uneducated eye the prairie is often seen as a monotonous habitat with little to offer humankind, a sentiment often shared by early settlers who were quick to plow it up and turn it into fields of corn. But prairies are complicated plant

Less than one percent of our native prairies still remains. This remnant at Frenchman's Bluff Scientific and Natural Area in northwestern Minnesota is a Nature Conservancy project that supports a mix of both tallgrass and mixed prairie species.

communities filled with intricacies that reflect the differences in available moisture, soil types, region of origin, and the vast array of plant species they include. This ecosystem often contained two to three hundred species of plants, millions of soil microorganisms, and an abundance of animals, all working together in a complex association. As with all native plant communities, prairies and the plants and animals that evolved in them play an important role in supporting the cycle of life, and consequently the survival of humankind.

Our native prairies once covered over 200 million acres in the middle United States and south-central Canada; today less than one percent remain. No other natural habitat has been so devastated in so short a time period. Once destroyed, prairies do not regenerate themselves. It is up to us to do what we can to hold on to this last glimpse of our national treasure, be it through preservation and restoration or the use of prairie plants in our gardens and landscapes.

Prairie Types

Prairie-type communities are found in other areas of the continent, including coastlines on the Gulf of Mexico, in the far Northwest, and in the desert Southwest, but the majority of the prairies of North America existed in an almost unbroken expanse in the middle of the continent extending from Texas into central Canada. Although there are many distinct ecosystems within this prairie region, the broadest classification roughly divides the region into three bands, running north to south, labeled shortgrass, mixed, and tallgrass prairies. Obviously these natural plant communities did not develop in distinct areas bounded by straight lines, as the maps might lead you to believe, but rather along a gradient that was often in a state of flux. There is much overlap in species between prairie types, making it difficult to always say just where one type began and one type ended. Generally the height of grasses and frequency of trees increased with the increase in rainfall amounts as you moved from west to east, giving rise to this classification system.

Shortgrass prairie is found just to the east of the Rocky Mountains and is the most arid of the three main prairie habitats. It is dominated by grasses that stay less than 2 feet tall and can survive the low rainfall amounts, as little as 10 inches a year, and grow in the often shallow, unfertile soil. Most months of the year the shortgrass prairie appears drab and lifeless, but once spring rains come it turns into a lush green carpet dotted with wildflowers. Shortgrass prairie grasses include buffalograss and blue grama, the two dominants, as well as western wheatgrass (*Pascopyrum smithii*), green needlegrass (*Nassella viridula*), sideoats grama, and needle and thread (*Hesperostipa comata*). Prominent forbs include blackfoot daisy (*Melampodium*), broom snakeweed (*Gutierrezia sarothrae*), common sunflower, deathcamas (*Zigadenus*), hairy false goldenaster, Indian paintbrush (*Castilleja*), sego lily (*Calochortus nuttallii*), blue flax (*Linum perenne*), and Indian breadroot (*Pediomelum*).

As you move farther east and rainfall levels increase, shortgrass prairies blend into mixed prairies, which have a deeper soil higher in organic matter. As the name implies, the plants of the mixed prairie overlap with both shortgrass and tallgrass prairies. The grasses are generally in the 2- to 4-foot range and include the often-dominant little bluestem as well as western wheatgrass, green needlegrass, blue grama, sideoats grama, needlegrasses (*Stipa*), Indian ricegrass (*Achnatherum hymenoides*), prairie sandreed (*Calamo-vilfa longifolia*), threadleaf sedge (*Carex filifolia*), needle and thread, and prairie Junegrass. The more than one hundred species of forbs include many species of asters, milkweeds, penstemons, evening primroses, dotted blazing star, and sunflowers.

The mixed prairie segues into the tallgrass prairie, which has the richest soil and most abundant rainfall of the three types. Dominant grasses in the tallgrass prairie grow up to 12 feet tall, with big bluestem and Indiangrass most prevalent.

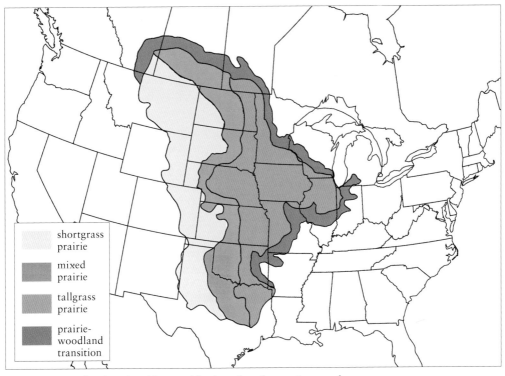

shortgrass prairie

mixed prairie

tallgrass prairie

prairie-woodland transition

American grasslands existed in roughly three bands running north to south. The tallgrass prairie emerged from the deciduous forest in the east, changing into mixed prairie as it moved west, and eventually grading into shortgrass prairie at the foot of the Rocky Mountains.

Well-known prairie plants such as blazing stars, purple coneflowers, asters, black-eyed Susan, and sunflowers were prevalent here. The tallgrass prairie is often referred to as the "true prairie."

Since it would be an overwhelming task to cover all three major prairie types in one book of this size and the plants of the tallgrass prairie are best suited to a wide range of garden and landscape use, the plants of the tallgrass prairie are the focus of this book. A list of prominent tallgrass prairie plants that are appropriate for gardens and landscapes is found in the appendix.

Savannas

Savannas occurred in transition areas where grasslands met forests, mainly along the outside borders of the prairies. These open, parklike plant communities had an understory of prairie grasses and forbs with occasional shrubs and an intermittent canopy of trees. They developed on sites where there was enough moisture for forest species to survive but fire, either set naturally or by indigenous peoples, was frequent enough to prevent an abundance of trees and shrubs from taking hold and forming closed canopies. Once established, savannas required regular fires to maintain the balance of woody and herbaceous species, with some help from grazing animals such as bison and elk.

Trees in a savanna were distributed evenly or in scattered small groves, with the canopy ranging from 10 to 50 percent closed. The dominant trees in North American savannas were oaks that grew as large, open-grown trees bearing fires scars or clusters of spindly sprouts growing from a common root system. The species of oaks changed across the country based on climate, rainfall amounts, soil type, and topography. Bur oak (*Quercus macro-*

Blue grama (*Bouteloua gracilis*) was a dominant grass in the drier soils of shortgrass prairies.

carpa) was a common sight in savannas bordering the tallgrass prairies, especially on drier sites. White oak (*Q. alba*) often dominated the eastern edge of the tallgrass prairie, the prairie/woodland transition, where soil moisture was the highest. Black oak (*Q. velutina*) and pin oak (*Q. palustris*) adapted to more acidic soil. As you moved farther south, Texas live oak (*Q. fusiformis*) and post oak (*Q. stellata*) replaced bur oak on the drier sites. Other savanna trees were rare, but included hickories (*Carya*), black cherry (*Prunus serotina*), and various pines (*Pinus*).

Shrubs were rare in savannas, and those that adapted to this habitat had to be able to resprout readily after fire. In areas where fire or grazing animals couldn't reach, such as in ravines along cliffs, shrubs often formed thickets, which were important sources of food and habitat for birds and other wildlife. Leadplant was

The tallgrass prairie was home to familiar prairie plants such as big bluestem, Indiangrass, sunflowers, silphiums, and blazing stars.

one semi-woody species that was almost always present in a savanna as well as an established tallgrass prairie. Other savanna shrubs include New Jersey tea, gray dogwood, smooth sumac, American hazelnut, and Carolina rose.

Because it straddles both grassland and woodland biomes, the understory of a savanna is often richer in plant species than either the neighboring prairie or forest. Herbaceous vegetation in savannas was dominated by species typi-cal of nearby prairie types, with plants typical of oak woodland and oak forest also present beneath the tree or shrub canopies. Some familiar woodland wild-flowers found in savannas included early meadow-rue (*Thalictrum dioicum*), wild blue phlox, bloodroot, zigzag goldenrod (*Solidago flexicaulis*), trilliums (*Trillium*), Mayapple (*Podophyllum peltatum*), wood anemone, baneberries, and Jacob's ladder. Savanna grasses included almost all the prairie grasses, both cool- and

Savannas were characterized by widely spaced oak trees with wide-spreading canopies.

Both prairie and woodland plants, including occasional shrubs, were found in savannas.

warm-season types. Several species of sedges were usually present, with Pennsylvania sedge often forming large patches. A list of shade-tolerant savanna plants suitable for garden and landscape use is found in the "Shaded Sites" section in chapter 3.

The fertile soils of savannas have been widely converted to agricultural uses. And with the suppression of prairie fires, most remaining savannas succeeded to close-canopied forests within two to three decades. Today, as with the prairies, less than one percent of our native savannas remain; the savanna and the tallgrass prairie are among the most threatened plant communities in the world.

The Prairie Ecosystem

Prairies were more than just the plants that grew there. As in all plant communities, all life forms, including plants, animals, and soil microorganisms, were interdependent.

Tallgrass prairie soils owe their genesis to the glaciers that covered most of America's heartland thousands of years ago. As they retreated and melted, the glacial till they scraped up was washed away and deposited throughout the area. The powdery, high-mineral material that resulted from the scraping and depositing by the strong winds is called loess, and it is a common component of many tallgrass prairie soils. This well-drained, neutral to slightly alkaline, fertile soil set the stage for the growth of the grasses that began to inhabit it. As grasses die and rot they help form a mollisol, a deep soil layer that is dark in color and rich in organic matter.

One important feature of tallgrass prairie soils is that the subsoil remains moist year-round. Another feature is that even when the soil surface dries, it remains soft rather than forms a hard crust.

The initial soil type definitely had an influence on what plants established themselves in certain areas, but precipitation levels, wind, warm summer temperatures, and fire are the natural forces that keep prairies as grassland communities rather than seceding into neighboring plant communities such as woodlands and deserts. The climate of the Great Plains is characterized by moist springs, hot, dry, windy summers, and cold, windy, dry winters. Precipitation can range from 10 to 20 inches in the shortgrass prairie to 25 to 39 inches in the tallgrass prairie, with over half falling during the growing season. There can be great variations in yearly precipitation, however, and drought is a frequent occurrence.

Tallgrass prairies are classified according to the soil's ability to hold moisture, ranging from dry or xeric to mesic to wet. Dry prairies are typically found at the highest elevations on gravelly, sandy, or sandy loam soils. Most had an abundance of little bluestem, along with sideoats grama. Mesic prairies are the most common prairie type, occurring on sites that are relatively well drained but have moisture available throughout most of the growing season. Here you'll find healthy stands of little bluestem along with big bluestem, switchgrass, prairie dropseed, and Indiangrass. On soils saturated during most of the growing season or often flooded during winter and spring, the vegetation is taller and denser than on mesic sites. Sedges come into the picture, as well as bluejoint, prairie cordgrass, mat muhly (*Muhlenbergia richardsonis*), and northern reedgrass (*Calamagrostis stricta* ssp. *inexpansa*). Wet prairies often blend into neighboring wetlands, which were a natural part of most grassland habitats.

Fires were common in the tallgrass prairie, caused by fierce storms and by indigenous peoples who used them to drive game, to clear the land, or as a weapon against other tribes. Fire was important to the prairie ecosystem for several reasons. Fires reduced the litter layer in a prairie, which would become very thick without periodic removal. After a prairie fire the remaining black ashes absorbed the warmth of the sunlight in early spring and the bare soil allowed rain to soak in, giving plants and seeds a quick start. The fires unleashed nitrogen from the dead

Plants that tolerated drier prairie soils include little bluestem, hoary verbena, and prairie clovers.

plants, and the ashes contributed potash, phosphorus, and calcium to the soil. Fires also inhibited the growth of woody species and helped prevent these grasslands from turning into forests.

Animals were abundant on tallgrass prairies and an important part of this sustainable ecosystem. White-tailed deer, bison, elk, and other grazing animals consumed large amounts of plants, including shrubs and trees, and then moved on, allowing the grazed areas to recover. Burrowing animals such as pocket gophers, badgers, and ground squirrels churned the soil and exposed seeds to bare soil and sunlight, which aided germination. Mound-building ants mix and aerate soil as they build their tunnels, bringing up nutrients and clay particles from the subsoil. Birds that rely on prairie habitats include the prairie chicken, upland sandpiper, meadowlark, and

Spotted Joe-pye weed (*Eupatoriadelphus maculatus*) was common in prairies with higher soil moisture.

bobolinks, with hawks and owls playing important predatory roles. Amphibians and reptiles include many species of frogs, toads, snakes, and salamanders.

Prairies are also home to thousands of species of insects, which are important pollinators, predators of other insects, and food sources for many birds and mammals. Grasshoppers and crickets are also important grazers, and their burrowing helps loosen the soil. Other insects are decomposers, playing an important role in reducing and recycling the abundance of vegetation.

Life also teems beneath the surface. Prairie soils rely on a large number of microscopic organisms that are important for decomposition of the vast amount of plant material generated by a healthy prairie ecosystem. Many prairie plants have a symbiotic association with mycorrhizal fungi, which act as an extension of the root

Wild lupine (*Lupinus perennis*) responds favorably to fire, often blooming profusely a few weeks after a burn.

Nitrogen-fixing legumes such as leadplant (*Amorpha canescens*) form symbiotic relationships with soil bacteria, which are able to take nitrogen from the air in the soil and make it available to plants. When these plants die and decompose, this essential element goes into the soil and is available for other nearby plants.

system, increasing nutrient uptake by the plants. Prairie legumes fix nitrogen in their roots, which helps replenish soil nitrogen.

Prairie Plant Adaptations

The prairie ecosystem is not always a kind one, with its drying winds, droughty conditions, long, cold winters and hot summers, regular invasion by fire, and insistent munching by bison and other grazers. In order to survive these conditions, prairie plants have evolved certain characteristics that enable them to live and reproduce effectively.

Most prairie plants are long-lived perennials, but some are annuals, evolved to move in when the soil is disturbed and laid bare. They germinate, flower, and set seed quickly in an effort to complete their life cycle and guarantee reproduction before their shallow roots succumb to drought. These annual species can be prolific in areas for a while, but the long-lived perennial plants will eventually move back in.

In general, there is an increase in plant height from spring to fall in the tallgrass prairie. Spring plants such as violets, prairie smoke, and pasque flower are usually less than a foot tall, just tall enough to find sunlight above the new grass shoots. Summer forbs such as rattlesnake master, fringeleaf wild petunia, and black-eyed Susan stretch a couple of feet higher to avoid the shade of the growing grasses. The tallest prairie plants tend to be the fall grasses, which reach 7 to 10 feet or more. Some of the latest blooming forbs, including goldenrods, asters, nodding

Bird's-foot violet (*Viola pedata*) and other violets are among the earliest prairie plants to bloom, creating a welcome splash of color against the mostly brown grasses.

Black-eyed Susan (*Rudbeckia hirta*), a short-lived perennial, is often prolific in young prairies and then takes a back seat once slower-to-establish plants fill in.

lady's tresses, and gentians, are shorter than the grasses to take advantage of increasing light levels as grass leaves turn brown in fall.

Two characteristics prairie grasses and forbs have that enable them to withstand fire and grazing are growing points underground or at the soil surface and extensive root systems. Since growth occurs from the plants' base rather than the leaf tips, growth is not impaired when plants are bitten off by grazing animals or burned off by fire. Many grasses send out side shoots of reproductive stems, either rhizomes or stolons. Rhizomes are underground stems that produce new stems and rootlets as they grow. Stolons grow along the surface of the ground putting down rootlets as they go. These help stabilize the plant and keep them from being pulled out of the ground when grazed. It also helps them spread to form dense sod,

Late-blooming compass plant (*Silphium laciniatum*) is among the tallest of prairie forbs, often rising several feet above surrounding plants.

which deters woody plants from becoming established.

Prairie plants are also adapted to withstand dry conditions and high daytime temperatures. Prairie grasses have narrow leaves that lose less water to evapotranspiration than flat, broad leaves. They are arranged vertically so that less surface area is exposed, but they still can collect as much sunlight as possible. During long dry spells, the leaves curl in on themselves to prevent further moisture loss. Their tough stems are resilient and slender and offer less resistance to wind than broad leaves. The roots of these grasses, which form thick networks beneath the prairie extending 5 to 7 feet or more, effectively absorb moisture during dry periods.

Most tallgrass prairie forbs also have deep, extensive roots systems to help them survive dry conditions, some reaching down 20 feet. As these extensive root systems decay they contribute greatly to the organic content of the soil. Some have finely divided or narrow leaves to prevent overheating and offer less resistance to wind. Many have hairy leaves to deflect sunlight and wind, or leathery or waxy leaves to prevent water loss. Milkweeds and other plants have sticky resinous sap that minimizes evaporation. Prairie rosinweed traps evaporated moisture in tiny hairs on the leaves. The taller flowers rely on neighboring grasses to provide shade and natural support to help keep them from falling over in the strong winds.

Prairie plants have several adaptations that help them in seed dispersal. Most prairie plants are pollinated by wind

Indiangrass (*Sorghastrum nutans*) and other prairie grasses have evolved to grow upright and narrow, with flowers high above surrounding plants to catch pollinating breezes.

rather than insects since not many insects enjoy visiting prairies in the heat of the summer when pollen is set. The seeds are often small and lightweight and easily dispersed. Grasses hold their flowers high above the stems to catch the breezes. Some, such as needlegrasses, have developed seeds that have barbed spears that readily attach to any passing animal's fur coat for a ride to a further destination. The flowers of most forbs are at the top of the plants to attract the few insects that brave the heat and to take advantage of every available wind gust.

Prairie Communities as Models

The key to success in any type of gardening using native plants is to look to nature for inspiration. Basing your prairie garden or landscape planting on a natural plant community will help ensure that it has a natural look, is appropriate for the site, and will include suitable plants with similar requirements.

That said, it's your garden, and it's up to you how literally you want to interpret a natural prairie. Obviously most people won't have the space or inclination to exactly replicate a prairie community. Unless you are creating a large habitat garden, chances are you will use local prairies as models rather than try to exactly reproduce what you see when you visit them. The main purpose of your visits should be to see what and how plants grow together naturally and get a feel for what this plant community once looked like. Note which forbs tend to grow as scattered individuals throughout the prairie and which are

mainly found in large patches. Carry this idea into your home landscape, choosing some plants to be used as individual accent plants and others to be grown in larger groups of five or more.

It's almost impossible to see a pure native prairie anymore, but there are many places to see restorations, large prairie gardens, and remnants. Check out your state's Department of Natural Resources Web site to find public places to see prairie plants in natural settings, which will include state and county parks and scientific and natural areas. The Nature Conservancy (www.nature.org) manages prairie remnants and restorations in almost every state in the Midwest, and they are open to the public. Other places where small remnants may have survived the plow are along railroad rights of way and in old cemeteries. Many botanical gardens and arboretums have restorations or large prairie gardens. A list of some places to see prairie plants is included in the resources at the back of this book (see page 284). If you have shady areas or transition areas that bring you up to the north or east side of your house or buildings, try to find a savanna habitat to visit so you can see which plants tolerate these conditions.

When visiting these natural plant communities and gardens, always respect the plants and animals that live in these areas and never dig plants or harvest seeds. Although prairie plants tend to be quite resilient (they were regularly trampled by bison, after all), it is still a good idea to stay on marked paths if they are available. If there are no paths tread carefully, both for your own safety as well as for the sake of the plants. The terrain may be uneven and you may come upon large holes made by burrowing animals. Poison ivy (*Toxicodendron radicans*) is also often found in native prairies. Sturdy shoes, long sleeves, long pants, a hat, and insect repellent are good ideas.

Use a good field guide to help you identify the plants you see. Make notes of plant combinations based on what is blooming at different times during the growing season. Unlike woodland gardens, where plants often grow in large colonies, most prairie forbs grow somewhat randomly among the grasses, only occasionally occurring in solid stands or large colonies. The forbs usually grow to about the same height or shorter than the surrounding grasses, but some, such as silphiums, tower above the grasses, creating accents or focal points. Bring your camera

In this natural prairie some plants grow in large patches while others, such as butterfly milkweed (*Asclepias tuberosa*), grow as widely scattered individual plants.

so you can bring information home with you to use for future reference.

Prairie Restoration and Reconstruction

Restoration, or rehabilitation, is the process of bringing back an existing prairie remnant. Since it is rare to find a remnant in today's world, most people end up doing more of a reconstruction, which is re-establishing a prairie community on plowed ground. The long-term goal of both is to create a working plant community.

Restoring or reconstructing a prairie is a wonderful gift to the world. However, it is challenging, frustrating, and often

The Minnesota Landscape Arboretum prairie garden and other public gardens that provide plant identification labels are great places to get ideas for your own prairie garden and landscape plantings.

expensive. It is usually outside the realm of the average landowner and requires professional expertise. The basic steps in restoration are identifying existing species, getting rid of problem species, reintroducing fire, and adding plants as needed. With reconstruction you start with a clean slate by getting rid of all existing vegetation, preparing the soil, and replanting. It is actually more like prairie gardening, but on a larger scale.

If you have the land, resources, desire, and most of all patience, the creation of prairie on your property will bring you many rewards. I know from personal experience. Start by reading up on the prairie types that would have occurred in your area. Many states publish this

Scientific and natural areas, such as the Black Earth Prairie just west of Madison, Wisconsin, are wonderful places to see what natural prairies would have been like.

information or offer references on their Department of Natural Resources Web site. Good information about suitable plants as well as the process can be found in restoration and nursery catalogs, in books, and on Web sites. An excellent reference is *The Tallgrass Restoration Handbook* (Packard and Mutel 2005).

Keep in mind that to successfully restore or recreate a prairie, you really need a minimum of one acre of land in order to effectively produce a working plant community. You should stick with local genotypes, only planting species and varieties that would have been native to about within two hundred miles of your location. The greatest challenge of restoration or reconstruction is dealing with invasive plants. The more effort you make to rid your site of nonnative weedy plants before you plant, the better. Most of all, be patient. These ecosystems took thousands of years to evolve, and they won't be recreated overnight.

The Curtis Prairie at the University of Wisconsin Arboretum is the oldest restored prairie. It covers sixty acres and contains over two hundred native species.

Silphiums are accent plants in natural prairies. Here we see wholeleaf rosinweed (front left) and the tropically large leaves of prairie rosinweed (back right).

CHAPTER 2

Creating a Prairie Garden

A garden devoted to all or almost all prairie plants is a very rewarding endeavor and one that is within the realm of most gardeners. A habitat garden such as this is a wonderful way to not only study and enjoy the seasonal changes of native plants but also the interactions between native flora and fauna. When compared to the common alternatives—an area of turfgrass or a patch of weeds—a garden of prairie plants is a much healthier, and often lower-maintenance, choice.

My definition of a prairie garden is a tended plot of land less than a quarter acre in size but often much smaller, typically in the 1,000- to 5,000-square-foot range, that features native tallgrass prairie plants—the prairie type best suited to most landscape situations, as it is home to

A prairie garden is a beautiful sight in midsummer, when tallgrass prairie forbs such as butterfly milkweed, stiff tickseed, and pale purple coneflower are at their peak bloom.

39

a nice mix of showy flowers and attractive grasses. If your site is larger than a quarter acre, it will be difficult to maintain without professional help or large-scale garden equipment. Not that I want to discourage planting large areas to prairies. I just want to be honest in saying a large-scale prairie planting is usually outside the realm of most homeowners' expertise, not to mention equipment, time, and finances.

Planning a Prairie Garden

Before you put shovel to the soil, it's a good idea to give a little thought as to why you want a prairie garden. Are you trying to re-establish a natural plant community? Provide habitat for wildlife? Create a showy patch of wildflowers? Stabilize a slope or cover an infertile piece of ground? Create a low-maintenance garden? All are good reasons for creating a garden of prairie plants, but they may call for different plants and different techniques, so it is helpful to have an idea of what you want to accomplish before starting.

If you want to try to re-establish a native plant community, you'll want to do some research into what prairie type would have been native in your area and the species and varieties that grew there (local genotypes). Some states have Natural Heritage Programs on their Department of Natural Resources Web sites where you can find information about native plant communities. Natureserve. org has also developed a national classification system. Keep in mind that these plant communities evolved over thousands of years; your soil conditions are probably quite removed from their original state, so it may take a bit more work up front to get the appropriate conditions for the prairie community you choose to recreate. It may be easier to model your garden after another prairie community that is better suited to your current soil conditions.

If your main goal is to provide habitat for birds, butterflies, pollinating insects, and other wildlife, you'll want to put more emphasis on choosing plants that are higher in wildlife value. The lists found later in this chapter and the information on wildlife attraction included in each Plant Profile will help you with this.

If you are looking for a showy splash of color in your landscape, you'll want to include more forbs and use fewer grasses and make sure your garden includes plants with interest year-round. Most tall-grass prairie plants bloom from mid- to late summer. Refer to the list on page 52 for good spring- and fall-blooming plants to include in your garden. Allowing your plants to remain standing through the winter provides interest in that season.

If your prairie garden is to be more functional, such as stopping erosion on a slope, you'll want to consider fast-growing rhizomatous plants to hold the soil. Most prairie plants tend to be on the low-maintenance side, especially once established, but some are more resilient than others. These are good choices if you are looking for a "plant it and leave it" approach. The maintenance information in each Plant Profile points out plants that are better suited to naturalized situations and tough sites.

I suspect most readers will be looking to incorporate several or all of these concepts into their prairie garden to a certain extent, the result being an attractive, environmentally friendly alternative to a traditional perennial border or patch of lawn that satisfies your green thumb as well as provides much-needed habitat for native fauna.

Choosing a Site

Obviously tallgrass prairies are full-sun plant communities, so top priority is choosing a spot that gets a minimum of six hours of sun a day. It's okay to have some small areas of partial shade, such as under the canopy of a large deciduous tree. These are good places to incorporate

The tallgrass prairie is an all-American ecosystem not found anywhere else in the world. A garden of prairie plants will bring a true sense of place to our lives in a world that has become increasingly global and homogenized.

savanna plants, listed on page 108, which do well in light shade.

You can be a little more flexible with the soil conditions; most tallgrass prairie plants are pretty adaptable to a range of soil types and soil pH. You will have the greatest palette of plants to choose from if you have a mesic, well-drained soil with a pH between 5.5 and 7.0. Heavier soils and drier soils can be improved before planting by incorporating organic material such as compost to bring them more into the desirable range. However, it is usually easier to select plants that are better suited to dry or moist soil conditions. Prairies did exist on seasonally wet sites and low areas, but if your site is wet all year long, you should probably consider a wetland garden rather than a prairie garden.

Most people think of a prairie as being an open, flat expanse of land, but prairie communities also evolved on hillsides and

This prairie garden at the University of Wisconsin Arboretum is planted along a hillside, offering visitors a good way to see a wide variety of plants from the path.

Prairie plants that are well suited to moist soil conditions found along water features include cardinal flower, spotted Joe-pye weed, white turtlehead, and brown-eyed Susan.

Paths are important in any garden, both as a pleasant way to bring you and your guests close to your plants and as a way to access your plants for maintenance. Mown paths provide a comfortable, natural way to move through a large garden. If your garden is small, stepping stones make an attractive path.

slopes. Prairie gardens are actually beautiful on hillsides where you can see the patches of flowering plants better. Stay away from steep north-facing hillsides, however, which are protected from the sun and are not well suited to most tallgrass prairie plants.

If possible, locate your prairie garden adjacent to an open field to increase the effective size of the habitat and make it more attractive to prairie birds and other wildlife. Try to keep it away from woodlands. Trees and shrubs along the periphery, especially along south and west sides, will reduce available sunlight and buffer the wind, which are both important to prairie habitats. Wooded areas can also be home to aggressive trees and shrubs, such as quaking aspen, gray dogwood, and smooth sumac, which will try to invade your garden.

If your prairie garden is on the large side and there is a chance you may be burning it at some point, be sure to keep it at least 30 feet away from buildings and other ignitable structures. Install some kind of buffer strip, such as mown turf grass or gravel, between your prairie garden and areas of the landscape that you don't want harmed by fire.

Lastly, you may want to consider proximity to neighbors and the public. Despite the growing popularity of natural gardening, not everyone appreciates the beauty of these tall grasses and flowers, especially in winter when they turn brown. You may want to avoid the potential hassles by placing your prairie garden away from property lines or in your backyard, if you have the option.

Preparing the Site

As with all gardening, proper site preparation is key with prairie plants. Some people believe that native plants are so tough that all you have to do is scatter seeds or place an abundance of plants and they will take over an area and thrive. This misconception couldn't be further from the truth. Native plants established themselves in an area over thousands of years; they can't simply be planted and expected to grow just anywhere, especially when the soil in many landscapes is very far from its natural state and covered with aggressive nonnative plants (i.e., weeds).

Chances are the site you have selected is already covered with some type of existing vegetation, most likely turfgrasses or field weeds. If this is the case, you must take the time to get rid of all existing vegetation before you put plants or seeds in the ground. This preparation will pay off significantly. The main source of frustration I encounter among people trying to grow native plants is that they have trouble fighting the weeds while the plants get established. Many prairie plantings, especially those that were seeded, take several growing seasons before they really look like much since these plants put a lot of early energy into establishing their strong root systems. It's easy to become frustrated when your new garden looks worse than it did before you planted because the weeds have moved in and taken over before prairie plants have had a chance to become established.

There are several ways to get rid of existing vegetation, the main methods being digging, smothering, and using a herbicide. How you go about it depends on what plants are there, how strong your back is, how much time you have, and how you feel about using chemical herbicides.

You can manually dig up the garden or use a sod cutter if it is covered with turf-grasses. Just be sure to get rid of all the existing plant roots. Even tiny pieces of tough perennial-weed roots can grow into big bad weeds in no time. A major disadvantage with this method is that you lose substantial amounts of topsoil. To avoid this, if you have the time, you can simply turn the sod over and allow it to decay on site for a full growing season.

If you don't want to dig, you can get rid of the existing vegetation by smothering it. Start by mowing closely in spring, then covering the area with a thick layer of newspaper (ten sheets or more). Wet down the newspaper to hold it in place. If it is a windy site, you may need to anchor the paper with stakes of some sort. Cover the newspaper with about 6 inches of organic mulch, such as shredded straw or leaves, compost, or a mixture. You can also mix in some sand to add weight. You can go ahead and plant container-grown plants

Large prairie gardens should be mowed and the existing woody vegetation removed before spraying with an herbicide.

right into the layers. The roots should grow through the newspaper and into the soil. If you plan to sow seeds, it is a good idea to give this method a full growing season before sowing. This method works best on lawn areas rather than areas with lots of deep-rooted perennial weeds.

Another option is to use a nonselective glyphosate-based herbicide, such as Roundup, which kills tops and roots of herbaceous plants. If you follow directions exactly, aim carefully, and use only when necessary, these products should kill invading plants without causing undue harm to the environment. It is usually a good idea to make two applications of herbicide, waiting about two weeks before the second. Once the vast majority of existing vegetation is dead (usually ten days to two weeks after the second spraying) and removed, you can turn the soil by hand or use a mechanical tiller to cultivate down 6 to 10 inches.

Avoid using a mechanical tiller without killing all existing vegetation first. While it may look like you've created a bare planting area, all you've done is ground the roots into smaller pieces, which in turn sprout into many more plants than you started with. Even after multiple tillings spaced weeks apart, you'll be haunted by these root pieces.

Chances are that at least part of your prairie garden will butt up to an area of lawn. Where this is the case, you'll want to establish some sort of edging method to keep lawn grasses from invading your garden. The two main options are hand edging twice a year using a sharp, flat spade to cut a neat edge around your garden or installing a barrier of some type. When it comes to barriers, it's usually worth paying more for a material. Consider a high-quality metal edging, buried 4 inches or more into the soil, completely surrounding areas where turf can sneak in.

Working with the Soil

It's definitely worth it to take some time up front to get to know your soil. A good place to start is having your soil tested by a soil-testing laboratory; check with your local university extension office for labs in your area. A soil test will provide you with information on existing soil texture and fertility, along with recommendations on what to add to improve it.

In general it is best to choose plants adapted to your existing soil texture, pH, and moisture conditions. However, if your soil has been drastically changed by construction or other factors, you will want to do all you can to improve it before planting.

Most prairie plants grow better in less-fertile, drier soil than traditional garden plants do; if the soil is too rich, plants may grow too lush and flop over. However, some—especially those that are native to moist-soil prairies—do require a heavier, richer soil. Most prairie plants are adaptable to soil somewhere in the pH range of 5.5 to 7.0. Drier calcareous prairie plants require a soil pH from 7.0 to 8.0 and acidic-soil plants prefer a soil pH less than 5.5.

If the soil in your chosen site is on the heavy side and you want to plant a wide range of tallgrass prairie plants, adding organic matter is the best way to loosen the soil. It also adds valuable nutrients at a slow and steady pace, and it has a buffering effect on soil pH. The best source of organic matter for gardeners is compost. Composting materials such as cow or horse manure, grass clippings, and leaves ensures they will be in optimum condition to work into the soil. Other good sources of organic matter are chopped straw and hay. Avoid using peat-based products as soil amendments. The process of extracting peat from bogs is environmentally harmful to these threatened natural habits.

Harebell (*Campanula rotundifolia*) is a prairie plant that can tolerate a higher soil pH, making it a good choice among these limestone boulders.

The easiest time to add organic matter is before planting. Loosen the soil with a spade or digging fork to a depth of 6 to 10 inches. Spread a layer of compost or well-rotted manure 2 to 4 inches deep over the entire bed. Use a fork to mix it thoroughly into your soil. If your soil is very heavy (high in clay), you may want to add an inch or two of sharp builder's sand along with the compost or manure. Sand alone will only make matters worse, but when it is added with organic matter to heavy soil, it does help loosen the soil.

Once you improve the soil and get suitable plants established, you usually don't need to add amendments again. However, keep your eyes open for signs that plants may not be well suited to their conditions, such as discoloration of leaves or overall lack of vigor, and be prepared to make some corrections or find a plant better suited to the spot.

Selecting and Purchasing Plants

Once your garden bed is virtually weed-free and the soil is prepared, the fun begins: selecting plants. A typical tall-grass prairie had about 80 percent grasses and 20 percent flowering plants. If you want a natural-looking prairie garden you should stick somewhat close to this ratio. Most people will want to go heavier on the showier forbs, at least at the start. Don't discount the beauty and value of grasses, however. They provide interesting

PRAIRIE PLANTS WITH SOIL pH PREFERENCES

Tolerant of higher soil pH

Allium species (wild onions)
Bouteloua species (grama grasses)
Campanula rotundifolia (harebell)
Dodecatheon meadia (prairie shooting star)
Echinacea paradoxa (Bush's purple coneflower)
Gentiana andrewsii (closed bottle gentian)
Gentianopsis crinita (greater fringed gentian)
Liatris mucronata (cusp blazing star)
Oenothera species (evening primroses)
Sisyrinchium species (blue-eyed grasses)
Symphyotrichum sericeum (western silver aster)
Yucca glauca (soapweed yucca)

Like a slightly acidic soil pH

Carex pensylvanica (Pennsylvania sedge)
Helenium flexuosum (purplehead sneezeweed)
Lilium philadelphicum (wood lily)
Lupinus perennis (wild lupine)
Symphyotrichum ericoides (white heath aster)
Viola species (violets)

contrast to the flowering plants. They bring a lot of late summer, fall, and winter interest. They are sources of food and shelter for birds. They provide natural support for flowering plants, reducing the need for artificial staking. In general, the larger your prairie garden, the more grasses you can and should include.

A native prairie may have had up to four hundred different species. Obviously you won't come close to that in your home prairie garden, but you should try to include as many species as possible. Not only will it make your garden more interesting, it will also help your garden survive natural challenges such as drought and extremely cold winters, and it will attract a greater variety of wildlife. A good goal for a typical home prairie garden may be to have thirty to fifty different species. You don't necessarily have to plant them all right away, however.

Be sure to include plenty of plants with spring and early summer interest. Prairies are showiest from midsummer into late fall, when the warm-season forbs and grasses really come into their own. That's fine in the natural world, but most gardeners are looking for color and interest throughout the growing season. Use the

If you want a more natural-looking prairie garden, go heavier on the grasses.

To ensure your prairie garden has interest in spring, plant plenty of prairie smoke and cool-season grasses. Although not a true tallgrass prairie plant, *Aquilegia canadensis* (Canada columbine) is an early-blooming native plant that does well in prairie gardens.

list below as a guide to help ensure you have something showy in your prairie garden starting in early spring and continuing through late fall.

Many prairie plants have adapted to set seeds—and lots of them—as a means of self-preservation. While a certain amount of spontaneity should be welcome in a prairie garden, too many self-sown seedlings can definitely be a problem. The easiest way to avoid this is to stay away from the prolific self-sowers. However, this

PRAIRIE PLANTS FOR SEASON-LONG INTEREST

Early to midspring

Anemone canadensis (Canadian anemone)
Anemone caroliniana (Carolina anemone)
Antennaria species (pussytoes)
Carex pensylvanica (Pennsylvania sedge)
Claytonia virginica (Virginia spring beauty)
Deschampsia cespitosa (tufted hairgrass)
Dodecatheon meadia (prairie shooting star)
Geum triflorum (prairie smoke)
Heuchera richardsonii (prairie alumroot)
Hypoxis hirsuta (common goldstar)
Koeleria macrantha (prairie Junegrass)
Penstemon grandiflorus (large beard-tongue)
Phlox bifida (sand phlox)
Pulsatilla patens (pasque flower)
Sisyrinchium species (blue-eyed grasses)
Thalictrum dasycarpum (purple meadow-rue)
Viola species (violets)
Zizia species (alexanders)

Late summer into fall

Andropogon gerardii (big bluestem)
Boltonia asteroides (white doll's daisy)
Chelone glabra (white turtlehead)
Gentiana species (gentians)
Gentianopsis crinita (greater fringed gentian)
Helenium autumnale (autumn sneezeweed)
Helianthus salicifolius (willowleaf sunflower)
Liatris aspera (tall blazing star)
Panicum virgatum (switchgrass)
Physostegia virginiana (obedient plant)
Schizachyrium scoparium (little bluestem)
Silphium terebinthinaceum (prairie rosinweed)
Solidago species (goldenrods)
Sorghastrum nutans (Indiangrass)
Sporobolus heterolepis (prairie dropseed)
Symphyotrichum species (asters)
Vernonia species (ironweeds)

Closed bottle gentian (*Gentiana andrewsii*) is a great plant for bringing
a touch of purple to the late-summer prairie garden.

greatly reduces your plant choices as well as takes away some of the fun of natural gardening. A better approach is to get to know the seedling stages of these plants and be ready to weed some of them out or transplant them as soon as they reach a suitable size. You may also want to deadhead some of the more prolific seeders before they get a chance to set seed. Obviously this will reduce their value to seed-eating birds and mammals, but it may be a compromise that is worth considering in some cases.

You may also want to avoid some of the more aggressive-spreading prairie plants, especially if your prairie garden is on the smaller side. The list below includes tallgrass prairie plants that can get out of control or reseed prolifically if they are too happy. It is best to limit their numbers or restrict their use to sites with extremely poor conditions such as very dry hillsides.

In chapter 3 I talk about using cultivars of native plants. While I advocate this in certain landscape situations, I advise people to try to stay away from them in habitat gardens. Since cultivars are propagated vegetatively rather than sexually, they lack the genetic diversity that results from reproduction by seed. And cultivars are often selected because of their different flower color, shape, or size, or foliage

PLANTS TO USE WITH CAUTION IN SMALL PRAIRIE GARDENS

Achillea millefolium (common yarrow)
Allium canadense (meadow garlic)
Anemone canadensis (Canadian anemone)
Arnoglossum atriplicifolium (pale Indian plantain)
Artemisia species (sageworts)
Asclepias species (milkweeds) other than *A. tuberosa* (butterfly milkweed)
Castilleja species (Indian paintbrushes)
Chelone glabra (white turtlehead)
Coreopsis palmata (stiff tickseed)
Coreopsis tripteris (tall tickseed)
Eryngium yuccifolium (rattlesnake master)
Eupatorium species (bonesets)
Euphorbia corollata (flowering spurge)
Filipendula rubra (queen of the prairie)
Helianthus species (sunflowers)
Lobelia species (lobelias)
Monarda fistulosa (wild bergamot)
Monarda punctata (spotted beebalm)
Oenothera species (evening primroses)
Packera species (ragworts)
Panicum virgatum (switchgrass)
Physostegia virginiana (obedient plant)
Pycnanthemum species (mountainmints)
Ratibida pinnata (gray-headed prairie coneflower)
Rosa species (wild roses)
Silphium species (rosinweeds)
Solidago species (goldenrods)
Vernonia species (ironweeds)

color, which can change leaf chemistry. These characteristics can make them unattractive or even unpalatable to native fauna that rely on them for food. It can also reduce a plant's value as a source of pollen. So unless you have a small prairie garden where you need to be careful about plant size and aggressiveness, try to stick with the pure species.

The term "local genotype" refers to a plant that has evolved to have special characteristics that make it especially well adapted to a specific site. These characteristics include height, hardiness, coloring to attract pollinators, and drought tolerance. Just what is "local" is debatable, but most experts consider a radius of about two hundred miles to be within a local

Monarda fistulosa (wild bergamot) is great for bringing pale lavender color to summer prairie gardens, but it spreads by rhizomes and reseeds and so is best used in large gardens, with other tough plants that can stand up to it.

genotype. Obviously the closer your seed source is to your location, the better your chances are of obtaining local genotypes.

Plants with local genotypes that differentiate them from the general species are

If you want to add aggressive plants such as *Helianthus tuberosus* (Jerusalem artichoke) to your prairie garden, plant them in buried nursery containers to restrict root growth.

classified into subspecies (abbreviated as "ssp.") and varieties ("var."). A subspecies has a characteristic that isn't quite different enough to make it a separate species. This characteristic may occur over a wide range or in a geographically isolated area. Varieties have minor recognizable variations from the species, such as flower size or leaf color, but are not distinct enough to be labeled subspecies. Having a goal of using only local genotypes is certainly advisable if you are doing a restoration or even a large-scale prairie garden. It helps to perpetuate these special characteristics as well as increases your chances of success.

Many native plant advocates stress the need to use only local genotypes in gardens and landscapes, but most home gardeners are not willing to invest the time and effort to research and seek out local genotypes. It's your garden, and it should be a space that suits your level of gardening interest. You don't even have to stick with all prairie plants. You may want to include semishade woodland plants or even some nonnative plants. Just be sure to give some thought to how the plants will grow in your conditions and how they will look with your prairie plants. And most importantly, be sure to avoid any exotic invasive plants that can escape to nearby natural areas and become pests there.

After land clearing, exotic plants are the second greatest threat to natural areas. The U.S. Fish and Wildlife Service estimates that 42 percent of our endangered and threatened species have declined as a result of exotic plants and animals. Unfortunately many of these harmful plants have been introduced, albeit without malice, by the horticultural industry. There are some exotic invasive plants that should not be planted in landscapes, especially those that are at all near natural areas. For information on potentially invasive plants, go to www.invasiveplantatlas.org.

When it comes to finding sources for your plants the best thing for the environment and for the success of your prairie garden is to purchase seeds and plants from a native plant nursery that grows its own seed stock. You can find a list of native plant nurseries for your state on the PlantNative Web site at www.plantnative. org. Many state Department of Natural Resources Web sites and native plant

Whenever possible, use local genotypes in your prairie garden. Choosing plants that have evolved in conditions similar to your planting site not only helps ensure greater success for you, it also serves local pollinators and other wildlife and helps preserve genetic diversity within a species.

The naturally occurring *Ratibida columnifera* var. *pulcherrima* shows a major variation in petal color from the all-yellow petals of the typical species.

Buy plants from a reputable native plant nursery to ensure you are getting only nursery-propagated plants that are suitable for your area.

organizations also publish lists of native plant nurseries. Never dig plants from the wild unless you are part of a plant rescue group that is authorized to save a population that is slated to be destroyed. The truth is, usually the time and effort spent digging native plants is not worth it. Very few survive the move to a new site.

I also discourage you from collecting seed and cutting flowers. As we lose more and more of our native populations of prairie plants, it becomes more and more important that we allow the remaining plants to set ample seed to ensure their reproduction and survival in natural areas. If too much seed is collected from these remaining natural areas, it will be difficult for these plant communities to sustain themselves. Remember also that seeds are important food sources for wildlife.

Choosing Plants to Attract Wildlife

As much as you will get from your prairie garden, it will benefit our native fauna even more, providing food and shelter necessary for their survival in a world where their natural habitats are quickly being destroyed. Even a small prairie garden will have great benefits for insects and in turn birds and other wildlife farther up the food chain.

Beneficial insects prefer a less-manicured landscape, so a prairie garden is a natural attraction for them. Many overwinter in leaf litter or rotting wood and will be looking for organic matter. Wood chip mulched paths will provide overwintering sites. Ground-dwelling bees and wasps will look for bare patches of soil. Other beneficial insects like to hide under stones and fallen logs. It goes without saying that you should refrain from using insecticides if you want to attract native insects, birds, and other wildlife.

Thickets of mixed shrubs and small trees along the borders of your prairie garden will provide nesting sites and shelter as well as food for many birds and small mammals. Thickets also provide opportunities for more creatures, all of which will help make your prairie garden more of a functioning plant community that keeps problem insects in check. Good savanna thicket shrubs and small trees include gray dogwood, downy arrowwood (*Viburnum rafinesqueanum*), hazelnuts (*Corylus*), chokecherry, wild plums (*Prunus*), snowberry, willows, raspberries (*Rubus*), wild roses, and hawthorns (*Crataegus*). If possible, separate your thicket from the prairie proper with a mown path to help keep these suckering shrubs from moving into your prairie garden. You can also just be diligent about hand cutting any woody stems that make their way into your garden. Do not treat the cut stumps with herbicides, however, or you will kill the entire thicket as the poison moves through the connected root system.

In addition to plants, there are items you can add, such as nesting boxes and feeders, and techniques you can practice that will increase your garden's attractiveness to wildlife. Consider creating a small brush pile in one corner of your garden. Rock walls or rock piles will also be favorite sunning spots for dragonflies, snakes, lizards, and salamanders in

Creating a garden of prairie plants is a cooperative venture with nature, where native fauna has an active role in the overall success, including maintenance.

summer and provide overwintering sites. Just about all animal species will benefit in some way from a water feature such as a pond, but dragonflies and damselflies will especially thank you. You will also provide habitat for frogs, salamanders, and snakes.

Obviously the larger and more diverse your prairie garden, the more types of wildlife you will attract. Many good books, including the excellent *Birdscaping in the Midwest* (Nowak 2007), deal specifically with this topic, if you are interested in learning more.

BUTTERFLIES

Prairie gardens are natural havens for everyone's favorite insects, butterflies, which love open sunny habitats. Most butterflies are on their way somewhere else when you see them in your garden; for these vagabonds, your garden is a crucial rest stop, a place where they can linger for a while to enjoy food, water, and shelter. If you want to provide a complete butterfly habitat you will have to include the proper host plants for butterflies to lay eggs, keeping in mind that these are not always the showiest plants and that they become even less attractive when they have been eaten by the newly hatched caterpillars. These host plants are important, however, since without them butterflies will not lay eggs.

Make sure you have plants available all growing season, from spring (when butterflies first arrive) to late fall. Early-blooming prairie violets are occasionally weighed down with butterflies, as are late-blooming asters and Joe-pye weeds.

As more and more natural areas are lost, birds, butterflies, and other insects must more and more rely on city and suburban gardens featuring the native plants they depend on for survival.

PRAIRIE PLANTS TO ATTRACT BUTTERFLIES AND THEIR CATERPILLARS

Allium cernuum (nodding onion)
Amorpha canescens (leadplant)
Andropogon gerardii (big bluestem)
Antennaria species (pussytoes)
Asclepias species (milkweeds)
Baptisia species (wild indigos)
Boltonia asteroides (white doll's daisy)
Bouteloua species (grama grasses)
Callirhoe species (poppymallows)
Camassia species (camases)
Carex pensylvanica (Pennsylvania sedge)
Ceanothus americanus (New Jersey tea)
Chelone glabra (white turtlehead)
Coreopsis species (tickseeds)
Dalea species (prairie clovers)
Deschampsia cespitosa (tufted hairgrass)
Echinacea species (purple coneflowers)
Eryngium yuccifolium (rattlesnake master)
Eupatoriadelphus maculatus (spotted Joe-pye weed)
Eupatorium species (bonesets)
Gaillardia species (gaillardias)
Geum triflorum (prairie smoke)
Helenium autumnale (autumn sneezeweed)
Helianthus species (sunflowers)
Heliopsis helianthoides (smooth oxeye)
Heterotheca villosa (hairy false goldenaster)
Heuchera richardsonii (prairie alumroot)
Houstonia species (bluets)
Hypoxis hirsuta (common goldstar)
Liatris species (blazing stars)
Lilium species (lilies)
Lobelia species (cardinal flower, lobelias)
Lupinus perennis (wild lupine)
Monarda fistulosa (wild bergamot)
Monarda punctata (spotted beebalm)
Panicum virgatum (switchgrass)
Penstemon species (beardtongues)
Phlox species (phloxes)
Pycnanthemum tenuifolium (narrow-leaf mountainmint)
Ratibida species (prairie coneflowers)
Rudbeckia species (coneflowers)
Schizachyrium scoparium (little bluestem)
Silene regia (royal catchfly)
Silphium species (rosinweeds)
Solidago species (goldenrods)
Sorghastrum nutans (Indiangrass)
Symphyotrichum species (asters)
Thalictrum dasycarpum (purple meadow-rue)
Verbena species (vervains)
Vernonia species (ironweeds)
Veronicastrum virginicum (Culver's root)
Viola species (violets)
Yucca glauca (soapweed yucca)
Zizia species (alexanders)

Monarch butterfly caterpillars rely on members of the genus *Asclepias* (milkweeds) for their food. The more milkweeds you have in your garden, the greater the chance you will see monarch butterflies.

Blazing stars are among the top prairie plants for attracting butterflies, including monarchs.

In addition to host plants, butterflies need mud puddles or other wet areas, and they need shelter—shrubs, trees, and bushy flowers where they can hide from birds, find shade at midday, and rest at night. They also look for basking stones, where

Attract even more birds to your prairie garden by installing birdhouses.

they can build up enough body heat to fly, and windbreaks to temper the wind.

BIRDS

Birds have three basic requirements for survival, and many prairie plants provide them with some aspect of the food, water, and shelter they need. Some prairie natives, such as cup plant, provide all three. Hummingbirds are attracted to its bright yellow flowers, and goldfinches and other birds seek out the seeds for food; the leaves form cups that collect and hold rainwater for drinking and bathing; and the large, stiff plants offer shelter. Most prairie gardens won't be large enough to attract nesting birds, which prefer a minimum of an acre of habitat, but studies show that even small native landscapes serve as mini stopover refuges for migratory birds, helping to compensate for the loss of large expanses of natural habitats (Tallamy 2007).

Liatris, *Echinacea*, *Symphyotrichum*, *Rudbeckia*, *Helianthus*, and *Solidago* species are important food sources for goldfinches and other seed-eating birds. But remember that most birds are insectivores. You want to be sure to have a diversity of plants to attract a diversity of insects, aka food, for birds.

Ideally your prairie garden will have nearby trees and shrubs for birds to nest and where they can roost and find shelter from the elements. You can also supplement nesting sites by erecting nesting boxes in your prairie garden. Have fresh water available for drinking as well as for bathing.

Among the favorite feathered friends

PRAIRIE PLANTS TO ATTRACT HUMMINGBIRDS

Asclepias species (milkweeds)
Baptisia species (wild indigos)
Campanula rotundifolia (harebell)
Ceanothus americanus (New Jersey tea)
Chelone glabra (white turtlehead)
Dalea purpurea (purple prairie clover)
Echinacea species (purple coneflowers)
Gaillardia species (gaillardias)
Heliopsis helianthoides (smooth oxeye)
Heuchera richardsonii (prairie alumroot)
Liatris species (blazing stars)
Lilium species (lilies)
Lobelia cardinalis (cardinal flower)
Lupinus perennis (wild lupine)
Monarda fistulosa (wild bergamot)
Oenothera species (evening primroses)
Penstemon species (beardtongues)
Phlox species (phloxes)
Physostegia virginiana (obedient plant)
Pulsatilla patens (pasque flower)
Ruellia humilis (fringeleaf wild petunia)
Silene regia (royal catchfly)
Silphium perfoliatum (cup plant)
Symphyotrichum species (asters)
Thalictrum dasycarpum (purple meadow-rue)
Verbena species (vervains)

visiting any garden is the hummingbird. Most hummingbird-attracting flowers are tubular in shape and many are red, though certainly not all. A successful hummingbird planting provides nectar sources from spring through the first frost.

Cup plant (*Silphium perfoliatum*) is one of the best plants for birds, providing food, water, and shelter.

Planting Your Garden

Planting a prairie garden really isn't different from planting a traditional garden. Your biggest decision will be seeds vs. plants, or perhaps you will use both in combination. Most grassland plants are relatively easy to start from seeds. Others are best as transplants; these include *Sporobolus heterolepis*, *Veronicastrum virginicum*, *Heuchera richardsonii*, and *Gentiana* and *Lilium* species. If you plan to use both seeds and plants, place your potted plants first, then seed around them.

Obviously seeds take longer to produce a showy end product, but they are less expensive and there are often more choices available than with plants. If you will be seeding a large area you may want to consider a suitable seed mixture developed by a reputable native plant propagator in your area. Absolutely stay away from nationally available "meadows in a can," which often contain nonnative plants that end up becoming weeds. Nonnative plants that can be found in these mixes include *Chicorium intybus* (chicory), *Daucus carota* (Queen Anne's lace), *Hesperis matronalis* (dame's rocket), *Leucanthemum vulgare* (oxeye daisy), *Lotus corniculatus* (bird's-foot trefoil), *Lupinus succulentus* (hollowleaf annual lupine), *Papaver rhoeas* (annual poppy), *Saponaria officinalis* (soapwort), and *Securigera varia* (crown vetch).

Seeding can be done in spring or fall. The main thing is to avoid the heat of summer, when rainfall is less and the seeds may not germinate. If you seed in spring, wait until all danger of a hard freeze is past so you won't lose tender seedlings to frost. Many seeds won't germinate until the soil has warmed a little. Fall seeding, which is more like what happens in nature, can be done from about mid-September until the ground freezes. Another option is dormant seeding, which is done after the ground freezes and allows the seed to stratify naturally over the winter. One drawback of this method is that the exposed seeds may be eaten by birds and rodents. Plan to increase your seeding rate if you use this method.

Seeding rates vary depending on the species you are including, the ratio of grasses to forbs, the quality of the seed, and the time of year you are seeding. The nursery you purchase your seeds from will provide information about seeding rates based on the make-up of their individual mixes. In general a diverse, high-quality mixture of forbs and grasses should be sown at a rate of about 12 pounds per acre. This translates to about 3 pounds per 10,000 square feet of garden, or about 80 seeds per square foot if you know a seed count. If you go too light you will have a lot of bare ground for weeds to move in. If you go too heavy you may just be wasting seed because the seedlings will crowd each other out.

Broadcast the seed right after the final cultivation or rototilling on a calm day so you don't lose seeds to wind. Mix the seed with an inert carrier such as clean sand to bulk it up and make it easier to spread. Divide the seed in half and make two passes over your garden, one going north to south and one going east to west, to ensure good coverage of the site. If you are including some species in small quantities, sow that seed separately in random areas to make sure it gets evenly distributed in your garden. Rake the seed bed gently by hand to shallowly incorporate the seed into the soil. Walking across your newly planted bed a few times will also help with soil to seed contact. Cover the newly seeded garden with 1 to 2 inches of an organic, fine-textured mulch of shredded leaves, clean little bluestem straw, or compost to help hold seeds in place, retain moisture, and reduce weed competition.

Many prairie plants germinate readily with sufficient water and contact with the soil. Others need some sort of cold-moist stratification, which is supplied naturally over winter. Seeds with tough seed coats need to be scarified, or have their coats physically broken before

Largeleaf wild indigo (*Baptisia alba* var. *macrophylla*) is a prairie plant that requires nitrogen-fixing soil bacteria to grow successfully.

Unfortunately, many nonnative plants found in "meadows in a can," such as dame's rocket (*Hesperis matronalis*), are pretty, so people think it's not so bad to have them in their landscapes. But all too often these prolific plants escape to nearby natural areas where they displace native plants, thereby eliminating important food and habitat sources for native fauna.

germination occurs. Some prairie legumes require nitrogen-producing soil bacteria before growing. These include leadplant, milkvetches, wild indigos, showy tick-trefoil, roundhead lespedeza, wild lupine, and prairie clovers. Some garden soils may have these bacteria in them, but as added insurance it is a good idea to purchase the necessary companion inoculum from your seed source. Commercial seed producers often take care of these germination requirements, another good reason to start with a commercially available mix.

More and more prairie plants are becoming available as potted plants, and this is the best way to go if you can afford it. Container plants become established quickly and give you a better-looking garden sooner. The best time to put most plants in the ground is spring, which gives them ample time to become established before they have to endure their first winter in the ground. Summer- and fall-blooming flowers and most woody plants can be planted in spring or fall—actually all season long if you are diligent about watering when needed. You may also need to provide shelter from the sun for a few weeks. Plant or transplant early-blooming species after they flower, usually in late spring. Bare-root plants shipped by mail-order nurseries are another option. These should be planted in spring.

Plant spacing depends on each individual species and how long you want to wait for your garden to fill in, but 9 to 12 inches is good for most plants. Obviously the more plants you can afford, the sooner your prairie garden will be attractive and the fewer weed problems you will

It's a good idea to place labels near your newly planted seedlings to help you identify them and differentiate them from any weeds that may sneak into your garden.

Careful thought should be given to placing silphiums and other plants that don't like to be moved once they are established.

have. However, as with seeding, planting too densely can be a waste of money and effort.

One of the nice things about planting a prairie garden is that you don't typically have to exactly plan where to place each plant. It's more of a random planting, with the plants moving around and establishing themselves as they see fit.

It's still a good idea, however, to have a general idea of where you want certain plants. You may identify an area toward the back where you'd like to place some taller plants. Or, if you have a range of soil moisture types or pH, you will benefit from choosing plants suited to these conditions. And some plants (silphiums, leadplant, milkweeds) have extensive or

The purples and yellows in this midsummer prairie garden are nature's way of providing complementary colors.

deep root systems and don't like to be moved once they are established. Careful thought should be given to placing these plants since they don't respond well to transplanting.

Even though established prairie plants are drought tolerant, young seedlings and new transplants will require watering their first growing season if rainfall is inadequate. One to two inches of water every three days for the first month is a good goal, with additional watering as needed the first growing season. After the first year most plants won't require additional water except in the cases of an extreme dry spell. One thing your newly planted garden won't need is fertilizer. This will only encourage weeds.

Prairie Junegrass (*Koeleria macrantha*) is a cool-season grass that greens up before most prairie grasses. However, it usually turns brown by midsummer, something to keep in mind when using it in a prairie garden.

Prairie Garden Dynamics

In traditional garden design, experts like to remind you to carefully plan for complementary colors, contrasting forms and textures, focal points, and repetition when selecting plants. One of the nice things about using native plants is that nature takes cares of a lot of this for you. Plant communities have evolved to have a diversity of species that have varying characteristics. By choosing plants that have evolved together in a plant community, you end up with a diversity of bloom time, flower color, and plant type.

In natural gardening you are guaranteed changes from year to year, and you'll need to allow for plant movement, dormancy, and even the lack of a species to appear some years. One of the greatest joys of

In general, the more you can allow prairie plants to settle in and develop an interactive community, the more successful your garden will be.

gardening with native plants is being able to observe the changes the plants go through. Native plants can change rapidly—sometimes overnight!—and by growing them in your own landscape you are able to enjoy these changes, which you'd miss if they were occurring miles away in a park or natural area.

If possible, you should try to embrace the natural dynamics of your prairie garden and allow nature to take its course. Some plants, such as black-eyed Susan, gray-headed prairie coneflower, and wild bergamot, are quick to establish and often bloom the first or second year from seed. They usually reseed with abandon, becoming almost weedy in their second or third year; however, they eventually lose ground to slower-to-establish perennials and become a smaller part of the overall planting. Some of the slower-to-establish plants such as prairie shooting star, Culver's root, prairie alumroot, gentians, and compass plant may not contribute much to your garden until they have been in the ground three years or more. And some plants (prairie shooting star, wild lupine, common goldstar, Atlantic camas, prairie violet, Virginia spring beauty, and pasque flower) will go dormant, especially during dry seasons. It's a survival mechanism, and it doesn't mean the plants won't show up again next year. Knowing some of these characteristics of natural plant communities will help you appreciate and enjoy each plant, when it is present, for what it has to offer your garden.

CHAPTER 3

Prairie Plants in Traditional Landscapes

As beautiful as a garden of prairie flowers is, most city and suburban gardeners don't have a large expanse of open, sunny land to devote to such an endeavor. Fortunately, many prairie plants adapt well to traditional landscape use, and many are actually much better suited to the conditions found in urban settings than our typical, overused landscape plants. They tolerate less-fertile soils, reducing the need for synthetic fertilizers. They thrive on less water, reducing water use. And they don't require heavy fossil-fuel input from mowing and trimming.

Prairie plants in a landscape also greatly benefit native fauna. As we lose more and more of our natural areas, landscape plantings become important refuges for our native insects and other wildlife. A University of Delaware study showed that native landscaping reduced biodiversity losses in human-dominated landscapes and positively influenced both avian and lepidopteran communities on six pairs

Drought-tolerant, low-growing prairie plants such as prairie smoke and pussytoes are perfect choices for hot, dry strip gardens.

of suburban properties in southeastern Pennsylvania. Not only were there more caterpillars (and caterpillar species) on the native properties, but "greater bird abundance, diversity, species richness, biomass, and breeding pairs of native species." In particular, "bird species of regional conservation concern were eight times more abundant and significantly more diverse on native properties." (Burghardt, Tallamy, and Shriver 2009)

The goal of this chapter is to encourage you to add prairie plants to your already established landscape and help you do it in a way that is pleasing to you and acceptable to your neighbors. All successful landscapes have certain things in common: plants are tended and cared for, in scale with their surroundings, and suited to the site. When these things are taken into consideration, native plants can be used successfully in any landscape situation.

Native Plants in a Nonnative World

Even with all the benefits of using native plants there are still people who have a

Purple coneflowers, Joe-pye weeds, coneflowers, and monardas are all popular landscape perennials that originated in the tallgrass prairie.

Many well-behaved prairie plants can be used in even the smallest city garden. Pictured here are fringeleaf wild petunia, butterfly milkweed, rattlesnake master, and Michigan lily.

hard time appreciating them in traditional landscape settings, and city and suburban gardeners will be most successful if they keep this in mind. It is usually best to start small and go slow. Try to let your neighbors know beforehand what you are planning. Nothing will turn them off faster than tilling up the entire front yard one day and seeding it in prairie plants. Start by incorporating native plants into existing landscaped areas and then move on to larger areas and entire gardens. Follow nature's lead and let your native plantings evolve slowly.

Education is key. Take every chance you get to teach your neighbors about this intricate plant community. Any time you see a neighbor outside, invite them over to look at a flower or butterfly in your yard. Encourage them to walk through your landscape so they can see some of the important details that may be missed from the outside. An easy way to educate people about what you are doing is to install a sign indicating that this is a native plant landscape; Wild Ones (www. for-wild.org) and many native plant nurseries are sources of such signs. Some people even install "welcome to my garden" signs to invite visitors to enter and walk around. If you do this, make sure to include plenty of obvious pathways to welcome people and help them experience these plants. A bench placed along a path will tell visitors it is okay to stop and enjoy your landscape.

Be sensitive to the people around you and approach any conflict calmly and reasonably. Many of your neighbors may have lived in their homes for decades and are used to a certain look and feel in their neighborhood. An attitude of self-righteousness and arrogance will only make things worse. Be aware of city ordinances, and get to know the laws in your city or township. If they don't allow for the use of native plants, go through the proper channels to try to obtain a variance or get an ordinance changed.

Showing Intent

When it comes to acceptably incorporating prairie plants into traditional landscapes, the most important thing is to show intent rather than neglect. If you live in an urban area and need to be cognizant of what your neighbors and city officials think, or if you just prefer a more traditional, well-tended look, there are many things you can do to make prairie plants look less "wild." By incorporating traditional design principles and maintenance practices that illustrate that your landscape is cared for and intentional, you'll show people you haven't just allowed "weeds" to move in and take over. I have seen many examples of people who have used native plants successfully in urban settings and just as many examples of misuse of these plants. Of course, the same can be said for landscapes using traditional exotic plants.

CHOOSE THE RIGHT PLANTS
Most prairie plants will bring a relaxed, natural look to traditional landscapes. It's just their nature. They've evolved to be survivors and haven't been bred and hybridized to always stand up straight, be

Wild Ones provides its members with signs that identify native plantings as a maintained and cared-for landscape or garden.

constantly covered with showy flowers, or stay green all winter long. The result is that some prairie plants are just too aggressive, tall, coarse, or floppy for traditional landscape situations.

If you want a traditional-looking landscape or are using prairie plants in your front yard you'll want to stick with plants with a more controllable growth habit. These tend to be clump-forming plants rather than spreaders. You'll probably also want to avoid using excessively tall plants; the front yard is probably not the place for cup plant or Indiangrass.

USE TRADITIONAL PLANTING METHODS

Another way to help your landscape look more tended is to use traditional planting and design methods. Plant in groups of three, five, or seven plants as is more typical of nonnative landscapes. Limit your

Clump-forming bunchgrasses such as *Schizachyrium scoparium* (little bluestem) have a nice, neat, mounded form and are better choices for small landscapes than rhizomatous, spreading grasses.

number of species, and maybe even consider a simple planting of one species, such as a planter devoted to little bluestem. Use "upscale" mulches such as cocoa bean hulls or shredded bark. For a more planned look, repeat a few specific plant groupings or color schemes at intervals throughout the landscape. Include some areas of visual calm where the eye can rest momentarily from stimulation. Green lawns, a small grouping of silver-leaved plants, or a simple green-leaved deciduous or evergreen shrub all create spots of calm.

CUT BACK TALLER PLANTS IN FALL

Although it's not something I usually advocate because of their benefits to wildlife, consider cutting back at least some of your taller plants in fall. This won't harm the plants. The truth is, prairie plants are

Use traditional landscaping practices such as mulching, limiting your number of species, and equal spacing to introduce familiarity and predictability into a native plant landscape.

brown in winter and not everyone finds this attractive. One of the biggest objections city officials and neighbors will have about using prairie plants is that they look "dead" and "weedy" in winter. And, as you are probably realizing, natural gardening in urban settings is all about compromises. So if it gets you through the process without too many issues, it may be worth cutting back your taller plants in fall, especially those growing in the front yard. In time your neighbors may come to appreciate the benefits your natural landscape has in all seasons, including winter.

INCORPORATE STRAIGHT LINES

Most landscape designers will tell you to incorporate curved lines, especially when designing garden beds. They do this to encourage a natural look and they are right—there are very few perfectly straight lines in nature. And that is precisely why including some in your landscape will help give it a tended look. Native plants won't mind growing in linear gardens. Chances are your landscape already has several straight edges in it in the form of fences, driveway edges, and hedges. If you are installing a patio or

Not everyone finds prairie plants attractive in winter when they are brown and often flopping over. It may be worth cutting back taller plants in late fall to help appease cranky neighbors.

In this urban landscape, a fence and small square area of lawn both
bring straight lines to the otherwise natural-looking plantings.

deck, consider a square or rectangular form to bring a more-controlled look to your native plants.

INSTALL A BUFFER

It's a good idea to keep taller plants away from public areas such as sidewalks and entry areas. People get nervous when they have to walk by herbaceous plants—especially grasses—that are taller than they are. Use a buffer of lawn or mulch between planted areas and sidewalks and streets so plants don't flop over onto the paved areas and make visitors and passersby uncomfortable.

PLAN FOR YEAR-ROUND INTEREST

Prairie habitats peak in summer and fall, so it can be challenging to get year-round interest when using these plants in the landscape. Choose plants with varying

A border of traditional turfgrass separates these taller prairie plants from the driveway.

Many prairie plants, especially warm-season grasses such as little bluestem, don't have much to offer the landscape in early spring. Make sure to include some plants that green up early in spring, such as prairie smoke, nearby.

bloom times to ensure that there is something happening in your landscape all year long. Incorporate spring bloomers such as prairie smoke, violets, and pasque flower as a distraction from the brown hummocks of the grasses. Many fall bloomers survive several degrees of frost, prolonging the growing season. Evergreens are great for setting off the seed heads of grasses in the winter landscapes. Allow goldenrods, milkweeds, rattlesnake master, Joe-pye weeds, and grasses to remain through the winter so their dried flower heads can provide visual interest as well as food for birds. Remember that there are other qualities, such as persistent fruits and seedpods, that offer interest year-round. Place an emphasis on plants with interesting foliage shapes and textures, since foliage is usually decorative for much longer than flowers.

Prairie Plants as Design Elements

Most of what I've advocated in this book focuses on using prairie plants in groupings or small communities. However, some prairie plants have strong architectural qualities that allow them to be used as accent plants in unconventional ways. Others work well as groundcovers or austere plantings using only one or two species. While this may not be as beneficial to native fauna, it is still a better option than turning to nonnative plants. Here are some examples of ways to use prairie plants as design elements in traditional landscapes.

Amorpha canescens (leadplant) can be pruned into interesting shapes.

Anemone cylindrica (candle anemone) has interesting seed heads.

Baptisia australis var. *minor* (blue wild indigo) has good structure; bold, blue foliage; and large, dark-colored seedpods.

Bouteloua species (grama grasses),

A mono-planting of one prairie grass, such as little bluestem (*Schizachyrium scoparium*), has a strong contemporary look in the landscape.

Heuchera richardsonii (prairie alumroot), *Opuntia* species (pricklypears), *Schizachyrium scoparium* (little bluestem), and *Sporobolus heterolepis* (prairie dropseed) make interesting mono-plantings or groundcovers.

Carex pensylvanica (Pennsylvania sedge) can be used as a fine-textured groundcover in shade.

Eryngium yuccifolium (rattlesnake master) and *Yucca glauca* (soapweed yucca) make interesting bold-textured focal points.

Monarda punctata (spotted beebalm) has uniquely colored bracts.

Silphium laciniatum (compass plant), *S. terebinthinaceum* (prairie rosinweed), and *Veronicastrum virginicum* (Culver's root) make interesting focal points for their cutleaf foliage, tropically oversized leaves, and strong, upright presence, respectively.

A single plant of rattlesnake master (*Eryngium yuccifolium*) is a focal point in this mixed border.

Using Cultivars

As native plants become more popular, many are being selectively cultivated to produce different varieties. These cultivated varieties, or cultivars, are usually chosen for certain characteristics (flower color, larger or double flowers, leaf color, compact growth habit) and are propagated vegetatively to maintain the traits.

CULTIVARS TO CONSIDER

Asclepias incarnata (swamp milkweed): 'Cinderella', 'Ice Ballet', 'Soulmate'

Boltonia asteroides (white doll's daisy): 'Nana', 'Pink Beauty', 'Snowbank'

Coreopsis grandiflora (largeflower tickseed): 'Domino', 'Early Sunrise', 'Flying Saucers', 'Robin', 'Sundance', 'Sunray'

Coreopsis lanceolata (lanceleaf tickseed): 'Double Sunburst', 'Goldfink', 'Sterntaler'

Gaillardia ×*grandiflora* (hybrid blanketflower): 'Arizona Sun', 'Burgundy', 'Dazzler', 'Goblin', and others

Helenium autumnale (autumn sneezeweed): 'Crimson Beauty', 'Dakota Gold', 'Helena Gold', 'Helena Red Shades', 'Indian Summer', 'Moerheim Beauty', 'Rubinzwerg' [Ruby Dwarf], and others

Heliopsis helianthoides (smooth oxeye): 'Prairie Sunset', 'Summer Nights', 'Summer Sun'

Liatris spicata (dense blazing star): 'Kobold'

Panicum virgatum (switchgrass): 'Amber Wave', 'Dallas Blues', 'Heavy Metal', 'Northwind', 'Rotstrahlbusch', 'Shenandoah'

Penstemon digitalis (foxglove penstemon): 'Husker Red'

Penstemon hirsutus (hairy beardtongue): 'Pygmaeus'

Physostegia virginiana (obedient plant): 'Miss Manners', 'Olympus Bold', 'Variegata', 'Vivid'

Rudbeckia hirta (black-eyed Susan): 'Becky', 'Cherokee Sunset', 'Indian Summer', 'Prairie Sun', and others

Schizachyrium scoparium (little bluestem): 'The Blues'

Symphyotrichum ericoides (white heath aster): 'Blue Star', 'Esther', 'Pink Star', 'Snow Flurry'

Symphyotrichum lateriflorum (calico aster): 'Lady in Black', 'Prince'

Symphyotrichum novae-angliae (New England aster): 'Andenken an Alma Pötschke', 'Hella Lacy', 'Honeysong Pink', 'Purple Dome', 'Roter Stern' [Red Star], 'Wedding Lace', and others

Symphyotrichum oblongifolium (aromatic aster): 'October Skies', 'Raydon's Favorite'

Native plant purists will argue that cultivars are not truly native and should not be used in native landscaping. Because they are vegetatively propagated and each plant is exactly alike, they do not contribute to genetic diversity like seed-grown plants. They may also lose some of their attractiveness to native fauna. Pollinating insects may no longer be attracted to a new flower shape or color, and chewing insects may not feed on leaves if the leaf chemistry has been changed. These cultivars also run the risk of escaping and contaminating natural stands, where they

Liatris spicata 'Kobold'

Penstemon digitalis 'Husker Red'

Panicum virgatum 'Rotstrahlbusch'

can alter the genetic make-up of the original species.

My thought is that while many prairie plants have a lot to offer the landscape, the truth is that there are certain native species that are just too coarse and unrefined to be used in traditional landscape settings. There are a lot of improved cultivars that are better behaved. I'd rather have people use cultivars of native plants instead of continuing to use the same old exotic plants, many of which are proving to be serious problems for our remaining natural areas and require high inputs of fossil fuels, water, and chemicals.

Incorporating Hardscapes and Ornaments

The hardscape includes all the nonplant elements in a landscape. It is made up of functional features such as patios, decks, pathways, driveways, sidewalks, fences, compost bins, and other storage structures as well as more-decorative items such as containers, arbors, and pergolas. Native plants don't mind growing next to these nonplant items, so don't be afraid to use them with your prairie plants. A well-designed, attractive hardscape is one of the best ways to show intent rather than neglect in your native plant landscape.

Chances are most of your hardscape is already in place, but if it isn't, or if you are looking to enhance it, you have a wonderful opportunity to create a backdrop for native plants. Put an emphasis on developing a hardscape that is just as good for the environment as your native plants are. Stay away from plastics, which not only rely on fossil fuels but also just don't look as natural with prairie plants.

Stones, found in many native prairies, are good materials to use with native plants. Stone looks good as a flooring

Symphyotrichum novae-angliae 'Purple Dome' with *Solidago rugosa* 'Fireworks'

material on patios and paths, and it makes very attractive walls and fences. You can even include stones in your garden beds. Just be sure to snuggle them down into the ground at least halfway so they look natural. Refrain from just placing a large prized rock out in the middle of the lawn or at the end of the driveway.

Wood is another good material for hardscapes in natural landscapes. Wood benches and decks look right at home with prairie plants. The wood you use should come from managed forests or plantations where it is sustainably harvested. Use cedar, oak, or other naturally rot-resistant woods whenever practical. If you want to use treated wood, stick with those treated with copper-based products rather than the highly toxic chromium- or arsenic-based chemicals, which can leach into the soil and persist for a long time.

For accent and embellishment, rusted

Planting prairie plants close to a home and patio area allows you to get a close look at these plants and the butterflies and other insects they attract.

Gravel and stone are nice materials to use with prairie plants.

This rustic upright sculpture is the perfect accent piece in this prairie
garden at Shaw Nature Reserve in Gray Summit, Missouri.

iron sculptural pieces blend nicely with the casual look of a prairie landscape. Sundials are nice additions to gardens featuring these sun-loving plants. Birdbaths made of ceramic or stone are practical as well as beautiful. But don't be afraid to add anything that makes you happy and adds to your enjoyment of the space, including gazing balls, handmade decorations, wind chimes, and even pink flamingos!

Xeriscaping

Xeriscaping is landscaping that promotes water conservation by using drought-tolerant, well-adapted plants within a landscape carefully designed for maximum use of rainfall runoff and minimum care. It is most common in western and southern states where rainfall is lower and water use is more regulated, but it is good to follow the principles

The well-designed prairie garden at the Minnesota Landscape Arboretum provides many examples of how to incorporate prairie plants with various hardscapes.

Most prairie plants are more tolerant of hotter, drier conditions than typical landscape plants but some, such as purple coneflowers and rattlesnake master, are tougher than others and are good choices for xeriscaping.

behind water-wise gardening in any landscape. Prairie plants are naturals for xeriscaping since many of them tolerate the hot, dry conditions required for these water-efficient landscapes.

There are other things to keep in mind besides plant selection for effective xeriscaping. Before planting, determine whether soil improvement is needed for better water absorption and improved water-holding capacity, and mix compost or peat moss into soil before planting to help retain water. Reduce water runoff by building terraces and retaining walls.

Use high-maintenance turfgrasses as a planned element in the landscape. Avoid impractical turf use, such as long, narrow areas, and use it only in areas where it provides functional benefits. Plant groundcovers and add hard-surface areas like patios, decks, and walkways where practical. Raise mower blades to get a higher cut. Taller grass encourages grass roots to grow deeper, making stronger, more drought-resistant plants.

Properly timed pruning, weeding, pest control, and irrigation all conserve water. Install drip or trickle irrigation systems in those areas that need watering, and use timers and water-control devices to increase their efficiency even more. Apply organic mulch to reduce water loss from the soil through evaporation and to increase water penetration during irrigation.

Lawns in Native Landscapes

Nothing says "tended landscape" better than a carpet of turfgrass. But keep in mind that a lawn is a monoculture with little to offer the environment. It is best to think of lawn areas as part of the hardscape rather than part of the greenscape. Give a lawn the same consideration you give a patio or deck, and consider the high maintenance costs, both to you and to the environment.

Remember that "lawn" doesn't necessarily have to be made up of high-maintenance Kentucky bluegrass. There are some native prairie grasses that withstand occasional mowing and can be used as substitutes for the traditional turfgrasses so often turned to for certain activities, such as a children's play area or a spot for the family pet. These grasses can't take weekly mowing like traditional turfgrasses, but they do make environmentally friendly groundcovers in areas where the main objective is to cover the ground with something that can withstand use by people and pets. This list includes *Bouteloua* species (grama grasses and buffalograss), Pennsylvania sedge, prairie Junegrass, little bluestem, and prairie dropseed.

A few prairie plants can be allowed to naturalize in a lawn, creating more of a meadow effect. These are Virginia spring beauty, longleaf summer bluet, and common goldstar.

Trees, Shrubs, and Vines in Prairie Landscapes

Most landscapes require more than just grasses and flowers. Although it is true our native prairies did not support a large number of woody species, those species that were found in scattered areas (listed in the appendix) should be considered for landscape use with prairie plants where appropriate. Tree and shrub species increased as prairies blended into neighboring savanna communities and woodlands. Many of these native woody species do well in conditions similar to prairie plants and have a lot to offer in terms of function, beauty, and wildlife attraction.

No tree is more indicative of America's prairies than the oak, and it is a wonderful choice for landscape use. Not only are oaks beautiful but they are long-lived, and they support more species of butterflies (and thus provide more bird food) than any other plant (Tallamy 2007). Unfortunately most oaks are just too big for urban situations. If you have the space, dwarf chinkapin oak (*Quercus prinoides*) and

'Mo-Buff' buffalograss (*Bouteloua dactyloides*) used as a lower-maintenance turfgrass at Shaw Nature Reserve.

pin oak (*Q. palustris*) are good choices for landscape use. Other good native tree to consider for larger sites are Kentucky coffeetree (*Gymnocladus dioicus*) and river birch (*Betula nigra*).

Most landscapes require smaller trees, however. They are in better scale in city and suburban settings, and they don't threaten overhead power lines and create problems of too much shade as they get older. Good small trees for use with prairie plants are hophornbeam (*Ostrya virginiana*), American hornbeam (*Carpinus caroliniana*), and prairie crab apple (*Malus ioensis*).

Native shrubs, especially those native to prairie edges and savannas, tend to be suckering plants. This is a survival method for these plants, which were continually eaten by grazing and chewing

Oaks are wonderful trees for prairie gardens, especially large gardens and open landscapes where they have room to fully develop their canopy.

Serviceberries (*Amelanchier*) are excellent native woody shrubs for landscape use, and the larger species are easily pruned into attractive small trees.

animals. While suckering shrubs can be an asset in natural plantings and on problem sites, suckering is not a trait that carries well into most traditional landscapes. If you want to use a prairie or savanna shrub, you probably will have to commit to doing some annual pruning of suckers if you want your shrubs to maintain a certain shape. Personally, I find dormant pruning to be an enjoyable winter task—a way to keep my green thumb busy during the winter months. However, it is definitely a maintenance issue and not one that everyone wants to add to their list.

If you'd prefer a shrub that is a little better behaved in the landscape, there are several North American shrubs to consider. Some that do well in conditions similar to prairie plants include chokeberries (*Photinia*), junipers (*Juniperus*), ninebarks (*Physocarpus opulifolius* cultivars), serviceberries (*Amelanchier*), shrubby cinquefoil (*Dasiphora fruticosa* ssp. *floribunda* cultivars), and *Viburnum* species and cultivars.

Vines were rare in prairies, but several vines native to other natural habitats are good choices if you are looking for something to cover a wall or climb up an arbor. Consider *Aristolochia macrophylla* (Dutchman's pipe), *Campsis radicans* (trumpet creeper), *Celastrus scandens* (American bittersweet), *Parthenocissus quinquefolia* (Virginia creeper), and *Wisteria frutescens* (American wisteria).

If you want to use exotic trees and shrubs in your landscape, avoid planting species known to be invading local natural areas and causing habitat destruction.

This list includes such familiar landscape plants as *Acer ginnala* (Amur maple), *A. platanoides* (Norway maple), *Ailanthus altissima* (tree of heaven), *Ampelopsis brevipedunculata* (porcelain berry), *Berberis* species (barberries), *Caragana arborescens* (Siberian peashrub), *Celastrus orbiculatus* (Oriental bittersweet), *Elaeagnus angustifolia* (Russian olive), *Euonymus alatus* (burningbush), *E. fortunei* (winter creeper), *Ligustrum vulgare* (European privet), *Lonicera* species (honeysuckles), and *Sorbus aucuparia* (European mountain ash). For an up-to-date list of invasive species (including natives that are invasive outside their natural ranges), refer to the Invasive Plant Atlas of the United States at www.invasiveplantatlas.org.

Prairie Plants for Special Situations

As pointed out in chapter 1, the prairie ecosystem is not always a kind one, and many of the plants that evolved there tend to be strong of stature and resilient, characteristics that don't always translate well to formal landscape situations. These characteristics do, however, lend themselves to use in some of the more challenging or functional areas of a landscape.

BOULEVARD OR PARKING STRIPS

As prevalent as they are in urban landscapes, boulevard or parking strips (also known as hell strips or tree lawns) are often neglected when it comes to landscaping. This is unfortunate since these narrow areas between the sidewalk and the street are in plain view of anyone who visits or passes by on the sidewalk.

There are many reasons to garden on boulevard strips. (Many of these same principles can be applied to other areas in the landscape that are long and narrow, such as the area between the house and the driveway or a foundation planting on the south or west side of a building.) From a gardening standpoint, they offer extended opportunities for space-starved urban gardeners. From an environmental standpoint, they can be very effective at keeping grass clippings out of the street and storm sewers.

But boulevard strips are among the most challenging spots to grow and maintain plants. The soil is usually compacted and low in fertility and often gets bombarded with road salt in winter. They are

Prairie plants that are great choices for strip gardens include prairie alumroot, prairie smoke, and pussytoes.

usually hot, dry, and sunny—unpleasant conditions for tending, and often the garden hose doesn't reach that far, creating maintenance issues. Consequently, most strips remain covered with poorly grown turfgrasses or weeds. If they are gardened, they are typically filled with high-maintenance annual plants that often end up looking worn and tattered by midsummer and can actually be worse

PRAIRIE PLANTS FOR A SUNNY STRIP GARDEN

Allium cernuum (nodding onion)
Allium stellatum (autumn onion)
Amorpha canescens (leadplant)
Anemone cylindrica (candle anemone)
Antennaria species (pussytoes)
Asclepias tuberosa (butterfly milkweed)
Bouteloua species (grama grasses)
Callirhoe species (poppymallows)
Campanula rotundifolia (harebell)
Ceanothus americanus (New Jersey tea)
Coreopsis grandiflora (largeflower tickseed)
Coreopsis lanceolata (lanceleaf tickseed)
Dalea purpurea (purple prairie clover)
Gaillardia ×grandiflora (hybrid blanketflower)
Geum triflorum (prairie smoke)
Heterotheca villosa (hairy false goldenaster)
Heuchera richardsonii (prairie alumroot)
Houstonia longifolia (longleaf summer bluet)
Hypoxis hirsuta (common goldstar)
Koeleria macrantha (prairie Junegrass)
Liatris cylindracea (Ontario blazing star)
Liatris mucronata (cusp blazing star)
Liatris punctata (dotted blazing star)
Liatris squarrosa (scaly blazing star)
Lupinus perennis (wild lupine)
Monarda punctata (spotted beebalm)
Oenothera macrocarpa (bigfruit evening primrose)
Penstemon gracilis (lilac penstemon)
Penstemon hirsutus (hairy beardtongue)
Phlox bifida (sand phlox)
Phlox pilosa (prairie phlox)
Pulsatilla patens (pasque flower)
Ratibida columnifera (upright prairie coneflower)
Rudbeckia hirta (black-eyed Susan)
Ruellia humilis (fringeleaf wild petunia)
Schizachyrium scoparium (little bluestem)
Sisyrinchium species (blue-eyed grasses)
Sporobolus heterolepis (prairie dropseed)
Symphyotrichum ericoides (white heath aster)
Symphyotrichum novae-angliae (New England aster, dwarf cultivars)
Symphyotrichum sericeum (western silver aster)
Verbena stricta (hoary verbena)
Viola species (violets)

from an environmental standpoint than the weeds.

Many prairie plants, with their ability to withstand these hot, dry, and often sunny conditions, are a good choice for these strips, but it is best to stick with low-growing clumping plants. Try to stay away from prolific self-seeders because even a couple extra plants can make this small space look weedy. Any plant growing over a foot in height will probably need to be cut back in fall, and plan on cutting back any remaining plants in spring and raking off the debris.

Soil preparation takes a little extra thought in a strip garden. Good soil drainage is key since you need the water to percolate down rather than run off. You want your soil line slightly below the sidewalk and curb heights to make sure no soil washes away. This usually means that you will have to remove some of the soil before planting. Cover your new bed with a 1- to 2-inch layer of mulch to hold the soil and reduce weed competition while the prairie plants become established. Don't mulch too thickly or you run the risk of the mulch washing away.

Many wet-soil and mesic prairie plants are good choices for use in rain gardens.

Parking strip gardeners must also consider public safety and civic issues. Install a path clearly in sight, of ample width, and free of vegetation so people can see where to cross the strip. Make sure your plants don't block people's ability to see at intersections. Be aware of any city ordinances that govern the boulevard strip. In most communities, homeowners own the space between the sidewalk and the street but the city has the legal right to enter this utility-filled area. Be aware that the city may need to dig up the strip or sidewalk to repair and upgrade utilities, and you will be responsible for repairing any damage.

RAIN GARDENS

By now everyone should be aware of the environmental benefits of trying to keep rainwater on site to replenish groundwater supplies rather than allowing it to wash away down storm sewers and into nearby wetlands. A well-designed rain garden absorbs 30 percent more water than turf lawns and puts it to work on your property. It will hold excess water for a short time so that it can slowly soak into the

Culver's root (*Veronicastrum virginicum*) is a good choice for rain gardens.

soil within a few days after an average storm.

Entire books have been written on rain gardens, and you should refer to these for specific information about where to place your rain garden and how to plant and maintain it. Deep-rooted prairie plants, especially those native to mesic or wet soils, are naturals for rain gardens.

Even though a rain garden is primarily

PRAIRIE PLANTS FOR RAIN GARDENS

Allium cernuum (nodding onion)
Andropogon gerardii (big bluestem)
Anemone canadensis (Canadian anemone)
Asclepias incarnata (swamp milkweed)
Asclepias sullivantii (prairie milkweed)
Baptisia alba var. *macrophylla* (largeleaf wild indigo)
Boltonia asteroides (white doll's daisy)
Camassia scilloides (Atlantic camas)
Carex species (sedges)
Chelone glabra (white turtlehead)
Coreopsis tripteris (tall tickseed)
Deschampsia cespitosa (tufted hairgrass)
Eupatoriadelphus maculatus (spotted Joe-pye weed)
Eupatorium perfoliatum (common boneset)
Filipendula rubra (queen of the prairie)
Gentiana species (gentians)
Helenium autumnale (autumn sneezeweed)
Liatris ligulistylis (northern plains blazing star)
Liatris pycnostachya (prairie blazing star)
Liatris spicata (dense blazing star)
Lilium michiganense (Michigan lily)

Lobelia species (cardinal flower, lobelias)
Panicum virgatum (switchgrass)
Penstemon digitalis (foxglove penstemon)
Phlox glaberrima (smooth phlox)
Physostegia virginiana (obedient plant)
Pycnanthemum tenuifolium (narrowleaf mountainmint)
Ratibida pinnata (gray-headed prairie coneflower)
Rudbeckia subtomentosa (sweet coneflower)
Rudbeckia triloba (brown-eyed Susan)
Schizachyrium scoparium (little bluestem)
Silphium laciniatum (compass plant)
Silphium perfoliatum (cup plant)
Solidago rigida (stiff goldenrod)
Sorghastrum nutans (Indiangrass)
Symphyotrichum novae-angliae (New England aster)
Thalictrum dasycarpum (purple meadow-rue)
Tradescantia species (spiderworts)
Verbena hastata (swamp verbena)
Vernonia species (ironweeds)
Veronicastrum virginicum (Culver's root)
Zizia aurea (golden alexanders)

a functional aspect of a landscape, it can still be attractive both to you and to the butterflies, birds, and beneficial insects that visit it. Vary the height, shapes, and textures of plants to give the garden interest. Consider bloom time, with a goal of creating color all season long. Rather than one of everything, site species in groups of three to seven plants to give a bolder splash of color and texture. Incorporate grasses and sedges, both for natural support and to add interest. And don't be afraid to ornament your garden with appropriate accent pieces.

SHADED SITES

Most established landscapes have some areas of shade, from trees on their property or on the neighbor's side of the fence, or along the north and east sides of buildings. Shade can be an asset or a challenge in a landscape depending on how you look at it. You definitely have fewer choices when it comes to showy flowering plants, but shady spots are a welcome respite in summer and a wonderful showcase for spring wildflowers.

Obviously prairie ecosystems are full-sun habits, so they aren't going to be the best choices for shady spots. Remember, though, that bordering oak savannas were home to many prairie plants that tolerated the partial shade under tree canopies and among the shrub thickets. The oak savannas segued into oak woodlands, and these are good plant communities to emulate if

Bloodroot (*Sanguinaria canadensis*) is a very showy, spring-blooming savanna plant that can tolerate the dry shade found under large trees.

you have the dry shade often found under large trees and near buildings.

Don't rule out experimenting with sun-loving prairie plants in semishade areas. Most will grow fine as long as the soil conditions are suitable. Be prepared for fewer flowers, and most plants will grow a little taller and lankier with less sunlight. You'll still get the advantages these plants have to offer, in terms of wildlife attraction, seasonal interest, and habitat creation.

SAVANNA AND OAK WOODLAND PLANTS FOR SHADY AREAS

Actaea pachypoda, A. rubra (baneberries)*

Anemone quinquefolia (wood anemone)*

Aquilegia canadensis (Canada columbine)*

Aralia nudicaulis (wild sarsaparilla)*

Arisaema triphyllum (Jack in the pulpit)*

Asclepias purpurascens (purple milkweed)

Athyrium filix-femina (lady fern)*

Carex pensylvanica (Pennsylvania sedge)*

Chelone glabra (white turtlehead)

Claytonia virginica (Virginia spring beauty)

Cypripedium species (yellow lady's slipper)

Deschampsia cespitosa (tufted hairgrass)

Dicentra cucullaria (Dutchman's breeches)*

Dodecatheon meadia (prairie shooting star)

Elymus hystrix (eastern bottlebrush grass)

Geranium maculatum (spotted geranium)*

Hepatica species (hepaticas)*

Heuchera species (alumroots)

Lilium michiganense (Michigan lily)

Lobelia species (cardinal flower, lobelias)

Maianthemum canadense (Canada mayflower)*

Phlox divaricata (wild blue phlox)*

Polemonium reptans (Jacob's ladder)

Polygonatum biflorum var. *commutatum* (smooth Solomon's seal)*

Sanguinaria canadensis (bloodroot)*

Thalictrum dasycarpum (purple meadow-rue)

Thalictrum dioicum (early meadow-rue)*

Thalictrum thalictroides (rue anemone)*

Trillium grandiflorum (white trillium)*

Uvularia grandiflora (largeflower bellwort)*

Uvularia sessilifolia (sessileleaf bellwort)*

*plants that tolerate full shade

SEPTIC FIELDS AND MOUNDS

Prairie plants, especially grasses and forbs with shallower root systems, are good choices for planting on septic fields and mounds. Herbaceous plants actually enhance the operation of septic systems by removing the wastewater and nutrients from the soil and keeping them out of the groundwater, and their roots won't grow into the pipes like many woody plant roots do. Plant cover also helps reduce soil erosion from these sites.

Prairie plants are good choices because many grow well in sandy or gravelly soil and are tolerant of the higher soil pH that may result from some of the household

Pennsylvania sedge (*Carex pensylvanica*) is a wonderful groundcover for use in full to partial shade areas of landscapes.

chemicals that may make it into your system. The best choices are those plants that can become established and cover the ground while still offering an attractive alternative to turfgrasses, which have no wildlife benefits and require much more maintenance. Prairie plants are also good because they do not require supplemental irrigation, which can be harmful to a system.

There are a couple of things to keep in mind when planting over a septic field or mound. Don't till or double dig the soil. Remove any weeds before planting and then plant directly into the soil and cover the area with a mulch to keep weeds down until plants become established. In general, plan to plant the area and then let it fend for itself for the most part (another good case for prairie plants). This isn't a garden you're going to want to spend time in, tending high-maintenance plants. Always wear gloves when working with the soil to avoid direct contact with any harmful organisms that may be present.

Rhizomatous prairie grasses are good low-maintenance choices for covering the ground over a septic system.

PRAIRIE PLANTS TO PLANT OVER SEPTIC SYSTEMS

Allium cernuum (nodding onion)
Allium stellatum (autumn onion)
Andropogon gerardii (big bluestem)
Antennaria species (pussytoes)
Asclepias tuberosa (butterfly milkweed)
Boltonia asteroides (white doll's daisy)
Bouteloua species (grama grasses)
Callirhoe species (poppymallows)
Campanula rotundifolia (harebell)
Coreopsis grandiflora (largeflower tickseed)
Coreopsis lanceolata (lanceleaf tickseed)
Dalea species (prairie clovers)
Echinacea species (purple coneflowers)
Euphorbia corollata (flowering spurge)
Gaillardia species (gaillardias)
Geum triflorum (prairie smoke)
Helenium autumnale (autumn sneezeweed)
Helianthus species (sunflowers)
Heliopsis helianthoides (smooth oxeye)
Heuchera richardsonii (prairie alumroot)
Hypoxis hirsuta (common goldstar)
Koeleria macrantha (prairie Junegrass)
Liatris species (blazing stars)
Lupinus perennis (wild lupine)
Monarda fistulosa (wild bergamot)

Monarda punctata (spotted beebalm)
Opuntia species (pricklypears)
Penstemon species (beardtongues)
Phlox species (phloxes)
Pulsatilla patens (pasque flower)
Rosa species (wild roses)
Rudbeckia species (coneflowers)
Ruellia humilis (fringeleaf wild petunia)
Schizachyrium scoparium (little bluestem)
Silene regia (royal catchfly)
Sisyrinchium species (blue-eyed grasses)
Solidago species (goldenrods)
Sorghastrum nutans (Indiangrass)
Sporobolus heterolepis (prairie dropseed)
Symphyotrichum ericoides (white heath aster)
Symphyotrichum laeve (smooth blue aster)
Symphyotrichum oblongifolium (aromatic aster)
Thalictrum dasycarpum (purple meadow-rue)
Tradescantia species (spiderworts)
Verbena stricta (hoary verbena)
Viola species (violets)
Zizia species (alexanders)

CHAPTER 4

Maintaining Prairie Plants

For a lot of people, the initial appeal of using native plants in the landscape comes from their desire to go "no maintenance." And a long-term goal of creating a prairie garden is often to create a sustainable community that requires little or no effort on your part. This is in great contrast to a traditional landscape or garden, where human intervention is constant and necessary to keep things looking as planned.

Any experienced gardener knows there is no such thing as a no-maintenance garden or landscape. That said, once a prairie garden or native landscape is established, it should not need nearly as much care and tending as a traditional garden or landscape. Because these plants have evolved in and adapted to North America's grasslands, one of the toughest ecosystems out

A well-maintained prairie planting adds beauty and interest to a neighborhood as well as fostering a greater appreciation and understanding of this native plant community.

there, they tend to be cold hardy, wind resistant, and drought tolerant.

The need to water is all but eliminated once these plants are established, and the need for pesticides to kill insects or diseases is absent or rare. If you go one step further and use prairie plantings to replace areas of traditional lawn, you will reduce your need for weekly mowing and all the other maintenance issues that come with growing turfgrasses. This leaves you time for the more pleasurable gardening tasks such as grooming, transplanting and moving plants, and adding new plants. Your end goals when it comes to maintenance should be to have a garden or landscape that is pleasing to you, is good for the environment, and is easily maintained at a level that suits your time and interest.

Weeding

Keeping out unwanted plants, be they exotic weeds or native plants that are a bit too prolific, is the biggest maintenance task in prairie gardens and native landscapes. The most effective way to fight weeds is to do all you can to eliminate them before you put any plants or seeds in the ground. Once a garden or landscape is planted, it is important to get the desirable plants established and covering the ground as quickly as possible. A dense planting definitely reduces the potential for invasion by weeds.

Weeds come in from many sources, including neighbors' yards, surrounding fields, visiting birds, and even the wind. Without their natural controls to keep them in check, these weedy species

quickly take hold and often take over. Humans brought the majority of these weeds to our gardens, and human intervention is definitely needed to keep them in check.

An important first step in the war with weeds is to be able to identify which plants are weeds as early in their life cycle as possible. This is challenging, especially for new gardeners who are afraid to pull seedlings because they think they may be desirable plants rather than weeds. Experience will help overcome this fear. Invest in a good weed identification guide and use it regularly. *Weeds of the Northern U.S. and Canada* (Royer and Dickinson 1999) is a good choice because it includes color photographs of weeds at various stages of their life cycle, including the seedling stage.

Remember, weeds are easiest to pull when they are young and the soil is moist. A weekly weed-pulling walk through your garden should be enough to keep most weeds under control. You want to pull them before they go to seed or overtake desirable plants. Be sure to remove the entire root system or rhizome but be careful not to uproot neighboring prairie plants. Use a weeding tool to get leverage if needed.

Annual and biennial weeds can usually be controlled by making sure they aren't allowed to reseed. This means removing flowers before they go to seed. In a small garden and in landscape plantings, hand pruning every couple of weeks should suffice. In a large garden, a properly timed mowing is usually quite effective in the first year or two of establishment. Most seeded prairie plants don't grow much taller than 6 inches in their first year, so if you have an abundance of annual weeds you can mow or weed-whip them before their flowers go to seed without doing too much damage to your prairie plants.

Although you may use mowing as a method of weed control in the early years of a garden, mowing should be done only once a year after the first or second year. If you mow too often, you will hinder the growth of the warm-season grasses and perennial forbs (see "Burning or Mowing" later in this chapter for more information).

Perennials and woody weeds are much more difficult to control. Learn to spot perennial weeds (including prolific reseeding prairie plants) in their seedling stage so you can get them out while they are young and easy to pull, and definitely before they go to seed. If you are dealing with persistent perennial weeds such as Canada thistle (*Cirsium arvense*) or quackgrass (*Elymus repens*) and hand pulling has not been effective, you may

Most weeds have their origins in Europe or Asia, but not all. Certain genera of native plants, such as *Solidago*, *Eupatorium*, *Heliopsis*, and *Helianthus* (shown here), include species that can become weedy in small gardens and landscapes.

want to consider spot treatments with a nonselective herbicide such as Roundup. To apply it without harming yourself or nearby desirable plants, choose a calm day; protect yourself with long sleeves, safety glasses, and gloves; and carefully but thoroughly spot spray individual weeds.

The only good thing about woody weeds is that they are obviously easier to identify at a young age. They should be pulled as soon as you see them. It only takes one growing season for most woody plants to become hard to eradicate by hand pulling.

Mulching

Mulching is a good way to keep weeds out of your landscape plantings and can also be effective in smaller prairie gardens. However, mulching is effective only when placed on soil where the existing weeds have been removed. Organic mulch also holds water in the soil and improves fertility at a slow and steady pace.

Mulch prairie gardens at planting time with a light layer of chopped, weed-free straw 1 to 2 inches deep. Avoid shredded bark or wood chips, which can be too coarse and take a long time to break down. Once prairie gardens are established, they can be left unmulched, but it certainly won't hurt to top dress with compost annually.

Landscape plants will grow best with an organic mulch such as shredded leaves, but they can be mulched with materials such as shredded bark or cocoa bean hulls if you want a more decorative look. Avoid

black plastic and rock mulch, which is not a good choice for any landscape plant.

About the only time you'll need to winter-mulch prairie plants is if you are growing plants that aren't reliably hardy in your area (or the first winter after planting if you planted in fall). Winter mulch offers added protection from cycles of freezing and thawing, which can result in frost heaving of plants. It should be laid down after the ground has frozen to keep the cold in. If you put it down too early it acts as an insulator, and the ground can remain warm too long. Winter mulch should be removed in early spring just as the plants begin poking above ground.

Watering

One of the main attractions of using native prairie plants is to reduce or even eliminate the need for supplemental watering. If you've chosen plants correctly for your conditions, established plants will rarely need supplemental watering. In fact, since most prairie plants are adapted to soil on the drier side, too much water often leads to problems such as root rot and the rampant growth of moisture-loving weeds. Some of your established prairie plants may go dormant during extremely dry conditions, but they should come back the next year. You may want to do some supplemental watering in the front yard during dry periods to keep things green and growing instead of going dormant, to appease the neighbors and passersby.

Almost all plants, drought-tolerant natives included, need supplemental water during establishment. Keep soil adequately moist until new plants have a full year of new growth on them. If you are planting in an established prairie garden, mark the new plants so you water them only as needed and don't end up overwatering the entire planting.

Any trees, shrubs, or vines you include in your prairie garden or landscape need to be watered regularly for at least the first full year after planting. In hot weather they may need supplemental water once or twice a week. If autumn is dry, continue watering until the first hard frost. An organic mulch spread from near the trunk to at least as far as the drip line will help hold soil moisture as well as reduce competition from weeds for available moisture. Once fully established, after three to four years, most native woody plants should not need supplemental watering.

Fertilizing

Possibly one of the best arguments for growing prairie plants is their ability to grow in soils lower in fertility than most exotic landscape plants require. Most soils will be able to support a wide array of prairie species without the need for additional fertilizers or soil amendments. Soil that is too fertile is usually more of a problem, since fertile soils favor the establishment of weedy species and can also cause prairie species to grow too lush and lank.

Unless a soil test indicates that your soil is significantly lacking in one or more of the necessary nutrients, you shouldn't need to add fertilizers. Incorporating organic matter into the soil before planting and on an annual basis in established gardens should be all your prairie plants need in the way of added fertilizers.

Use a stake to mark newly planted seedlings so you can find them later in the summer to provide the supplemental water they may need.

An upside-down tomato cage was put around *Heliopsis helianthoides* 'Summer Nights' when it was still small to provide support for this tall plant.

Grooming

Obviously native plants don't receive any grooming in the wild, and they survive just fine. However, there are a few tasks that will help plants grow better and keep your landscape looking more tended, which is especially important if you have a front-yard garden in the city. The amount of grooming you do will depend on which prairie plants you are growing, where you are growing them, and how much time you like to spend tending your plants.

STAKING

In the natural world, prairie grasses create natural support for taller forbs such as gray-headed prairie coneflower and autumn sneezeweed. In landscape situations some artificial help may be in order, however.

Many support systems using hoops and sticks of wood or metal are available from nurseries and home improvement stores. Use small tomato cages for bushy plants. Long-stemmed plants will need a stake for every blooming stem. Get stakes in the ground as early as possible to avoid root damage, and loosely tie plants to the stake with inconspicuous green or brown twine.

If you don't want the maintenance of staking, consider using lower-growing bushier plants or selecting dwarf or compact cultivars of taller growing species. A prime example is New England aster. The species itself can grow to 6 feet tall, and plants often topple over in garden settings before they've even had a chance to bloom. To enjoy the late summer color and insect-attracting traits offered by

Symphyotrichum novae-angliae, select one of its many dwarf cultivars, such as 'Andenken an Alma Pötschke', 'Purple Dome', or 'Roter Stern' [Red Star].

REDUCING PLANT HEIGHT

Although it definitely adds to your maintenance, cutting back taller summer- and fall-flowering prairie species in spring reduces plant height and encourages more compact growth, making these plants more suitable for landscape use. It will also reduce or eliminate the need for staking. Cutting back can also be used to stagger bloom times, extending the period of bloom for certain species. For gardeners, who typically enjoy tending and caring for plants, this extra effort greatly expands the list of prairie plants suitable for landscape use.

Cutting back of plants by one-half to two-thirds must be done early enough in the growing season so as not to delay flowering too long. This timing will vary in different areas of the country. In the Upper Midwest, for example, it is best not to do any cutting or pinching back after early June. Where the growing season is longer, you could cut back plants up to about mid-June. It is best to do a little experimenting each year to see how your plants react to cutting back. A good reference for these techniques is *The Well-Tended Perennial Garden* (DiSabato-Aust 2006).

These plants can be cut back in spring to reduce their overall height and make them better suited for landscape use in smaller spaces.

Part of this planting of smooth oxeye (*Heliopsis helianthoides*) was cut back by about half in midspring to stagger bloom time. The plants in the foreground will bloom a week or so later than those in the background, which were not cut back.

PRAIRIE PLANTS THAT CAN BE CUT BACK

Boltonia asteroides (white doll's daisy)

Eupatoriadelphus maculatus (spotted Joe-pye weed)

Helenium autumnale (autumn sneezeweed)

Helianthus salicifolius (willowleaf sunflower)

Heliopsis helianthoides (smooth oxeye)

Heterotheca villosa (hairy false goldenaster)

Physostegia virginiana (obedient plant)

Rudbeckia subtomentosa (sweet coneflower)

Symphyotrichum novae-angliae (New England aster)

Tradescantia species (spiderworts)

Vernonia species (ironweeds)

Veronicastrum virginicum (Culver's root)

DEADHEADING

Deadheading is a common maintenance task in traditional landscapes, especially those that rely heavily on annuals. Removing spent flower buds does help stimulate prolonged and repeated blooming on many prairie perennials as well. Cut back to the next set of leaves to encourage new buds to open. Think twice before deadheading plants that provide bird food and winter interest, however. A better option

than deadheading might be to try to select plants with varying bloom times so you have something else coming into bloom when one plant is finished.

Deadheading also reduces unwanted seed production on plants that tend to set a lot of seed and can become weedy. This is another one of those compromise situations that every gardener needs to decide for themselves. Obviously cutting off spent flower heads eliminates seeds that provide food for wildlife. However, if you allowed every flower to set seed you would be overwhelmed with seedlings in just one growing season. Again, I put forth the argument that it is still better to use native plants and have to deadhead some species rather than resort to non-native plants that have much less to offer native fauna and can become problems in natural habitats.

DIVIDING AND TRANSPLANTING

Most prairie plants growing in mixed borders and foundation plantings will benefit from being divided every three to four years. Dividing prevents overcrowding and keeps the plants healthy, vigorous, and more prone to flower production. It also provides a way to get more plants for your garden or to share. The best time to divide most plants is early spring, so they have a full growing season to recover. To divide herbaceous plants, unearth the plant with a spade or trowel, remove excess soil from roots, pull or cut apart rooted sections, and replant as soon as possible.

Some prairie plants with deep taproots do not respond well to attempts to divide or replant them. These include butterfly milkweed, silphiums, leadplant, and purple poppymallow. Be sure to give careful thought to site selection before planting. If they have outgrown their spot, do the best you can to get as much of the taproot as possible and move the plants in early spring.

Each Plant Profile includes a section on maintenance that talks about what plants benefit from dividing and which ones prefer to be left alone.

FALL CLEAN UP

Cutting back prairie plants in fall is definitely a point of controversy and another decision that each gardener must make based upon their own situation. There's no denying that a prairie planting can look a bit tattered and worn at the end of the growing season, especially when it's still in its developmental years. However, a lot of prairie plants offer winter interest as well as important food sources and shelter for birds and other wildlife.

Whether or not you decide to cut back your prairie plants in fall is really a matter of aesthetics. It doesn't affect how the plants grow. With many nonnative plants, a fall cutting back is recommended to reduce the chances of diseases and insects overwintering. This isn't as much of a factor with prairie plants since they aren't really plagued by pests and diseases that overwinter in plant parts. Some gardeners like to cut back some of the rougher-looking plants in fall and allow the showier plants to remain until spring. This also has the advantage of spreading out the maintenance.

Although beautiful, upright prairie coneflower (*Ratibida columnifera*) is a prolific seed producer. Consider deadheading landscape plants before they set seed to reduce unwanted seedlings.

Burning or Mowing

Two characteristics of natural prairies were that they were constantly under invasion by woody species and they generated a lot of organic matter each growing season. Fire, either started by lightning or set by indigenous peoples, was the natural solution to keeping both of these traits in check. Fire rejuvenated a prairie by reducing competition from weedy species, getting rid of dead plant parts, increasing available soil nutrients, and opening up the soil to sunlight so seeds could germinate and plants could start growing earlier in spring.

Some people find the natural fall browning of prairie plants objectionable, so it may be worth cutting back some of the taller plants—especially those growing in the front yard—to appease neighbors.

Prescribed burning is not a realistic option for most landscape situations, but if you do have a large enough garden in a rural area it will do wonders for your garden. Be sure to take precautions and enlist professional help if needed. Conservation groups in your area may offer burn courses or welcome your help as a volunteer where you can gain experience. As beneficial as they are to plants, fires can be very damaging to wildlife living in your prairie garden. Ideally you should burn only one-third of your prairie every three to five years and vary the time of year you burn to benefit both cool- and warm-season prairie plants as well as avoid total destruction of wildlife and habitat.

A better alternative to burning for most prairie gardeners is to remove the excess vegetation by mowing or using a string trimmer. The best time for this is spring, once any snow is gone and the soil and plants are dry enough to work with but before new growth is 10 to 12 inches tall.

You will probably need to hand cut some of the largest plants before mowing or trimming. Set the mower blade 4 inches above the soil level and slowly go back and forth to get an even cut. Don't cut all the way to the ground, or you may damage the plant crowns. Leave about 2 inches of stubble. If you use a mulching mower you can usually leave the small clippings right on the garden. If you are using a weed whip or scythe, you will

Prairie plants quickly recover and start growing after the soil has been warmed by a burn.

need to rake off the loose debris. If possible, make several small piles of the debris along the edges of your garden so that any beneficial insects or their eggs can continue their life cycle. The debris is also a great addition to the compost pile.

Although you may use frequent mowing as a method of weed control in the early years of a prairie garden, mowing should be done only once a year after the first or second year. If you mow too often, you will hinder the growth of the warm-season grasses.

Possible Problems

This is where prairie plants have a definite advantage over nonnative plants. If you've spent some time preparing your site and matching plants to it, your problems should be few and not serious, especially if you have beneficial insects in your landscape to offer natural pest control. Prairie grasses especially are rarely bothered by insects or diseases.

The key in pest management is to really get to know your gardens and the plants in them. Keep your eyes open on daily walks. If you spot a problem, identify it correctly (get help from a local expert, if needed), find out what is causing it, and decide if it is serious enough to warrant attention. Most pest problems are purely cosmetic and won't do any long-term damage to your plants. You have to decide what your level of tolerance is and determine whether you want to take action or live with the problem.

Keep in mind that many problems are due to cultural conditions rather than insects or diseases. Yellowing or browning foliage, stunted growth, and buds that rot before opening could be signs that you have poor soil drainage or your plants are overcrowded. Once again, making sure you have the right plant for the site and the appropriate soil conditions is the best way to avoid such problems.

DISEASES AND VIRUSES

Diseases are rare on prairie plants. If they do occur, they are rarely serious and can usually be prevented the next year by altering cultural practices, such as changing watering habits or thinning out some plants. Prevention in the form of good site selection and proper planting distance is the best way to avoid disease problems. If disease problems become severe, you'll need to pull up the infected plants and choose another plant for that site.

Aster yellows can be a problem on several genera of prairie plants, including *Gaillardia*, *Echinacea*, and *Symphyotrichum*. It is caused by a viral-like organism that is spread by leafhopper feeding. Plants become discolored and have irregular, stunted growth and often flowers do not open. There is no cure for plants infected with aster yellows. It is usually best to dig up infected plants and find something else better suited to the location. *Rudbeckia* species can be afflicted with several leaf spot diseases, especially when they are grown in landscapes and gardens where overhead watering is used and the disease organisms are easily splashed from plant to plant. While these diseases rarely kill plants, they can make the foliage quite unsightly. Here again, there is probably a better plant choice for these garden situations.

Powdery mildew is often seen on native plants, both in the wild and in gardens. To reduce chances of infection, increase air circulation by pruning out inside branches and removing some nearby plants. If you want to make the effort to control this disease on landscape plantings, try the baking-soda-based spray developed at Cornell University: mix 1 tablespoon baking soda and 1 tablespoon horticultural oil with 1 gallon of water; spray each plant completely about once a week, starting before infections appear. It's a good idea to test the spray on a few leaves before spraying the entire plant to make sure the spray won't do more damage than the disease.

Angular leaf spot is a common problem on the popular *Rudbeckia fulgida* var. *sullivantii* 'Goldsturm'.

Powdery mildew is one of the few diseases that afflicts prairie plants, and it can leave the leaves of wild bergamot (*Monarda fistulosa*) looking pretty sad by the end of summer.

INSECTS

The first thing to keep in mind when talking about insects in a garden is that most are not only harmless but are vital to the health of a garden or landscape. Tallamy (2007) points out, "Of the 9 million or so insect species on earth, a mere 1 percent interact with humans in negative ways.

Avoid using insecticides of any kind in your landscape. They not only kill beneficial insects, but they also disrupt the ecological balance you are trying to create by using native plants.

The other 99 percent of the insect species pollinate plants, return nutrients tied up in dead plants and animals to the soil, keep populations of insect herbivores in check, aerate and enrich the soil, and . . . provide food either directly or indirectly for most other animals." He also makes the case that these beneficial insects can survive in a landscape or garden only if there are "enough different types of prey available for them at all stages of their life cycle."

In fact, some insect damage is a good thing. It shows that your garden is a bio-diverse habitat providing important food sources for the native insects that are the basis of our entire food chain. Consequently, the first thing you need to do with insects is accurately identify them as friend or foe. Some of the well-known "good guys" are predators such as lady beetles, walking sticks, wasps, and praying mantis. But the list of insects that should also be considered beneficial based on their importance as bird food includes such unlikely candidates as grasshoppers and locusts, plant bugs, lace bugs, leafhoppers, and spiders. Dragonflies are important mosquito eaters, and remember that those hungry caterpillars turn into beautiful butterflies and moths. Even tent caterpillars have a good side; they are a favorite food of many birds, including black-billed and yellow-billed cuckoos (Nowak 2007). If you can tolerate their unsightly "webs," the caterpillars may reward you by attracting some of these elusive birds to your own landscape.

Aphids and leaf miners are among the most prevalent insect pests on prairie plants. In most cases, neither will be life-threatening to your plants. They can be tolerated in larger gardens, but in landscape situations these insects will make your plants unsightly. Aphids tend to be bigger problems during hot, dry spells. They especially like smooth oxeye, asters, black-eyed Susan, and phloxes. If you see aphids on your plants, give them daily blasts of water with your garden hose to dislodge the insects before they can become too numerous.

Keep in mind that most prairie plants can tolerate quite a bit of insect feeding before they are actually harmed by it. As you increase the number of native plants in your landscape, you will eventually increase the population of birds and natural insect predators that will help keep the bad insects in check.

Most of the major garden insect pests' first choices for food are nonnative plants. Japanese beetle larvae feed on turfgrass roots. Hybrid tea roses are magnets for Japanese beetles and aphids. The bronze birch borer prefers European white birch (*Betula pendula*) to our native river birch.

Even if you do have a large population of Japanese beetles or another devastating feeder, it's still never worth it to use insecticides. Not only are they toxic to you and your garden guests, they destroy too many beneficial insects. If an insect problem becomes so bad that the health of your plant is questionable, you should consider replacing the plant with something better suited to the conditions. It's cruel to lure wildlife to your landscape and then use herbicides, insecticides, and other pesticides that can poison and destroy them.

OTHER ANIMAL PESTS

Deer and rabbits are usually more serious problems than any insects that may visit your native plant landscape or garden. They are also much more difficult to control. There are many repellents available. All are temporary solutions, however, and they require a lot of time and effort to be effective, especially against deer.

Owning a large dog can be effective in deterring deer. But the best long-term solution for a serious deer problem is to install some type of fencing, which must be at least 8 feet tall to be effective. You can also make plant choices based on deer feeding. For starters, plant a wide variety of plants so an entire section of your landscape won't be eliminated in one meal. Although no plant can really be considered "deer proof" under all conditions, deer generally avoid aromatic plants, plants with thorns, and plants with leathery, fuzzy, or hairy foliage. Rabbit fences should be 3 feet tall and made of a wire mesh too dense for them to squeeze through.

Planting patterns can deter deer as well. Deer do not like to cross hedges or solid fences where they can't see what's on the other side. They do not like to force their way through dense shrubs, or shrubs with thorns and firm branches. By massing plants, you will discourage deer from feeding in the center of the planting, where you can plant more-susceptible plants.

No plant can be counted on to be resistant to deer feeding, but these plants are less favored by deer and other herbivores.

Deer and other herbivores tend to stay away from plants with fuzzy leaves, such as hoary verbena (*Verbena stricta*).

PRAIRIE PLANTS LEAST LIKED BY DEER

Allium species (wild onions)
Andropogon gerardii (big bluestem)
Anemone species (anemones)
Asclepias species (milkweeds)
Boltonia asteroides (white doll's daisy)
Bouteloua species (grama grasses)
Carex pensylvanica (Pennsylvania sedge)
Chelone glabra (white turtlehead)
Echinacea species (purple coneflowers)
Eryngium yuccifolium (rattlesnake master)
Eupatoriadelphus maculatus (spotted Joe-pye weed)
Eupatorium species (bonesets)
Euphorbia species (spurges)
Filipendula rubra (queen of the prairie)
Gaillardia species (gaillardias)
Gentiana species (gentians)
Geum triflorum (prairie smoke)
Helenium species (sneezeweeds)
Monarda fistulosa (wild bergamot)

Monarda punctata (spotted beebalm)
Panicum virgatum (switchgrass)
Parthenium integrifolium (wild quinine)
Penstemon species (beardtongues)
Physostegia virginiana (obedient plant)
Pulsatilla patens (pasque flower)
Pycnanthemum species (mountainmints)
Rudbeckia species (coneflowers)
Schizachyrium scoparium (little bluestem)
Sisyrinchium species (blue-eyed grasses)
Solidago species (goldenrods)
Sorghastrum nutans (Indiangrass)
Verbena species (vervains)
Vernonia species (ironweeds)
Veronicastrum virginicum (Culver's root)
Viola species (violets)
Yucca glauca (soapweed yucca)

Keeping a Record

One of the real benefits of bringing native plant communities into your own landscape is that you will be able to observe bloom times, plant movement, and interactions between plants and the animals that visit your garden. Most gardeners enjoy keeping some sort of record of these activities and comparing them from year to year.

To be most effective, start your record-keeping before you even put a shovel in the dirt. Make a scale (or close to scale) drawing of your garden or landscape, and note what is growing on the site and where it grows. This will be very helpful with weed identification later on. Start with a clean drawing each spring, and note where things show up so you can track the movement of plants. Keep track of bloom times and plant combinations that you especially like. As the years go by, note what works well on your site and where you want to make changes.

Keep a list of everything you planted

and when you planted it, especially if you seeded. You may not see some plants for several years. It will help you with plant identification if you know what went into your garden. But remember that just because something wasn't on your initial plant list doesn't mean you may not see it there. There is always the chance that native prairie plants will move in and become established once you create this desirable habitat—definitely another one of the joys of gardening with native plants!

Keep track of all your maintenance, noting what you do, when you do it, and what chemicals and tools you use. Take

Part of the fun of growing prairie plants is watching the changes the individual plants go through in a growing season as well as noting yearly changes in the overall planting.

pictures of weed seedlings so you can identify them in future years. Note when weeds go to seed so the next year you can be ready to mow or cut off flower heads before they seed again. Include clippings from Web sites and magazines that will help with plant identification and care. Include notes about the wildlife you see and the plants it is attracted to.

Make sure your recordkeeping system is user friendly so you will use it regularly. As efficient as computers are at storing data, it is still not practical to carry one out with you into the garden. Get yourself a notebook small enough to fit in a pocket so you'll carry it with you on your walks through your garden or around your landscape. Transfer your notes at a later time to a database or spreadsheet so you can manipulate and sort the information and develop helpful reports such as a list of flowering dates and a maintenance calendar.

PLANT PROFILES

Every tallgrass prairie plant plays a role in the prairie ecosystem, and most of them can be used in prairie habitat gardens. This section focuses on tallgrass prairie plants that will do well in typical landscape situations.

All the plants presented here are native to the tallgrass prairie of North America. Some have ranges that extend into mixed and even shortgrass prairies; they are better suited to drier, leaner soils. Others have ranges that extend into eastern oak savannas; they are good choices for areas in the landscape that get less sunlight. None of the plants (except *Carex pensylvanica*) will do well in full shade, however.

Most of the plants profiled, whether flowers, or grasses, or sedges, are hardy perennials that will survive almost anywhere in zones 3 through 9, provided their soil, sunlight, and moisture requirements are met. There are a few annuals.

It was a difficult task to whittle down the list of species to what could be accommodated in the pages of this book. The

Many prairie plants are suitable for traditional landscape use, even in a small front yard.

plants included here were selected based on their suitability for a variety of landscape situations and their availability from typical outlets, including specialty native plant nurseries. Some genera, including *Andropogon*, *Silphium*, *Rosa*, *Opuntia*, *Pycnanthemum*, *Vernonia*, and *Filipendula*, may be limited in their use in traditional landscape situations but are included because of their importance in the tallgrass prairie and the niches they fill such as in rain gardens, in butterfly gardens, or for naturalizing on tough sites.

It should go without saying that all these plants will be suitable for use in prairie gardens. The appendix recaps these and additional species that should be considered for prairie garden use.

USING THE PLANT PROFILES

Plants are listed alphabetically by genus, in two separate sections, first flowers and then grasses and sedges. The most recognized common name is included. Family names are given so you can start to develop a feel for which plants are related. Plant taxonomy is a dynamic science, and botanists are always fine-tuning genera, species, and varieties as they learn more about these plants. My main reference for plant names was the PLANTS database at plants.usda.gov. Alternative botanical and common names are included as cross references in the index.

Hardiness information is based on my own experience, the plant's native range, and various gardening references. These zone listings should be used only as a guide, especially since many of these plants have not been used extensively in landscape situations and their hardiness is not fully known. Many factors besides temperature come into play when it comes to a plant's ability to survive in an area, including snow cover, soil texture, and annual precipitation.

Native habitat lists the typical soil conditions and plant communities where the plant grew before the natural landscape was substantially affected by European settlement. It is based on several sources, but mainly comes from the Native Plant Information Network (NPIN) found at www.wildflower.org/explore and *Tallgrass Prairie Wildflowers* (Ladd and Oberle 2005). I have opted to not waste space listing specific states where the plants were originally found. These state lists can be misleading, since often a plant was found only in a small part of the state. These plants evolved in ecological areas and don't acknowledge political boundaries. If you really want to find out which plants were native in your area, you should consult a reference specific to your area, such as your state's Natural Heritage Program or Department of Natural Resources Web site, or lists available from local native plant nurseries and regional native plant organizations.

Mature height, unless somehow qualified, is the typical height of the plant in flower after it is fully established in a garden or landscape. Remember that many factors can affect plant height, including available sunlight, soil moisture, and fertility levels.

Description includes the plant's growth habit, flowering and foliage characteristics, and seasonal interest.

Site requirements addresses sunlight and soil conditions and are mainly intended for landscape use but can be applied to differences within prairie gardens as well. Full sun means at least six hours of direct sun daily. Part sun is roughly three to six hours of direct sun a day. Terms such as "average," "lean," and "rich" refer to soil fertility and the amount of nutrients available to plants. "Well-drained" and "moist" refer to the soil's ability to hold moisture. Most prairie plants do best in a well-drained soil of average to lean fertility, but some like a little more soil moisture and higher fertility. Most prairie plants are adaptable to a soil pH ranging from roughly 5.5 to 7.0. When plants require soil pH outside of this range, it is noted.

Landscape use offers suggestions on how to use the plant in traditional landscapes and gardens. (It is a given that all these plants are good choices for prairie gardens!)

Wildlife attraction is gathered from various sources but mainly the NPIN and Illinois Wildflowers Web site at www. illinoiswildflowers.info/index.htm. Keep in mind that not all native fauna are found in all areas of North America.

Maintenance is for traditional landscape and garden situations. Maintenance of the plant in prairie gardens is given only when it differs from the general information in chapters 2 and 4. I have also included information about the plant's toxicity to humans when it is available.

Good companions are other North American native species, mainly other tallgrass prairie plants, that are good choices for planting with the featured species in landscapes and gardens. They are suggested because they complement the plant in some way, including bloom time, color, texture, and ability to provide a backdrop or fill in an area if the profiled plant goes into dormancy.

Cultivars, if any, are selections of the species with characteristics so different they warrant consideration for landscape use. Whenever possible, species and natural varieties indigenous to your area should be used, especially in prairie gardens, to ensure genetic diversity.

Other prairie species (usually of the same genus) may not be as well known or well adapted for landscape use as the profiled species but are certainly worth considering, especially in prairie gardens. Some species are just as good for landscape use as the main plant, and it was just a coin toss to decide which species got top billing.

FLOWERS

Using prairie flowers in the landscape is a wonderful way to enjoy these fascinating plants on more of an individual basis. Their showy blooms, various sizes and forms, and interesting leaves will bring color, seasonal interest, and contrasting shapes and textures to traditional settings. Many are attractive to butterflies, birds, and bees, and some are even good for cutting and drying. Others are more functional, offering erosion control on a slope or attractive ways to deal with other problem areas in the landscape.

Many prairie flowers are well suited to traditional garden and landscape use. Some you may already know and grow. Wild bergamot, butterfly milkweed, Joe-pye weed, asters, and black-eyed Susan are all commonly grown in perennial beds and mixed borders. Although most are hardy perennials, a few are annuals, and a few (leadplant, New Jersey tea, prairie roses) are shrubs that grow more like herbaceous perennials and are often best treated this way in the landscape.

Colorful and almost carefree, prairie flowers are suitable for a wide range of landscape situations.

137

The most common family represented in the tallgrass prairie is Asteraceae, the composite family, which includes asters, blazing stars, sunflowers, coneflowers, and silphiums. Other prominent families of prairie forbs are Fabaceae (bean, pea, or legume family) and Rosaceae (rose family). Families well represented but with fewer species include Apiaceae (parsley or umbel family), Asclepiadaceae (milkweed family), Campanulaceae (bluebell or harebell family), Iridaceae (iris family), Liliaceae (lily family), Orchidaceae (orchid family), and Scrophulariaceae (snapdragon family).

Prairie forbs are categorized as either cool- or warm-season plants, based on when they put on most of their growth and start blooming. Cool-season forbs typically bloom and set seed before midsummer, and warm-season forbs bloom between midsummer and frost.

Allium cernuum

NODDING ONION
Liliaceae
Zones 3 to 9

Native habitat: Mesic to dry prairies, open woodlands, and rocky outcrops, mainly in the eastern portion of the tallgrass region.

Mature height: 12 to 18 inches

Description: Nodding onion grows from bulbs that look like miniature versions of cultivated onions. The grasslike, flattened leaves grow about 12 inches long in neat clumps that resemble chives. The nodding flowers are held nicely above the foliage on slightly bent stems. They can be white to pink to lavender and bloom for about a month starting in midsummer. The papery seed heads are decorative in autumn. All parts of the plant have a mild oniony scent when crushed.

Site requirements: Average to rich, moist to dry, well-drained soil in full to part sun. Soil pH neutral to slightly alkaline.

Landscape use: Nodding onion adds a touch of lavender to summer gardens. Use it in rock gardens, in the front of mixed borders, along pathways, in rain gardens, and in containers. The foliage is attractive into late summer, and the papery dried seed heads are decorative in autumn. The leaves can be used in cooking similar to chives.

Wildlife attraction: Attracts hairstreak butterfly and pollinating bees. Deer usually avoid this plant but may feed on young shoots.

Maintenance: Nodding onion is easy to grow. Plants will naturalize by self-seeding and expand outward by bulb offsets in optimum growing conditions but rarely become pesky. Deadhead flowers before seeds set to control unwanted seedlings. Divide plants every third year or so in early spring or as they go dormant to promote better flowering.

Good companions: Nice companions include fringeleaf wild petunia, black-eyed Susan, blazing stars, purple coneflowers, and obedient plant. Rattlesnake master, little bluestem, and switchgrass are good background plants.

Allium cernuum

Other prairie species: *A. canadense* (meadow garlic) is native in open woods and prairies throughout most of the tallgrass region. It grows 8 to 12 inches tall and is sparser in leaf and flower than either nodding onion or autumn onion and blooms earlier, starting in late spring. It is also more invasive and difficult to control, so it should be used mainly in prairie gardens. It tolerates partial shade. Zones 3 to 8.

A. stellatum (autumn onion) is frequent in dry prairies and rocky sites, often associated with limestone, throughout most of the tallgrass region. It has smaller, rose to pink flowers that are more upward-facing when open and bloom a little later than *A. cernuum*. Plants grow 6 to 12 inches tall. It does well in cultivation when grown on a sunny exposure in a limy, rocky soil. Zones 3 to 8.

Amorpha canescens

LEADPLANT

Fabaceae

Zones 3 to 9

Native habitat: Loamy or sandy, moist to dry prairies, savannas, open woods, and barrens throughout most of the tallgrass region.

Mature height: 2 to 3 feet

Description: Leadplant is a semi-woody, loose shrub that has attractive flowers and foliage. The showy flowers consist of numerous spiked clusters of tightly packed, small, purple flowers with bright yellow anthers. It blooms from early to midsummer for about three weeks. The pinnately compound leaves and stems are covered in dense, woolly, gray hairs, giving plants a grayish color.

Site requirements: Prefers dry, average, well-drained soil in full to part sun.

Landscape use: Use leadplant in mixed borders and shrub plantings, where its attractive foliage can be enjoyed all season. It is also good for xeriscaping.

Mature woody plants can be pruned into various forms.

Wildlife attraction: Flowers attract bees and wasps. Butterfly and moth caterpillars eat the foliage, along with many other insects that are important bird food. Birds rely on it for perching and cover in treeless prairies. It is a favorite food of deer and rabbits.

Maintenance: Leadplant is easy to grow but slow to develop; flowers take at least four years to appear. Its deep-branching taproot makes it difficult to transplant. A wire fence or cage may be necessary to protect young plants from rabbits and other herbivores. Leadplant requires a nitrogen-fixing soil bacterium; if it is not present, use a commercial soil inoculant when planting. Mulch plants the first winter to prevent frost heaving. Plants can be rejuvenated in spring by cutting them to the ground or pruning out old wood. Leadplant is often treated more like an herbaceous perennial, especially when grown in a mixed border.

Good companions: Hot-colored summer bloomers such butterfly milkweed, prairie roses, and smooth oxeye.

Other prairie species: *A. nana* (dwarf false indigo) is native to dry prairies widely scattered throughout mainly the northern portion of the tallgrass region. It is a shrub growing 1 to 3 feet tall and has fragrant, pinkish flowers in early summer. Use and maintenance are similar to leadplant. Zones 3 to 7.

Amorpha canescens

Anemone canadensis

CANADIAN ANEMONE

Ranunculaceae

Zones 2 to 8

Native habitat: Moist prairies, open woodlands, and near water in the northern half of the tallgrass region.

Mature height: 12 to 18 inches

Description: This perennial has attractive foliage and showy flowers. The long-stalked, snowy white, 2-inch flowers have numerous gold stamens and are held well above the foliage for a nice show. They first appear in mid- to late spring and bloom well into early summer. Leaves are deeply divided into three to seven lobes with toothed margins.

Site requirements: Prefers moist, average to rich soil in full to part sun, but tolerates a wide range of soils. More moisture is required for growing in full sun. Slightly drier soil is tolerated with more shade.

Anemone canadensis

Anemone cylindrica

Landscape use: Despite its aggressive nature, Canadian anemone has its place in the landscape as a low-maintenance groundcover. A large colony is quite striking in bloom. Use it in place of nonnative goutweed (*Aegopodium podagraria*) to brighten up woodland edges and shady areas. It tolerates moist soil and can be used in bog gardens and rain gardens and for lakescaping. It will also survive in dry shade, where it will be much less aggressive. It provides early color in prairie gardens, and it makes a nice cut flower. All plant parts are poisonous if eaten in large quantities.

Wildlife attraction: May be used by waterfowl, muskrats, and small rodents. Deer do not like it.

Maintenance: Canadian anemone may need to be confined by edging strips buried in the soil or grown in a large bottomless container. The rhizomes are difficult to eradicate once established. Plants are less aggressive in drier soil and in partial shade. Divide crowded plants in spring or fall to encourage better blooming. Plants may go dormant during extremely dry conditions.

Good companions: Canadian anemone is often used alone as a groundcover. In large naturalized gardens, grow it with prairie roses, spotted geranium (*Geranium maculatum*), spiderworts, and bunchgrasses.

Other prairie species: *A. caroliniana* (Carolina anemone) is native to dry, often gravelly prairies throughout most of the tallgrass region. This 6- to 12-inch perennial blooms very early in spring for about two weeks. The terminal daisylike flowers range from white to pink to purple to deep blue and are quite large and showy. It will form small colonies but is not as aggressive as *A. canadensis*. It likes full sun and dry, well-drained soil. Plants are difficult to find in the nursery trade. Zones 6 to 9.

A. cylindrica (candle anemone) is native to dry, open woods, savannas, and prairies in the northern portion of the tallgrass region. It grows about 2 feet tall. The long, erect flower stalks are topped in midsummer by interesting greenish white flowers, which form tall "thimbles" that turn into showy dried seed heads in fall. The deeply lobed leaves are an attractive bright green. It can be grown in moist to dry soil in full to part sun. Use it in rock gardens, mixed borders, and boulevard or parking strip plantings. It is not as aggressive as Canadian anemone. Zones 3 to 8.

Antennaria plantaginifolia
PLANTAIN PUSSYTOES
Asteraceae
Zones 3 to 8

Native habitat: Dry soil in prairies, open woodlands, meadows, and barrens in the eastern portion of the tallgrass region.

Mature height: 3 inches (up to 16 inches in flower)

Description: This tough, low-growing perennial has grayish, woolly leaves and stems that grow only a few inches tall. The 4- to 6-inch-wide rosettes send out stolons that root and expand the colony.

Antennaria plantaginifolia

From mid- to late spring, dome-shaped clusters of fuzzy white flower heads appear on 12- to 16-inch stalks that usually flop over from the weight of the flowers. The flowers, which are sometimes tinged with pink, resemble compact tufts of white hair or cat's paws, hence the common name. Plants are dioecious, with male and the showier female flowers on separate plants.

Site requirements: Thrives in dry, poor, well-drained soil in full sun but tolerates part sun and heavier soil.

Landscape use: Plaintain pussytoes is good for bringing silver-gray color and soft texture to a spring garden. Use plants as groundcovers in sunny areas near hot pavement or on sandy banks, where they help control erosion. The flat, silvery foliage is attractive all season and is effective in twilight gardens. They can also be used in rock gardens, between paving stones, in sunny boulevard or parking strips, and in stone walls. Children will enjoy petting the soft paws of the "kittens."

Wildlife attraction: *Antennaria* species are larval food for the American painted lady butterfly, and small bees and flies pollinate the flowers. Plants may be browsed by deer and rabbits.

Maintenance: Pussytoes require little care once established. Divide in spring if you want more plants. Plants can be sheared back after flowering for a neater appearance.

Good companions: Grow plaintain pussytoes with other drought-tolerant, sun-loving plants such as pasque flower and prairie smoke for a nice spring display.

Other prairie species: *A. neglecta* (field pussytoes) is native to dry prairies, savannas, and meadows in most of the tallgrass region. It is similar to *A. plantaginifolia*, but its leaves are narrower and often more yellowish green. Plants are shorter in flower, usually about 12 inches. Zones 3 to 8.

A. parlinii (Parlin's pussytoes), native farther east, and *A. parvifolia* (small-leaf pussytoes), native farther west, are two similar species that are more difficult to find in the nursery trade. Probably hardy in zones 3 to 8.

Asclepias tuberosa
BUTTERFLY MILKWEED
Asclepiadaceae
Zones 3 to 8

Native habitat: Well-drained, sandy soils in prairies, savannas, and barrens throughout most of the tallgrass region.

Mature height: 1 to 3 feet

Description: Butterfly milkweed has dense clumps of leafy stems topped with broad, flat clusters of fiery orange, red, or sometimes yellow flowers in summer. Unlike other milkweeds, it has clear sap. The long, slender, 4- to 5-inch fruits are filled with seeds waiting to fly away on their silky "parachutes." Older plants will have larger and more flowers. Plants may send up additional stems from the crown as they get older, giving mature plants an almost shrublike appearance.

Asclepias tuberosa

Site requirements: Moist or dry soils in full to part sun. Mature plants can take full sun and dry soil.

Landscape use: Butterfly milkweed is a wonderful garden and landscape plant. It is particularly striking when planted with complementary purple and blue flowers. Plant it in perennial gardens, mixed borders, or butterfly gardens. It makes a nice cut flower, and the seedpods look nice in dried arrangements.

Wildlife attraction: As the common name implies, it attracts butterflies and their larvae, as well as hummingbirds, bees, and other pollinating insects. *Asclepias* species are the sole food source for the larval stage of monarch and queen butterflies. Plants tend to be avoided by deer.

Maintenance: Set out young container-grown plants in their permanent locations, as the deep taproot makes plants difficult to move. Good drainage is essential; plants may rot in overly rich or damp soil. Plants don't like competition during establishment. Plants are slow to emerge in spring, so cultivate carefully until new growth appears; you may want to mark the site each fall. Plants can get a little top-heavy and may require gentle staking. Aphids can be a problem on milkweeds in hot, dry weather. Be ready to spray plants with a garden hose. Apply winter mulch in cold areas to prevent frost heaving until young plants are established. Plants rarely need dividing, and they are not prolific seed producers.

Good companions: Plant butterfly milkweed with leadplant, purple prairie clover,

Asclepias incarnata 'Ice Ballet'

wild bergamot, fringeleaf wild petunia, spiderworts, and little bluestem for a spectacular summer show.

Cultivars: It's hard to improve on the species, but if you are looking for different flower colors, 'Gay Butterflies' is a seed-grown strain of mixed yellow, red, pink, and orange flowers, and 'Hello Yellow' is golden yellow.

Other prairie species: *A. incarnata* (swamp milkweed) is common in wet prairies, marshes, and along streams, ponds, and shores throughout the tall-grass region. It has flat, terminal clusters of pale rose to rose-purple, somewhat fragrant flowers on 2- to 4-foot, sturdy plants in summer. It grows best on con-stantly wet soils in full sun, such as in bog gardens, but it adapts well to the conditions in sunny perennial borders if it receives supplemental water. It has a clumping growth habit. It is a good plant for moist-soil areas in the landscape, including rain gardens. It does self-seed prolifically. 'Ice Ballet' has white flowers, and 'Cinderella' and 'Soulmate' have rose-pink flowers. These cultivars may be better choices for traditional garden use. Zones 3 to 9.

A. purpurascens (purple milkweed) is native to well-drained or rocky sites in prairie thickets, open woodlands, and along woodland edges. It is 1 to 3 feet tall in flower with very showy rose-purple blooms starting in late spring. It is less invasive than common milkweed (*A. syriaca*) but still may be too aggres-sive for formal gardens and is best used in naturalized areas and butterfly gardens. It prefers full sun and well-drained soil but is tolerant of a wide range of soils and light levels. Zones 3 to 9.

A. sullivantii (prairie milkweed) is native to moist to wet soils throughout much of the tallgrass region. It is among the better behaved milkweeds and so can be considered for garden use. Plants grow 2 to 3 feet tall, and the short-stalked umbels of pink, starlike flowers emerge from the axils of the upper leaves at the apex of the plant. The blooming period lasts about a month, from early to mid-summer. A rich loamy soil in full sun is best. Use it in borders, butterfly gardens, rain gardens, and naturalized areas as a nectar source for hummingbirds. Zones 3 to 7.

Baptisia australis var. *minor*
BLUE WILD INDIGO
Fabiaceae
Zones 4 to 8

Native habitat: Prairies and savannas in the southern tallgrass region.

Mature height: 1 to 2½ feet

Description: Blue wild indigo has attractive bluish green compound leaves on nicely shaped, almost shrublike, plants. The deep blue, pealike flowers occur on spikes up to 1 foot long in late spring and are very showy. They turn into ornamental charcoal gray seedpods that rattle in the wind. It is smaller than the true species, which grows 3 to 4 feet tall

Baptisia australis var. *minor*

and has a native range extending eastward in richer soils in woodland openings.

Site requirements: Average, dry to medium, well-drained soil in full to part sun. Tolerates drought and poor soils.

Landscape use: This is a very nice garden plant that can be used in formal borders, cottage gardens, or natural areas. It is best as a specimen or in groups of three on large sites. The true species is easier to locate than var. *minor*, but this smaller form is worth seeking out for landscape use. The dried seedpods are often used in floral arrangements.

Wildlife attraction: *B. australis* is the larval food source for the wild indigo duskywing butterfly. Hummingbirds seek its nectar, and chickadees eat the seeds in winter. Deer will eat the flowers and nibble back the foliage.

Maintenance: This long-lived perennial starts out slowly but eventually forms huge clumps that are difficult to transplant, so choose a site carefully. Plants rarely need dividing and resent disturbance. Trimming or shearing foliage to shape after bloom helps maintain the rounded plant appearance but eliminates the attractive seedpods. Peony hoops placed over plants in early spring will support larger plants or those grown in shadier spots. All *Baptisia* species are nitrogen-fixing legumes.

Good companions: Blue wild indigo doesn't really need any companions when in bloom. The blue-green foliage makes a nice backdrop for lower-growing, later-blooming plants such as butterfly milkweed, tickseeds, and gaillardias.

Other prairie species: *B. alba* var. *macrophylla* (largeleaf wild indigo) is native to moist to dry soils in prairies and savannas in both the tallgrass and mixed prairie regions. It grows 3 to 4 feet tall and has white flowers mid- to late spring. This stately plant takes a while to get established, but once it does it makes a bold statement in the perennial border, eventually becoming almost shrublike. It grows well in moist to dry, well-drained soil in full to part sun and can be used in rain gardens. Zones 4 to 8.

B. bracteata var. *leucophaea* (long-bract wild indigo) is native to mesic to dry prairies and open woodlands in all but the far northern part of the tallgrass region. It has a nice arching growth habit and grows only to about 2 feet tall. Flowers are cream-colored. It prefers a well-drained soil and full sun. Zones 4 to 9.

Boltonia asteroides
WHITE DOLL'S DAISY
Asteraceae
Zones 4 to 9

Native habitat: Wet prairies, marshes, and floodplain forests throughout the tallgrass region.

Mature height: 3 to 5 feet

Description: White doll's daisy is an erect plant with narrow, gray-green leaves. It has small heads of white, aster-like flowers with yellow centers. It starts blooming in late summer and continues well into fall.

Site requirements: Grows in a wide variety of soils from wet to dry in full sun.

Landscape use: This species provides much-needed white color in late summer, when yellows dominate borders and prairie gardens. Place it at the back of a large perennial border or cottage garden. It can be grown on wet or mucky soils and is good for rain gardens.

Wildlife attraction: Attractive to a wide variety of pollinating insects including butterflies, bees, wasps, flies, moths, and beetles. Deer usually avoid it.

Maintenance: Plants may need support to keep them from flopping over. Cut them back by one-half to two-thirds in spring to encourage compact growth. The large plants turn brown and become floppy, so front-yard plants may need to be cut back for winter to appease neighbors. Overgrown clumps are easily divided every three to five years in spring.

Boltonia asteroides

Good companions: Other tall, late-summer plants such as asters, goldenrods, fireweed (*Chamerion angustifolium*), Joe-pye weeds, and grasses.

Cultivars: 'Nana' is a more compact selection. 'Snowbank' is a widely available selection that stays in the 3-foot range and has sturdy stems smothered in white flowers. 'Pink Beauty' has pink flowers but grows quite tall and floppy.

Callirhoe involucrata

PURPLE POPPYMALLOW
Malvaceae
Zones 4 to 8

Native habitat: Dry, open soil in prairies, often in sandy or gravelly areas, mainly in the southern portion of the tallgrass region.

Mature height: 12 to 16 inches

Description: Purple poppymallow is a somewhat sprawling, mat-forming plant that is saved by its long-blooming flowers. The procumbent stems spread out 3 feet from the crown, forming a low foliage mound. The solitary, upward-facing, cup-shaped magenta flowers rise above this mound from late spring into early fall, revealing the white coloring inside the "cup."

Site requirements: Prefers full sun and well-drained, dry conditions, although a little shade and moister conditions are tolerated.

Landscape use: Its lax ivylike growth

Callirhoe involucrata

habit should be considered when choosing a site for this plant. If possible, allow it to weave its way through the garden, popping up its flowers at random. Or grow it over a rock wall or on a hillside as a groundcover. The very showy, 2-inch magenta flowers will lend a tropical feel to your native garden.

Wildlife attraction: Butterflies and bees like the flowers, and herbivores such as deer and rabbits enjoy the leaves.

Maintenance: The long taproot gives purple poppymallow drought tolerance but also makes it difficult to transplant, so choose a site carefully. It may self-seed in the garden in optimum conditions. Deadheading will prolong bloom, and plants can be trimmed back if they get too lanky. Crown rot may occur in poorly drained soils.

Good companions: Plant purple poppymallow with hot-colored prairie plants such as black-eyed Susan, tickseeds, gaillardias, evening primroses, and spiderworts for a splash of summer color. Interplant with flowering spurge to create a garden bouquet.

Other prairie species: *C. alcaeoides* (light poppymallow) is also found on dry soils in southern regions. It has a growth habit similar to *C. involucrata*, but flower color is white, light pink, or pale lilac rather than magenta. 'Logan Calhoun' has pure white flowers. Zones 4 to 8.

C. bushii (Bush's poppymallow) is native to dry areas in the central tallgrass prairie region. It is similar to *C. involucrata* and can be used in the same way. Zones 4 to 8.

C. digitata (winecup) is locally common on upland prairies in the southwestern tallgrass region. It is much more upright than the aforementioned species, growing to 4 feet in height. The lobed, finely dissected foliage also sets it apart. Flowers can be white to light rose to wine red with a white base and bloom for several months. It likes the same type of growing conditions as *C. involucrata* and can be used similarly in the landscape. Plants can be caged or staked to keep them more upright. Zones 4 to 8.

C. triangulata (clustered poppymallow) is native to sandy prairies and rocky clearings, often on acidic soils, in the east-central part of the tallgrass region. It grows 1 to 3 feet tall and is more upright than *C. involucrata*, making it better suited to traditional borders. Stems, leaves, and flower stalks are hairy, and basal leaves are triangular. The magenta flowers appear in one flush, so plants do not bloom as long. Zones 4 to 8.

Camassia scilloides

ATLANTIC CAMAS
Liliaceae
Zones 3 to 8

Native habitat: Common in mesic and dry prairies, savannas, and open woodlands throughout the eastern tallgrass region.

Mature height: 12 to 16 inches

Description: Atlantic camas grows

from a tuliplike bulb. The long, narrow, somewhat floppy basal leaves form a tight clump. The pale blue violet or white flowers appear in a loose raceme in late spring. The sweet-scented flowers have six petal-like segments and protruding yellow stamens and last for two to three weeks. The basal leaves turn yellow and wither away by midsummer.

Site requirements: A soil that is humusy and moist to wet is ideal, but plants do fine with drier conditions once they go dormant in midsummer. Best bloom is in full to part sun.

Landscape use: Atlantic camas is a very nice landscape plant. Use it in traditional perennial borders, in rain gardens, or as an accent near water. It is beautiful when allowed to naturalize in moist-soil areas.

Wildlife attraction: The flower nectar attracts bees, butterflies, and flies. The bulbs are usually safe from rodent feeding.

Maintenance: Atlantic camas is slow to develop but fairly long-lived. Vegetative growth and development occurs during the cool weather of spring, when adequate moisture is essential. Purchase as dormant bulbs in fall and plant immediately so roots can get established before winter. Plant four times as deep as bulbs are tall, in groups of five to seven or more.

Good companions: Surround Atlantic camas with moist-soil plants that will fill in once the plants go dormant in summer such as gentians, obedient plant, and cardinal flower.

Other prairie species: *C. angusta* (prairie camas) is native in the southern half of the tallgrass region. It is taller, growing up to 2½ feet, and the leaves are larger. Flowers are similar but usually smaller and lighter in color. The blooming period is a little later, from late spring to early summer. Zones 5 to 9.

Camassia scilloides

Campanula rotundifolia

HAREBELL

Campanulaceae

Zones 2 to 8

Native habitat: Dry hill prairies over limestone, exposed cliffs, savannas, and in shallow rocky soil along streams, mainly in the northern half of the tallgrass region.

Mature height: 6 to 18 inches

Description: Harebell blooms on wiry flowering stems that arise from the over-wintering rosette of small, roundish leaves. Once flowering begins the basal leaves start to wither away, so you are left with a wispy plant with nodding, bell-shaped flowers borne in loose clusters at the stem tips. The charming, blue-violet flowers begin blooming in late spring and continue sporadically well into fall.

Campanula rotundifolia

Site requirements: Prefers a well-drained soil in full sun and moist to dry conditions. It typically grows in shallow rocky soil but will flourish in ordinary garden soil if taller, more aggressive plants are kept away. It tolerates alkaline soil.

Landscape use: Plant harebell where the delicate flower won't be overpowered by nearby plants. It does well in rock walls and rock gardens, and between pavers on a terrace, where it will bloom all summer and into fall. It does send out seedlings, which helps ensure the future of this often short-lived perennial.

Wildlife attraction: Small bees and hummingbirds visit the flowers for nectar.

Maintenance: Despite its delicate appearance, harebell is surprisingly easy to grow. Add sand and organic matter to improve soil drainage if necessary. Avoid overly rich soils, which can encourage vigorous growth on nearby plants that can overtake harebell. In the right setting, the underground stems will spread, and plants do reseed, but not too prolifically. Plants may flop over from the weight of the flowers.

Good companions: Plant harebell with other diminutive, dry-soil plants such as pussytoes, autumn onion, prairie phlox, columbines (*Aquilegia*), prairie smoke, and penstemons.

Cultivars: 'Alba' is a rare white form.

Ceanothus americanus

NEW JERSEY TEA
Rhamnaceae
Zones 4 to 9

Native habitat: Prairie, dry, open woods, and thickets, mainly in the eastern half of the tallgrass region.

Mature height: 2 to 3 feet

Description: This low-growing, spreading shrub has dark green leaves with prominent veins. It tillers at the base, sending up multiple stems. The showy, creamy white flowers appear in upright, umbel-like clusters in midsummer, when not many shrubs are in bloom. The dried seed capsules add interest in late summer. Fall color is an unspectacular yellow-green.

Site requirements: A well-drained sandy soil in full to part sun; will not tolerate wet soils.

Landscape use: A durable small shrub once established, New Jersey tea can be used in mixed or shrub borders and foundation plantings. It makes a beautiful small hedge when planted 1 to 2 feet apart. It is a good cut or dried flower.

Wildlife attraction: The flowers attract bees, wasps, hummingbirds, and an abundance of butterflies and their caterpillars, and birds eat the seeds. Deer and rabbits will eat tender, young plant parts.

Maintenance: Young plants are easy to move, but older ones are hard to transplant because of the extensive taproot. New Jersey tea is often treated more like an herbaceous perennial, especially when grown in mixed borders. Occasional hard pruning in late winter will help keep plants looking neat. High humidity and heavy summer rainfall can be harmful to plants, especially if they are in heavy soils in partial shade. Some pruning of suckers may be necessary.

Good companions: Summer flowers such as butterfly milkweed, black-eyed Susan, and fringeleaf wild petunia.

Ceanothus americanus

Chelone glabra
WHITE TURTLEHEAD
Scrophulariaceae
Zones 3 to 9
   Native habitat: Wet prairies and other moist-soil habitats, mainly in the eastern half of the tallgrass region.
   Mature height: 2 to 3 feet
   Description: This perennial has terminal clusters of white, inflated, arching,

Chelone glabra

two-lipped flowers that are often tinged with pink or lavender. They appear in late summer, bloom for about six weeks, and are followed by attractive dried seed heads. Plants have an upright to slightly vase-shaped form and narrow, dark green leaves. The root system consists of a tap-root and rhizomes, which can form large colonies.

Site requirements: Prefers a rich, evenly moist soil in full to part sun but adapts well to most garden soils.

Landscape use: White turtlehead is a great plant for late-summer color. The ideal location would be alongside a stream or water feature. It can also be grown in borders and in rain gardens.

Wildlife attraction: White turtlehead is the preferred host for the caterpillar of the Baltimore skipper. Flowers are pollinated by bumblebees and are sometimes visited by the ruby-throated hummingbird. Deer and rabbits avoid the foliage.

Maintenance: Mulch garden plants well to conserve soil moisture. Plants will tolerate brief dry spells once they are established. Plants will spread by rhizomes but do not usually become invasive in drier garden soils. If needed, restrict growth by planting in large nursery containers.

Good companions: Other late-summer, moist-soil prairie plants such as cardinal flower, spotted Joe-pye weed, closed bottle gentian, and obedient plant.

Claytonia virginica
VIRGINIA SPRING BEAUTY
Portulacaceae
Zones 3 to 9

Native habitat: Rich-soil mesic prairies and woodlands, mainly in the eastern half of the tallgrass region.

Mature height: 4 to 6 inches

Description: Virginia spring beauty is one of the few spring ephemerals to be found in prairies. This dainty spring bloomer bears loose clusters of charming white or white and pink candy-striped flowers in early to midspring. The narrow leaves appear in basal clumps.

Site requirements: Prefers moist, rich soil in spring sun and partial shade in summer.

Landscape use: Virginia spring beauty makes a beautiful but short-lived spring groundcover. Plant it in masses to intermingle with other early prairie forbs, which will fill in once plants go dormant. It can be naturalized in lawns; plant a few plants, let them reseed, and do not mow the grass until they go dormant.

Wildlife attraction: Corms may be eaten by small rodents.

Maintenance: Virginia spring beauty grows from a small, tuberlike corm that is easily divided after flowering. It also self-sows. Be careful not to disturb the dormant clumps in summer. Plants can take considerable drought in summer but need consistent soil moisture in spring and fall. Plants will reseed, but usually it's

Claytonia virginica

a case of the more the merrier with this charming ephemeral.

Good companions: Plant with not-too-aggressive associates that will fill in after Virginia spring beauty goes dormant. Good choices include prairie phlox, long-leaf summer bluet, and pasque flower.

Coreopsis grandiflora
LARGEFLOWER TICKSEED

Asteraceae

Zones 4 to 9

Native habitat: Dry prairies in the southeastern part of the tallgrass region.

Mature height: 1 to 2 feet

Description: Largeflower tickseed is a short-lived perennial that has showy flowers and attractive foliage. It blooms for a long time beginning in early summer. The single composite flower is 2 inches or more across and has yellow ray florets surrounding golden yellow disk flowers. Each ray floret has four to five notches along the outer edge, giving the flowers an attractive pinked edge. The deeply lobed leaves appear at intervals along the stem and are somewhat coarse.

Site requirements: Does best in full sun and dry soil.

Landscape use: Largeflower tickseed has an old-fashioned look to it that makes it well suited to cottage gardens and cutting gardens. It can also be used in mixed borders and containers.

Wildlife attraction: Most *Coreopsis* species attract a wide range of insects, including bees and butterflies. Birds eat

Coreopsis grandiflora

the seeds. Rabbits, groundhogs, and deer occasionally consume the foliage.

Maintenance: This plant is very easy to grow in garden settings. Remove spent blossoms to keep it blooming all summer and to improve its appearance. It is not usually long-lived in gardens and should be replanted every year or two, or allowed to reseed a bit.

Good companions: Butterfly milkweed, spiderworts, flowering spurge, asters, purple coneflower, prairie phlox, and bunchgrasses.

Cultivars: 'Domino' stays 18 inches tall and has a burgundy flower center. 'Early Sunrise' is a common cultivar with semi-double flowers on compact 18-inch plants. 'Flying Saucers' is a compact selection with 2-inch sterile flowers that bloom a long time and don't require deadheading. 'Robin' has typical golden ray flowers with red markings in the disk flowers. 'Sundance' is a prolific bloomer with semi-double flowers. 'Sunray' is a double form that stays 2 feet or less in height.

Other prairie species: *C. lanceolata* (lanceleaf tickseed) is native to dry, sandy soil throughout most of the tallgrass region and beyond. It is similar to *C. grandiflora* in appearance and landscape use. Several cultivars have been selected. 'Double Sunburst' is a semi-double form. 'Goldfink' is a dwarf form with yellow ray flowers and an orange center. 'Sterntaler' is a 16-inch selection with a frilly center surrounded by a brown ring and a double row of yellow petals. Zones 3 to 8.

C. palmata (stiff tickseed) is native to dry prairies, open savannas, and rocky upland forests typically in sandy, gravelly, or rocky soil. It grows 2 to 3 feet tall and flowers earlier than other *Coreopsis* species. The 1½- to 2-inch composite flowers are pale to bright yellow and less ragged than either *C. grandiflora* or *C. lanceolata*. The leaves are medium to dark green and are distributed evenly along the stem. The foliage often has reddish tints in fall and usually remains in good condition until a hard frost. Plants spread by rhizomes and can form large colonies, which can be quite impressive when in flower. Grow it in moist or dry soils in full to part sun. Plants may sprawl if they get too much shade or the soil is too rich. It is a good choice for early color in a large prairie garden or for stabilizing dry, sunny slopes, but it is probably too aggressive for most landscape situations. Mature plants tolerate summer drought. Zones 3 to 8.

C. tripteris (tall tickseed) is native to moist to mesic prairies, often in deep soils, thickets, and moist sites. It is the tallest of the prairie tickseeds, growing 3 to 6 feet tall. It also blooms latest, midsummer through early fall. The slightly smaller flowers have yellow petals surrounding a brown disk and appear singly on the upper stems. Plants often form loose colonies, and this is another prolific seeder, so tall tickseed's landscape use is restricted to the back of large borders and rain gardens, where it provides a soft cloud of airy flowers. It does well with the taller prairie grasses, which offer natural support. Plants will be a bit less aggressive in drier soils, and deadheading will help reduce seedlings. It may need staking. Zones 3 to 8.

Cypripedium parviflorum ssp. *pubescens*

Cypripedium parviflorum ssp. *pubescens*

GREATER YELLOW LADY'S SLIPPER
Orchidaceae
Zones 4 to 8

Native habitat: Rich mesic prairies, savannas, and woodlands scattered throughout most of the tallgrass region.

Mature height: 12 to 18 inches

Description: Greater yellow lady's slipper has leafy stems bearing one or two flowers, each consisting of a pale yellow pouch 2 inches long flanked by two petals and two greenish brown, twisted sepals. It blooms in late spring for several weeks. Leaves are 6 to 8 inches long with parallel veins and smooth margins.

Site requirements: Moist to dry, high-humus soil in part sun.

Landscape use: This showy plant should be used as a specimen or massed in part sun to lightly shaded borders or woodland gardens in a spot where it can be enjoyed while in bloom. It is long-lived and resents transplanting, so choose a site carefully.

Wildlife attraction: Flowers attract small bees and various flies. Deer love the foliage.

Maintenance: Greater yellow lady's slippers are the easiest native orchids to grow, but they are still on the challenging side. Prepare the soil well before planting 12 inches apart in groups of three or randomly. Maintain a 1- to 2-inch mulch layer to keep the soil moist. Protect plants from deer. Plants will eventually form large clumps that can be carefully divided in spring. Exercise caution when obtaining plants: all lady's slippers are difficult to propagate, and many commercially available plants may have been collected in the wild.

Good companions: There aren't many prairie plants that require the same soil and light conditions as greater yellow lady's slipper and won't overwhelm it. It's probably best grown in an open area in a woodland garden with other shade-loving wildflowers.

Other prairie species: *C. parviflorum* (lesser yellow lady's slipper), the typical species, has a similar native range. It grows 10 to 14 inches tall and has two to four 1½-inch flowers per spike. The lip is darker yellow, and it blooms a week or two later than the profiled subspecies. Zones 4 to 8.

Dalea purpurea

PURPLE PRAIRIE CLOVER
Fabaceae
Zones 3 to 9

Native habitat: Dry to moist prairies, savannas, and open woods throughout the tallgrass region.

Mature height: 2 to 3 feet

Description: Purple prairie clover is a delicate-looking plant with unique rose-purple to crimson flowers. The densely packed, ½- to 2-inch flowers bloom in a ring around the flower head, starting at the bottom and working up to the top. It starts blooming in early summer and continues for a month or more. The foliage is pinnate and fine-textured and seed heads are attractive in winter. Older plants may tiller at the base and send up multiple stems, creating vase-shaped clumps.

Site requirements: Moist to dry soils in full sun. The soil can be quite poor, since *Dalea* species are nitrogen-fixers.

Landscape use: Purple prairie clover doesn't look like much in spring (including in the nursery container), but it will reward you in midsummer with its showy flowers. A mature plant is quite attractive in full bloom. Plant it in groups of three to five in perennial borders or butterfly gardens, or use a single plant as an accent in rock gardens. The fine-textured foliage remains attractive throughout the growing season, and the seed heads offer winter interest.

Wildlife attraction: The flowers attract honeybees and other bees, wasps, flies, small butterflies, hummingbirds, beetles, and plant bugs. Songbirds enjoy the seeds, and it is a favorite food of herbivores, especially rabbits.

Dalea purpurea and *D. candida*

Maintenance: Purple prairie clover is slow to develop, but once it settles in, it is a tough, low-maintenance garden plant. Be careful not to weed it out in spring. Mature plants tolerate summer drought, and clumps seldom need dividing. You may need to use an inoculant to help plants become established in some soils. It may self-seed in optimum growing conditions but rarely becomes a pest. Mulch the first winter to prevent frost heaving.

Good companions: Other summer-blooming flowers such as wild bergamot, leadplant, butterfly milkweed, tickseeds, mountainmints, autumn onion, and smaller grasses like little bluestem and prairie dropseed.

Other prairie species: *D. candida* (white prairie clover) is native to dry soil in similar habitats. It is taller, growing 3 to 4 feet, and has less-showy white flowers and sparser, lighter colored foliage. It can be used in similar landscape situations. The white color is good for balancing the hot colors of other summer prairie plants. It is a larval host plant for the dogface butterfly. Zones 3 to 9.

Dodecatheon meadia

PRAIRIE SHOOTING STAR

Primulaceae

Zones 4 to 8

Native habitat: Moist to dry prairies, open savannas, and open woods, mainly in the eastern half of the tallgrass region.

Mature height: 8 to 16 inches

Description: The fascinating flowers have five delicate, white to pink, strongly reflexed petals surrounding a yellow and red conelike center, giving them the appearance of "shooting stars." Native plant expert William Cullina (2000) also aptly describes them as looking "like tiny umbrellas torn violently inside out by some silent tempest wind." Plants blooms for a long time, starting in mid- to late spring. The lush green basal foliage has reddish tints at the base. The entire plant dies down when summer heat arrives, but the dried flower stalks persist somewhat longer. Offsets form slowly over time, but plants could never be called aggressive spreaders.

Site requirements: Any good soil, in full to part sun, but does best in a rich garden soil in part sun. Requires direct sun in spring, but summer shade is okay. It likes adequate soil moisture when actively growing. Avoid poorly drained, wet soils, particularly in winter.

Landscape use: Prairie shooting star is an adaptable plant that will be at home in rock gardens and perennial borders as well as semishade areas of woodland gardens. A large grouping makes a stunning show when in flower. Be sure to surround them with persistent foliage plants that will fill in once plants go dormant in midsummer.

Wildlife attraction: Bumblebees are the most typical visitors of the oddly shaped flowers, but other types of bees visit as well, all coming to collect pollen.

Maintenance: Plants need moisture

Dodecatheon meadia

while blooming but are drought tolerant after that. Plants develop slowly and take several years to bloom from seed. Fall transplanting is recommended, but planting in early spring is also fine. You may want to mark the spot so you don't disturb dormant plants in late summer and fall. Prairie shooting star tolerates higher pH soils.

Good companions: In sunnier sites and prairie gardens, it combines nicely with golden alexanders, prairie smoke, prairie phlox, and prairie violets. In shadier spots, plant prairie shooting star with Canada columbine (*Aquilegia canadensis*), spotted geranium (*Geranium maculatum*), Jacob's ladder (*Polemonium reptans*), and maidenhair fern (*Adiantum pedatum*).

Cultivars: 'Album' is a white selection. 'Goliath' is several inches taller than the species and has larger, lavender-rose blooms.

Echinacea purpurea

EASTERN PURPLE CONEFLOWER
Asteraceae
Zones 3 to 8

Native habitat: Occasional in tallgrass prairies, savannas, and open woodlands, usually in moister sites than other species.

Mature height: 3 to 4 feet

Description: This popular garden plant has showy, 3- to 4-inch, purple-pink petals and bristly orange center cones. It begins blooming in early to midsummer and often continues into fall. Plants are shrubby and branching with dark green leaves and fibrous root systems.

Site requirements: Full to part sun. Growth is best in fertile loam, but the soil can contain some gravel or clay.

Landscape use: The beautiful, well-behaved eastern purple coneflower can be used almost anywhere in the landscape, including natural areas, the perennial border, cottage and cutting gardens, and semishade areas of woodland gardens. The seed heads are attractive well into winter.

Wildlife attraction: All *Echinacea* species attract many species of bees, birds, and butterflies, including monarchs, fritillaries, painted ladies, swallowtails, skippers, sulfurs, and whites. Caterpillars feed on the foliage as well. Hummingbirds seek its nectar and insect visitors. Goldfinches eat the ripened seeds. It is not a favorite of herbivores such as deer and rabbits.

Maintenance: Eastern purple coneflower is very easy to grow if its requirements are met. It has some drought tolerance, but plants will wilt if the soil becomes too dry, particularly in strong sunlight. Deadheading doesn't really give more flowers and takes food from the goldfinches. Divide only when you have to, since divisions usually don't produce as many flowers. A better way to get more plants is to dig up seedlings in spring; they can be prolific when plants are happy.

Good companions: Other summer-blooming prairie flowers such as black-eyed Susan, leadplant, wild bergamot,

Echinacea purpurea

tickseeds, compass plant, blazing stars, butterfly milkweed, and gray-headed prairie coneflower, as well as native grasses.

Cultivars: The breeding of eastern purple coneflower has gotten a bit out of hand, and there are many cultivars available—some just a bit too far out, in my opinion (e.g., 'Razzmatazz'). The species itself is so beautiful, it's hard to see the need for anything else. And the increase in cultivars has put stress on native populations, which are suffering from genetic homogenization because of their cross-pollination with cultivars. If you are interested in a white-flowered selection, 'Alba', 'White Lustre', and 'White Swan' have white ray petals and coppery centers.

Other prairie species: *E. angustifolia* (blacksamson echinacea) was more common in prairies, found in mesic to dry to rocky soils and in oak savannas, but is rare in natural stands today. It grows 1½ to 2 feet tall and has stout, hairy, nearly leafless stems topped with paler rose-pink petals that are droopier and appear earlier (late spring) than *E. purpurea*. It is also more drought tolerant, and it will flop over in bloom if it gets too much water. Despite its somewhat limp appearance in native habitats, it looks quite nice in garden settings. Zones 3 to 8.

E. pallida (pale purple coneflower) is locally common and widely distributed in dry and mesic prairies and open savannas in western portions of the tallgrass region. It grows 2 to 4 feet tall with stout stems and flowers having lavender or (rarely) white rays drooping from a large, spiny, cone-shaped center, late spring through midsummer. It tends to be a bit more aggressive than other species so is best used in larger naturalized areas. Zones 4 to 8.

E. paradoxa (Bush's purple coneflower), native to prairies and exposed limestone slopes in Missouri and Arkansas, is rarely found in natural habitats anymore. It grows 2 to 3 feet tall. The flowers have droopy, golden yellow ray florets and dark purple disk florets. It requires full sun and well-drained soil to stay compact and upright. Plants that receive inadequate sunlight and overly fertile soil may become lax and require support. Zones 4 to 8.

Eryngium yuccifolium

RATTLESNAKE MASTER

Apiaceae

Zones 4 to 9

Native habitat: Mesic to dry prairies, savannas, and woodland openings mainly in eastern portions of the tallgrass region.

Mature height: 3 to 4 feet or more

Description: Rattlesnake master has clusters of small, greenish white, fragrant flowers from mid- to late summer. They are tightly packed among pointed bracts to form globular flower heads about ¾ inch wide in branched clusters atop the stems, which sometimes get 6 feet tall. The flowers have a honeylike scent in bright sunlight. The swordlike, blue-green leaves are large and narrow and can get up to 2½ feet long. They have pointed teeth and clasping bases, arising from a basal rosette similar to a yucca. Seed heads turn brown and remain on the plant for winter interest. Plants gradually die down after blooming, but one or more offsets will develop at the base, eventually forming a small clump of plants.

Site requirements: Prefers average to rich, moist but well-drained soil (gravel or sand okay) in full sun. Plants tend to open up and sprawl if grown in overly fertile soils or in anything less than full sun.

Landscape use: Rattlesnake master works well in large, sunny borders and naturalized areas. The distinctive yuccalike leaves and seed heads add interest when plants are not in flower. It can be used in a formal setting as an accent plant. Keep it away from traffic areas where the spiny leaves can harm passersby.

Wildlife attraction: Flowers attract many kinds of insects, including bees,

Eryngium yuccifolium

wasps, flies, butterflies, moths, beetles, and plant bugs, usually seeking nectar but also collecting pollen. Caterpillars of the rare rattlesnake master borer moth feed on the stem pith. Herbivores do not favor these prickly plants, but they may nibble leaves of young plants.

Maintenance: Choose a permanent site carefully for this taprooted plant, which transplants poorly and is best left undisturbed once established. Add sand or gravel to improve soil drainage if necessary. Young leaves may need protection from rabbits and deer in spring. Plants seldom need division. Rattlesnake master can be an aggressive self-seeder under optimum growing conditions. Remove seed heads to keep the plant in check. The seedlings can be moved when young. Taller plants may need support, which best comes from nearby grasses or tall perennials since staking is a difficult task with this plant. The spiny leaves make it difficult to weed around it, too.

Good companions: Combine bold rattlesnake master with flowering spurge, blazing stars, Culver's root, black-eyed Susan, coneflowers, goldenrods, and grasses.

Eupatoriadelphus maculatus
SPOTTED JOE-PYE WEED
Asteraceae
Zones 3 to 8

Native habitat: Moist prairies, sand prairies, sedge meadows, marshes, fens, and swampy thickets in the northern tallgrass region south to northwestern Missouri.

Mature height: 3 to 7 feet

Description: Spotted Joe-pye weed is a tall, unbranched perennial with whorls of four or five yellowish green leaves up to 8 inches long with serrated margins and conspicuous veins. Flat-topped, 4- to 5-inch clusters of feathery rose-purple to mauve flower heads appear on top of purple or purple-spotted stems, mid- to late summer into fall. The flowers are often fragrant.

Site requirements: Preference is full to part sun and wet to moist soil, but this species does well in all but extremely dry soils. Plants can tolerate occasional flooding.

Landscape use: Despite its affinity for moist soil, spotted Joe-pye weed is very well adapted to typical garden settings and can be used in borders and cottage and cutting gardens. It also does well in rain gardens and naturalized plantings, especially in low areas along lakes and streams.

Wildlife attraction: Joe-pye weeds are excellent sources of nectar for bees and butterflies (especially swallowtails), and some moth caterpillars feed on plants. The seeds are a food source for the swamp sparrow and wild turkey. The foliage is not a preferred food of herbivores, but it may be eaten by deer and rabbits on occasion.

Maintenance: Plants are late to emerge in spring, so don't forget where they are planted. Spotted Joe-pye weed is generally strong of stem and doesn't require

Eupatoriadelphus maculatus 'Gateway'

staking. Perennial expert Tracy DiSabato-Aust (2006) recommends pinching back when plants are about 3 feet tall to produce smaller but fuller flowers. She also suggests cutting plants back to about 6 inches in spring if shorter plants are desired. Bloom will be delayed about a week. Plants do reseed but usually not too prolifically in typical garden soils.

Good companions: The smoky purple color is a nice complement to yellow flowers such as gray-headed prairie coneflower, black-eyed Susan, autumn sneezeweed, and goldenrods.

Cultivars: 'Gateway' is a popular cultivar selected for its sturdier, richly colored stems and reduced height, but it still often gets 6 feet tall and is probably not really a better choice than the species.

Other prairie species: Until recently, Joe-pye weeds were in the same genus as the bonesets, *Eupatorium*, and many sources will still refer to this species as *Eupatorium maculatum*. Two *Eupatorium* prairie species can be considered for informal landscape use.

Eupatorium altissimum (tall thoroughwort) is native to mesic to slightly dry prairies and savannas. It grows 3 to 4 feet tall and has opposite dark green leaves. The rather flat inflorescence consists of numerous heads of small, dull white flowers and their buds. It prefers full to part sun and mesic to dry conditions. Drought tolerance is good, although plants may wilt.

Eupatorium perfoliatum (common boneset) is native to moist prairies and swamp margins. It grows 2 to 4 feet tall. The inflorescence is similar to *E. altissimum*, but the leaves have a wrinkled texture and the bases are fused, so stem appears to be pierced by a single long leaf. It requires consistently moist or wet soil in full sun, and it can withstand flooded conditions for short periods of time.

Both species have a tendency to spread via rhizomes and may become weedy. They flower in mid- to late summer and are popular nectar sources for many bees and butterflies. They can be grown in naturalized areas, where the white flowers offer a nice contrast to the yellows and gold that dominate late summer. Deer and rabbits avoid the bitter-tasting leaves of both species. Zones 3 to 8.

Euphorbia corollata
FLOWERING SPURGE
Euphorbiaceae
Zones 3 to 9

Native habitat: Open dry woods, savannas, and prairies in most of the tallgrass region.

Mature height: 2 to 3 feet

Description: Flowering spurge has clusters of small white flowers and pure white bracts that give it a look of a sturdy baby's breath. It blooms mid- to late summer for well over a month. The creeping, slender stems grow from slowly spreading rhizomes, and plants eventually form large clumps. The sparse, pale green leaves turn a very attractive orange-gold color in fall. *Euphorbia* plants bleed milky sap when picked or damaged.

Site requirements: Flowering spurge tolerates almost any kind of soil, including sandy, rocky, loamy, or clay, in full to part sun. Poor soil is actually preferred because of the reduction in competition from other plants.

Landscape use: This airy, delicate plant is easy to use in large borders and naturalized areas, where it will weave among plants and help tie the garden together. It is aggressive enough that you wouldn't want to use it in small gardens. Because it grows well on dry, clay hillsides and roadsides where few other plants thrive, it's often used for erosion control and restoration projects. It is a good substitute for nonnative baby's breath (*Gypsophila paniculata*), which is on invasive lists in many states.

Wildlife attraction: The flowers attract wasps, flies, and bees. Wild turkey, greater prairie chicken, bobwhite, mourning

Euphorbia corollata

dove, and other songbirds eat the seeds. The toxic white latex makes it unpalatable to deer, rabbits, and other herbivores.

Maintenance: This long-lived perennial tolerates drought and poor soil and needs little care once established. Plants grow slowly from creeping rhizomes to form dense stands. Mature plants prefer to be left alone, but clumps can be divided as needed to control spread or for propagating. The white latex that oozes from cut stems can irritate skin.

Good companions: Flowering spurge will do well with any prairie plant, especially summer bloomers such as butterfly milkweed, blazing stars, coneflowers, wild bergamot, and smooth oxeye.

Other prairie species: *E. marginata* (snow on the mountain) is native to dry soils in prairies and other habitats through much of the United States. It is one of few annuals and variegated plants found on tallgrass prairies. It grows 1 to 3 feet tall with light green bracts edged in white. It has white flowers, but they really take a back seat to the showier foliage. It will grow in full sun in poor to average soil. Use it in cutting and cottage gardens or as an accent plant in perennial borders, where it will provide great color in fall. As with flowering spurge, avoid contact with the toxic sap. Plants will self-sow.

Filipendula rubra
QUEEN OF THE PRAIRIE
Rosaceae
Zones 3 to 7

Native habitat: Moist prairies, seeps, and fens and along rivers in wooded areas in the northeastern part of the tallgrass region.

Mature height: 3 to 7 feet

Description: This tall, upright, clump-forming perennial is valued for its foliage as well as its tiny, pale pink flowers, carried for about three weeks in early to mid-summer, in large, astilbe-like panicles. The deeply cut, bright green leaves have seven to nine leaflets with an unusually large terminal leaflet. Flowers bloom from the bottom up and have little or no fragrance, but the leaves are slightly fragrant. Reddish fruits develop after the flowers.

Plants have a taproot and rhizomes and form colonies in moist soil.

Site requirements: Full to part sun and wet to moist soil. The soil should be high in organic content, but it can contain a little sand. This species will do best in the cooler climate of the northern tallgrass region rather than areas with hot, dry summers.

Landscape use: This plant almost didn't make the list of recommended landscape plants because of its aggressive tendencies. However, the beauty of the flowers kept it in. Queen of the prairie is a large plant for large gardens, where it can be spectacular, particularly when massed. It is best used in naturalized areas near wetlands and water features and in large rain gardens. Consider it for the back of large borders and cottage gardens, but be prepared to

Filipendula rubra

do a little digging of rhizomes each spring. It is a good replacement for nonnative invasive *Lythrum* species.

Wildlife attraction: Various species of bees, along with some beetles and flies, collect pollen from the flowers. The foliage doesn't seem to be bothered by deer or other herbivorous mammals.

Maintenance: Prefers consistently moist, fertile, humusy soils but does fairly well in most typical garden soils. It is intolerant of drought. It freely self-seeds and can form large colonies in optimum growing conditions. Flower panicles are best left in place after bloom since deadheading does not extend the bloom period. If foliage goes downhill in dry summers, it can be cut back hard to promote new growth. Though quite tall, this sturdy plant usually does not need staking.

Good companions: Plant this stately queen with other moist-soil plants such as sweet coneflower, New England aster, and autumn sneezeweed. It will compete well with shrubs.

Cultivars: 'Venusta' is a popular cultivar that doesn't really have much to offer over the species.

Gaillardia aristata
COMMON GAILLARDIA
Asteraceae
Zones 4 to 9

Native habitat: Mesic to dry prairies, mainly in the northern part of the tall-grass region.

Mature height: 2 to 3 feet

Description: This very showy perennial, which is also known as blanketflower, has 2- to 4-inch, golden yellow daisylike ray petals with a narrow band of burgundy at the base where they join the dark red disk flowers. It starts blooming midsummer and continues into early fall. The gray-green leaves are hairy and lobed or egg-shaped and appear in leafy clumps that will continue to increase in size but never become aggressive.

Site requirements: Well-drained soil and full sun. Avoid heavy soils.

Landscape use: Common gaillardia is a good addition to sunny perennial borders, butterfly gardens, and xeriscaped yards. It can also be used as a cut flower or container plant.

Wildlife attraction: Flowers attracts bees, hummingbirds, and butterflies, and some songbirds eat the seeds. Deer and rabbits avoid it.

Maintenance: Common gaillardia is very easy to grow and care for and is long-lived when it is happy with its site. It is drought, salt, and heat tolerant. The plant's fuzzy hairs can cause a skin irritation in susceptible people. You can deadhead to prolong bloom a bit, but you'll miss out on the attractive seed heads. Plants may get powdery mildew if conditions are right. Taller plants may need support of some sort.

Good companions: Set off the showy bicolor blooms by planting common gaillardia with single-colored summer bloomers such as upright prairie cone-flower, flowering spurge, snow on the mountain, tickseeds, butterfly milkweed, and wild bergamot.

Other prairie species: *G. pulchella* (firewheel) is an attractive annual species native in more southerly and westerly prairies. Flower color is highly variable in any population, ranging from shades of yellows to reds to purples with some bicolor. Plants grow about 2 feet tall. It grows in dry, lean soils and will reseed and naturalize.

G. ×grandiflora (hybrid blanket-flower) is a showy cross between *G. aristata* and *G. pulchella*. The resulting floriferous hybrids have orange and yellow flowers, often with dark red bands or eyes. Plants are short-lived perennials that are good choices for containers and landscape use. 'Arizona Sun' grows 12 inches tall and has large orange-red blossoms edged in yellow. 'Burgundy' has large wine-red flowers. 'Dazzler' has golden yellow flowers with maroon centers. 'Goblin' is a 12-inch plant with red-centered flowers with yellow edges. Zones 4 to 9.

Gaillardia ×grandiflora 'Arizona Sun'

Gentiana andrewsii

CLOSED BOTTLE GENTIAN

Gentianaceae

Zones 3 to 8

Native habitat: Mesic to moist prairies, open woods, savannas, and marshes, mainly in the northern half of the tall-grass region.

Mature height: 18 to 24 inches

Description: Closed bottle gentian has stunning, deep violet-blue flowers crowded into terminal clusters. It blooms late summer into fall, for about a month. The 1-inch flowers resemble oversized flower buds even when mature. Individual flowers in a cluster take on various shades of purple as they age. Plants are erect to sprawling with glossy, oval, 4-inch leaves. Multiple stems can emerge from the tap-root, and plants can grow into a good-sized clump with time.

Site requirements: Prefers a sandy loam high in organic matter that stays evenly moist throughout the growing season. Tolerates full to part sun; afternoon shade from summer sun is beneficial.

Landscape use: Closed bottle gentian's rich indigo blue color is a welcome sight in prairie gardens, borders, and cottage gardens when most plants are orange or yellow. It can be grown in moist soils along ponds and other water features. It is a good choice for rain gardens.

Wildlife attraction: Since the blossoms of closed bottle gentian never actually open, pollinating insects must burrow through the petals. Bumblebees are among the few insects strong enough to open the flower and pollinate it. Deer and rabbits do not like the older, bitter-tasting leaves,

but deer may chomp off the tender tops of plants before they have a chance to flower.

Maintenance: Closed bottle gentian is easy to grow and long-lived, requiring little care once established. Make sure the soil is high in organic matter, and mulch plants to conserve soil moisture. Plants seldom need dividing (in fact, they dislike root distur-bance) and tolerate higher pH soils.

Good companions: The beautiful purple color is a great complement to any late-summer prairie plant that can tolerate more soil moisture, including black-eyed Susan, New England aster, obedient plant, and blazing stars. It does not do well if there is too much competition, so keep it away from aggressive spreaders.

Other prairie species: *G. alba* (plain gentian) is native to dry to mesic prairies, savannas, and open woods throughout

Gentiana andrewsii and *G. alba*

most of the tallgrass region. It has creamy white flowers but is otherwise similar to closed bottle gentian. Zones 3 to 8.

G. *puberulenta* (downy gentian) is native in mesic to dry upland prairies and open savannas throughout most of the tallgrass region. It has blue-purple flowers that open wide over stiff plants about 15 inches tall. This plant is quite drought resistant, and it may form small loose colonies. Flowers are attractive to bumblebees, and some beetles may eat the seeds. Zones 3 to 8.

G. *saponaria* (harvestbells) is native on moist to mesic, sandy soils in savannas and prairies in the far eastern edge of the tallgrass region. It has pale violet or light blue, tubular flowers that open slightly at the top. Plants grow 14 to 18 inches tall. It grows in full to part sun in moist to mesic soil. Wildlife value and landscape use are similar to closed bottle gentian. Zones 5 to 9.

Gentianopsis crinita (greater fringed gentian) is native to moist or wet open sites, often in calcium-rich soil and mainly in the northern tallgrass region. This close relative of the gentians has stunning, upward-facing, fringed flowers of satiny blue-violet. The stiff stems grow 1 to 3 feet tall. It is one of the few gentians to have open flowers, blooming late summer through fall. This biennial doesn't reliably reseed and must be sown each year. It is a challenge to establish and grow but is rewarding when successful. It requires evenly moist soil with a neutral to slightly high pH in full to part sun. Zones 4 to 8.

Geum triflorum

PRAIRIE SMOKE
Rosaceae
Zones 2 to 7

Native habitat: Dry to moist prairies and savannas, mainly in the northern half of the tallgrass region.

Mature height: 6 to 16 inches

Description: Prairie smoke has pink- or rose-colored, nodding flowers that look like they never completely open. They begin blooming in early to midspring and continue well into summer. As each flower fades, the styles elongate (to 2 inches) to form upright, feathery gray tails that resemble plumes of smoke. The fernlike, pinnately divided, light blue-green leaves are covered with soft hairs.

Site requirements: Does best in dry, well-drained soil in full sun but tolerates part sun, and especially appreciates afternoon shade in hot summers. It will die out if subjected to wet soil in winter.

Landscape use: Prairie smoke is an excellent landscape plant, offering interest throughout the growing season. Use it for xeriscaping and in boulevard or parking strip plantings, perennial borders, and rock gardens. Mature plants frequently form dense mats, creating an attractive groundcover. The seed heads can be dried for flower arrangements.

Wildlife attraction: Butterflies will visit the flowers, and goldfinches and other songbirds eat the seeds. Deer and rabbits usually avoid it.

Maintenance: Prairie smoke is a tough plant that withstands bitter cold, high

Geum triflorum

heat, and drought. Rhizomes should be divided every third or fourth year to alleviate overcrowding (unless a dense groundcover is desired). It grows best where summers are cool.

Good companions: Combine it with other early bloomers (pasque flower, pussytoes, prairie violets) as well as later-blooming plants (blue-eyed grasses, golden alexanders, harebell) that will set off the showy plumes.

Helenium autumnale
AUTUMN SNEEZEWEED
Asteraceae
Zones 3 to8

Native habitat: Moist, open areas along streams and ponds throughout most of the tallgrass region.

Mature height: 3 to 5 feet

Description: Autumn sneezeweed has abundant daisylike flowers 1 to 2 inches wide with wedge-shaped, bright yellow rays and prominent, domelike, duller yellow center disks. It flowers for a long time beginning in late summer and continuing to frost. The bright green leaves are lance-shaped with toothed edges. Plants are erect, clump-forming perennials.

Site requirements: Does best in full

Helenium autumnale

sun. Prefers a dampish spot in gardens, perhaps a slight depression that can be given a good soaking during dry periods, but tolerates drier soils. It responds well to fertile soil.

Landscape use: Autumn sneezeweed provides nice late-summer color in perennial borders, cottage gardens, rain gardens, and naturalized areas. It does best in a low, moist area such as a bog or near streams, but it can be grown in many landscape situations. The fibrous root system is good for stabilizing stream banks and shorelines. The flowers can be used for cutting and in dried arrangements.

Wildlife attraction: Flowers attract butterflies, and the seeds are eaten by songbirds and upland game birds. Deer avoid it.

Maintenance: Although native to moist sites, autumn sneezeweed adapts readily to most garden soils. Plants in moist, rich soil are quite robust, while those grown in drier soils are shorter and less vigorous. Taller plants may need some sort of support to keep from flopping over. Mulch garden plants and give them extra water during dry times, especially in midsummer, to encourage good flowering. Prune plants back to about 12 inches in late spring to keep them smaller and more compact. Plants will bloom better if they are divided every three to four years. Sneezeweed does not derive its common name from the effects of its pollen.

Good companions: Plant autumn sneezeweed near ponds with ferns, New England aster, and ironweeds. In borders, use it with phloxes, asters, tickseeds, and gentians.

Helenium autumnale 'Rubinzwerg'

Cultivars: Several cultivars are available, selected for a more compact growth habit, different colored flowers, and double flowers, but they are not all easy to locate. 'Dakota Gold' stays under 2 feet tall. 'Moerheim Beauty' has bronze-red blossoms. 'Rubinzwerg' [Ruby Dwarf] has ruby red flowers on 2½-foot plants.

Other prairie species: *H. flexuosum* (purplehead sneezeweed) is native on dry to moist sites, often in acidic soils, mainly in the southern part of the tall-grass region. It grows 2 to 3 feet tall with clusters of flowers that have drooping yellow petals and much darker brown-purple centers. It is more adaptable to dry soils than *H. autumnale* but is more difficult to locate. Consider it for the perennial border if you can find it. Zones 5 to 9.

Helianthus salicifolius

WILLOWLEAF SUNFLOWER
Asteraceae
Zones 4 to 9

Native habitat: Dry prairies and savannas, often on limestone, in the central portion of the tallgrass region.

Mature height: 3 to 5 feet

Description: This perennial plant has attractive foliage as well as flowers. The showy flowers appear in 2- to 2½-inch clusters starting in late summer and continuing well into fall. They have the look of a traditional sunflower—yellow ray petals surrounding a dark brown center. The 8-inch, drooping, gray-green leaves cover the stems and offer nice color and texture when plants aren't in bloom.

Site requirements: Full sun and lean soil produce upright plants with abundant blooms.

Landscape use: The attractive foliage and late summer color make this an excellent addition to the back of a sunny border or naturalized planting. It also makes a nice cut flower.

Wildlife attraction: Butterflies visit the flowers, and many types of birds eat the seeds.

Maintenance: Willowleaf sunflower can get tall and lanky, especially when grown in part sun or in fertile soils. Plants may also bend with the weight of the flowers when in full bloom. Pinch or cut back plants in late spring to get shorter plants that won't flop over when in bloom. It is not as aggressive or as heavy of a seeder as other perennial sunflowers, but it will eventually spread by creeping rhizomes to form dense colonies. Divide every three to four years to control invasiveness and maintain vigor.

Good companions: Other tall, late-summer plants such as asters, blazing stars, and white doll's daisy. Prairie grasses such as big bluestem and Indian-grass will provide natural support.

Other prairie species: *H. annuus* (common sunflower) is native to mesic to dry prairies in most of the tallgrass region. It is an annual plant with a large and stout central stem, usually 3 to 9 feet tall but sometimes as short as 1½ feet. The large leaves are up to 8 inches long and 6 inches

Helianthus salicifolius. Photo by Merel R. Black, University of Wisconsin Freckmann Herbarium.

across. The 3- to 5-inch, daisylike composite flowers have numerous brown central disk florets surrounded by yellow ray florets. An average plant bears anywhere from one to ten of these flowers mid- to late summer for about six weeks. Pollinators include many types of bees. Other insect visitors include butterflies and a few beetles, mainly seeking nectar. The large, abundant seeds are nutritious and attract many animals, including upland game birds, songbirds, ground squirrels, tree squirrels, and mice. The main reason to plant the species in the landscape is to provide food for wildlife; the many available cultivars can be used in cutting gardens, containers, and mixed borders.

Most of the other perennial prairie species are a bit coarse or are too aggressive for most landscape situations. They are, however, great food for attracting birds and are good for naturalizing, screening, or use along woodland edges. The list includes *H. decapetalus* (thinleaf sunflower), *H. divaricatus* (woodland sunflower), *H. giganteus* (giant sunflower), *H. grosseserratus* (sawtooth sunflower), *H. hirsutus* (hairy sunflower), *H. maximiliani* (Maximilian sunflower), *H. mollis* (ashy sunflower), *H. occidentalis* (fewleaf sunflower), *H. pauciflorus* (stiff sunflower), *H. strumosus* (paleleaf woodland sunflower), and *H. tuberosus* (Jerusalem artichoke). Zones 4 to 9.

Heliopsis helianthoides

SMOOTH OXEYE

Asteraceae

Zones 3 to 9

   Native habitat: Prairies and dry, open woods throughout the tallgrass region.

   Mature height: 3 to 6 feet

   Description: Smooth oxeye has cheery golden yellow flowers starting in early summer and continuing well into fall. The daisylike composite flowers are 2 to 3½ inches across and held erect at the ends of the stiff stems. Leaves are dark green and usually have a rough texture, and plants have a rather coarse texture overall. The root system is fibrous.

   Site requirements: Easily grown in average, dry to medium, well-drained soil in full sun. Tolerates drought but does better if regularly watered. Also tolerates part sun, but plants grown in too much shade tend to require support.

   Landscape use: Smooth oxeye is an excellent landscape plant, providing summer-long color in perennial borders and cutting gardens. It is also great for naturalized plantings and in butterfly gardens. Do not confuse it with oxeye daisy (*Leucanthemum vulgare*), a weedy plant from Europe that should not be grown in North American landscapes.

   Wildlife attraction: The flowers attract several insects, including bees, butterflies, and soldier beetles. Hummingbirds visit the flowers for nectar, and goldfinches and other birds look for the seeds.

   Maintenance: Smooth oxeye adapts readily to garden culture. It is easy to grow from seed, often flowering the first summer if started indoors in winter.

Heliopsis helianthoides

Plants require watering during dry periods to prevent wilting. Plants may get floppy; pinch them back in late spring to reduce overall height. The named cultivars are less floppy. Smooth oxeye will self-seed, but the shallow-rooted seedlings are easily weeded out. Deadheading will extend the bloom period and prevent seeding, but leave some seed heads for the goldfinches. And plants tend to be short-lived, so you'll want some seedlings. It is occasionally attacked by aphids and powdery mildew, but neither does permanent damage.

Good companions: Plant smooth oxeye with other summer bloomers such as blazing stars, butterfly milkweed, prairie phlox, wild bergamot, and wild indigo. It also looks nice with prairie grasses.

Cultivars: Several cultivars are available, with 'Summer Sun' being the most popular and easiest to locate. It is more compact than the species, growing to about 3 feet with large flowers. 'Prairie Sunset' has bright yellow flowers with contrasting orange-red centers; plants grow to 6 feet with attractive purplish stems and purple-veined leaves. 'Summer Nights' has deep golden yellow flowers with mahogany centers and stems and foliage tinged with red.

Other prairie species: There are two distinct varieties of *H. helianthoides*: var. *scabra* is the western form with coarser leaves and a bushier growth habit; var. *helianthoides*, found farther east, has less-rough leaves, thinner stems, and a more open habit.

Heterotheca villosa
HAIRY FALSE GOLDENASTER
Asteraceae
Zones 3 to 8

Native habitat: Sandy soil in prairies, rocky slopes, and cliffs, mainly in northern and western portions of the tallgrass region.

Mature height: 1 to 3 feet

Description: *H. villosa* is a wide-ranging species with many natural varieties. Some are small, clumping plants, and others are taller and coarser. All have stiff, leafy stems and silvery gray leaves. The showy, yellow, asterlike flowers appear in clusters midsummer through fall.

Site requirements: Well-drained, dry soil in full sun.

Landscape use: For xeriscaping and in rock gardens and informal borders—wherever you need a tough, drought-tolerant perennial with late-summer color. Look for the smaller, clumping forms for landscape use.

Wildlife attraction: The flowers attract butterflies.

Maintenance: Hairy false goldenaster requires little care once established. It will self-sow when it's happy with its site. Deadhead plants to prolong bloom or prevent seedlings. Cut back plants by one-half in late spring or early summer to keep taller types more compact.

Good companions: The yellow flowers look nice with pink and purple flowers, such as asters and blazing stars, as well as with prairie grasses.

Heterotheca villosa

Heuchera richardsonii

PRAIRIE ALUMROOT

Saxifragaceae

Zones 3 to 9

Native habitat: Dry to mesic prairies, and sometimes gravel prairies and rocky woods, in all but the far southern part of the tallgrass region.

Mature height: 1 to 2 feet

Description: This tough, cold-hardy perennial produces a neat basal clump of heart-shaped, shallow-lobed leaves. They often show some white mottling or purple blush when young, maturing to a more uniform green. Tiny, greenish, bell-shaped flowers in open, airy panicles are borne on slender, wiry stems that extend well above the mound of leaves, typically to a height of 18 to 24 inches in spring to early summer. The flowers may have reddish tints.

Site requirements: The preference is for a well-drained, sandy soil in part to full sun, but it will grow in rocky soil as well as a heavier clay-loam. It prefers full sun in the northern part of its range but appreciates some afternoon shade farther south.

Landscape use: Prairie alumroot makes an excellent low-maintenance ground-cover in sunny, dry spots. The attractive foliage and airy flower panicles bring color and contrast to the rock garden, perennial border, or open woodland garden. It is a good plant for edging a sidewalk or driveway.

Wildlife attraction: Small bees pollinate

the flowers, and butterflies and humming-birds visit the flowers for nectar.

Maintenance: Prairie alumroot is drought tolerant once established. In cold-winter climates, a winter mulch applied after the ground freezes will help prevent root heaving. Divide clumps in spring every three to four years. As with other garden heucheras, the seed heads can be clipped off in midsummer to highlight the foliage.

Good companions: Prairie alumroot is best as a groundcover, but the clean green foliage will look nice with almost any other prairie plant.

Other prairie species: *H. americana* (American alumroot), although more of an eastern woodland species, does make its way into the east-central part of the tallgrass prairie. It grows 1 to 2 feet tall and has mottled, silvery green, 3- to 4-inch, heart-shaped leaves with scalloped edges. Long slender stalks rise above the mounds and end in airy sprays of tiny, cream-colored flowers. Leaves turn red to purple in fall. It is well behaved and does well in a wide variety of landscape situations, including perennial borders, shade gardens, and rock gardens. It does best in moist, rich, well-drained soil in part sun. Leaves may bleach out in too much sun, and foliage color is paler in shade. Zones 3 to 9.

Heuchera richardsonii

Houstonia longifolia
LONGLEAF SUMMER BLUET

Rubiaceae

Zones 3 to 9

Native habitat: Dry, gravelly prairies and barrens, mainly in the eastern portion of the tallgrass region.

Mature height: 5 to 10 inches

Description: Longleaf summer bluet is a delicate plant with a sort of old-fashioned look to it. The white to pale lavender flowers appear at the ends of erect stems, which have fine-textured, dark green leaves. Each small flower is made up of four slightly reflexed petals. What the flowers lack in size they make up for in abundance, appearing in crowded clusters and covering the small, mounded plants beginning in midspring and often well into autumn.

Site requirements: Full to part sun and dry, well-drained soils; tolerates infertile soils and summer drought.

Landscape use: Longleaf summer bluet

Houstonia longifolia

is a tough, durable plant despite it delicate look. It is the perfect native plant to naturalize in gravel patios and walkways and even in lawns. It will do well in rock gardens and as an edging plant in perennial borders or along stone patios and sidewalks.

Wildlife attraction: Flies, beetles, and butterflies visit the flowers for nectar, and small bees gather pollen.

Maintenance: Longleaf summer bluet does fine in low-fertility soils and requires very little maintenance once established. Individual plants may be short-lived, but plants do reseed. Learn to recognize seedlings so you can move them easily in spring or pull them if they are too prolific.

Good companions: Try autumn onion, harebell, blue-eyed grasses, prairie smoke, prairie violets, and lilac penstemon. They all like similar growing conditions, and none of these fellow dry-prairie denizens will overpower longleaf summer bluet, which doesn't like too much competition.

Other prairie species: *H. caerulea* (azure bluet) is native in moister soil areas along the eastern edge of the tallgrass region. It has bluer flowers with yellow centers, is smaller, only about 3 inches in flower, and blooms earlier, in late spring. It likes more soil moisture and a little more shade. Zones 3 to 8.

Hypoxis hirsuta. Photo by Merel R. Black, University of Wisconsin Freckmann Herbarium.

Hypoxis hirsuta
COMMON GOLDSTAR
Liliaceae
Zones 3 to 9

Native habitat: Dry to moist prairies and open savannas and woodlands throughout the tallgrass region.

Mature height: 6 to 12 inches

Description: This small perennial plant consists of a rosette of slender basal leaves and shorter flowering stems. The linear basal leaves are up to 1 foot long and ½ inch across. The flowering stems terminate in a rather loose umbel of two or more cheery yellow flowers. The bloom period is from midspring to early summer and lasts a month or more. Flowers may have a mild fragrance. The root system consists of small corms.

Site requirements: The preference is for full to part sun and moist to slightly dry conditions, but soil can be rocky or contain loam as well.

Landscape use: Common goldstar behaves a bit like a spring bulb in the landscape, but it blooms much longer. It can be massed at the front of a perennial border, used in a rock garden, and allowed to naturalize in lawns if mowing is delayed until early summer.

Wildlife attraction: The flowers attract bees, butterflies, flies, and beetles. Small rodents may eat the corms.

Maintenance: Common goldstar can spread to form loose colonies but is not particularly aggressive. If left undisturbed, large colonies will eventually form. Plants will go dormant without adequate summer moisture.

Good companions: Plant this species with other small late-spring bloomers, such as autumn onion, harebell, blue-eyed grasses, longleaf summer bluet, and lilac penstemon.

Liatris pycnostachya
PRAIRIE BLAZING STAR
Asteraceae
Zones 3 to 9

Native habitat: Common throughout the tallgrass region in seepage areas in upland prairies, moist prairie depressions, and mesic to dry prairies and moist savannas.

Mature height: 3 to 5 feet

Description: Prairie blazing star has very showy red-violet to mauve terminal flower spikes up to 20 inches long. It blooms midsummer through early fall. The alternate, grasslike leaves increase in size from top to bottom, reaching up to 10 inches in length. The root system consists of corms, which occasionally form offsets near the mother plant. The flowers of all *Liatris* species open from the top down and can be one of two general forms: spike or button. All species have strong stems with thin, closely set leaves whorled on the stem.

Site requirements: Best growth is in full sun and moist to mesic conditions, but this species is easily grown in drier soils. Once established it tolerates poor soils, drought, summer heat, and humidity but is intolerant of wet soil in winter.

Landscape use: Blazing stars are wonderful plants for perennial borders, butterfly gardens, cottage gardens, and other sunny areas of the landscape. Prairie blazing star is a good cut flower and holds its color well when dried. Some consider this species too tall and somewhat unmanageable for the border, but it can be a good replacement for invasive *Lythrum* species, and it does well in rain gardens.

Wildlife attraction: Bees, hummingbirds, monarchs, and other butterflies gather on the flowers all summer, and birds eat the seeds on all *Liatris* species. Younger plants may be eaten by rabbits and groundhogs, while mature plants are likely targets of deer. Pocket gophers, mice, and voles may eat the corms, and an abundance of these animals can make it difficult to get plants established.

Liatris spicata and *L. pycnostachya*

Maintenance: The tall stems usually need support, which can come from staking or nearby grasses and tall forbs. Plants reseed but never become weedy and seldom need dividing. Cut back plants in spring rather than fall, so birds can feast on the seed heads. Lower leaves may turn yellow and wither away if conditions become too dry. *Liatris* species may need a little pampering when young, but once established they are easy to maintain.

Good companions: Plant prairie blazing star with other summer prairie plants such as Culver's root, rattlesnake master, mountainmints, coneflowers, wild bergamot, goldenrods, and milkweeds.

Cultivars: 'Alba' has creamy white flowers.

Other prairie species: *L. aspera* (tall blazing star) is native on sandy, dry prairies, savannas, and woodland openings, usually on acidic soils, throughout most of the tallgrass region. It is a button form, having clusters of 1-inch, pale purple or pink flowers on short stalks on top of 3- to 5-foot stems. It blooms later (late summer to fall) than most other *Liatris* species. Individual flowers open somewhat at the same time, making it a particularly good fresh cut flower for floral arrangements. It will need staking or the support of nearby plants in gardens. Zones 3 to 9.

L. cylindracea (Ontario blazing star) is native to dry upland prairies, hill prairies, openings in rocky upland woods, and oak savannas, often associated with limestone or calcium-rich soils, mainly in the eastern tallgrass region. It is shorter, growing 8 to 24 inches with narrow clusters of pale purple flowers in open spikes in late summer. Zones 3 to 9.

L. ligulistylis (northern plains blazing star) is native to wet black-soil prairies and borders of marshes, mainly in the northern portion of the tallgrass region. It looks similar to Ontario blazing star but with dark violet flowers that are broader and more open. It grows 3 to 5 feet tall

Liatris aspera

and requires more soil moisture. Use it in heavier soils and alongside streams and ponds. Zones 3 to 8.

L. mucronata (cusp blazing star) is native on dry prairies in the southern portion of the tallgrass region. It grows about 2½ feet tall and has tight clusters of ½-inch-wide purple flower heads. It needs a well-drained soil in full sun; too much water will lead to root rot. It is tolerant of alkaline soils. Zones 6 to 9.

L. punctata (dotted blazing star) is native to dry prairies throughout the western tallgrass region. It grows 8 to 14 inches tall with pink-purple wands of dense flowers and silvery gray leaves. It has a deep taproot rather than a corm, making it tolerant of hot, dry conditions. It is good in rock gardens, xeriscaping, and other well-drained, sunny sites. Zones 4 to 8.

L. spicata (dense blazing star) is native to moist woodland openings, mesic to wet prairies, and marsh edges in the eastern part of the tallgrass region. It is similar to *L. pycnostachya* but smaller in size and flower, usually staying under 3 feet in height. It does best in full sun and is somewhat tolerant of poor soils but prefers moist, fertile ones. 'Kobold' is a very popular compact cultivar that is less likely to need staking than the species and is great for perennial borders, cutting gardens, rain gardens, and cottage gardens. Zones 3 to 9.

L. squarrosa (scaly blazing star) is native to dry, sandy prairies and upland, open woods in the southern half of the tallgrass region. It is a button type, growing 2 to 3 feet tall and blooming earlier than most *Liatris* species. Zones 5 to 9.

Lilium michiganense

MICHIGAN LILY
Liliaceae
Zones 4 to 8

Native habitat: Moist prairies, openings in floodplain forests, along waterways, and open seepage areas in most of the tallgrass region.

Mature height: 4 to 5 feet

Description: Michigan lily has nodding, deep orange flowers with strongly recurved petals flecked with brown in midsummer for about a month. The 2- to 3-inch flowers are held nicely above the stems, and the whorled leaves have smooth margins.

Site requirements: Prefers full to part sun, rich loamy soil, and moist conditions, but established plants can withstand some drought.

Landscape use: Borders, cottage gardens, near water features, and bogs. A grouping is much more effective than a single plant.

Wildlife attraction: The large, showy flowers attract hummingbirds as well as moths, bees, and butterflies. Deer and rabbits will eat plants, and small rodents often eat the bulbs.

Maintenance: Bulbs should be planted 5 to 6 inches deep in fall. Michigan lily likes a deep, rich soil, so add lots of

Lilium michiganense

organic matter before planting. Mulching will help keep the root zone cool and soil moist. It is a slow-spreading stoloniferous plant, with bulbs growing at the ends of the rhizomes. Plants usually need support from staking or neighboring plants. Deter rodents by surrounding planted bulbs with 1 to 2 inches of gravel.

Good companions: Other moisture-loving natives such as white turtlehead, northern plains blazing star, purple meadow-rue, and spotted Joe-pye weed.

Other prairie species: *L. philadelphicum*

(wood lily) is native to moist to dry prairies, barrens, and savannas, often on acidic sites, throughout most of the tallgrass region. It grows 1 to 3 feet tall, has whorled leaves, and is topped by upright-facing, red-orange flowers early through midsummer. It is a stoloniferous plant that will form colonies with time. It likes moist to dry, well-drained, acidic soil in full to part sun. Plants are difficult to establish and tend to be short-lived. Birds and hummingbirds visit the flowers. Zones 3 to 9.

Lobelia cardinalis
CARDINAL FLOWER
Campanulaceae
Zones 3 to 9

Native habitat: Moist to wet soils in open woods, swamps, and sandbars as well as marshy depressions in prairies and savannas.

Mature height: 2 to 4 feet

Description: Cardinal flower gets its name from the brilliant rich red flowers that grow in an elongated cluster atop the stems midsummer through early fall. The finely toothed, dark green, lance-shaped leaves get about 4 inches long. It is a somewhat short-lived, clump-forming perennial. Tubular flowers are two-lipped, with the three lobes of the lower lip appearing more prominent than the two lobes of the upper lip. White- and rose-colored forms can be found.

Site requirements: Moist to wet, average soil in part sun. It will tolerate full sun as

long as the soil is always at least slightly damp.

Landscape use: Cardinal flower is one of the few native plants with true red flowers, and they are a welcome addition to late-summer landscapes. Plant it in groups of five to seven in a moist area of perennial borders or semishade areas of the landscape and in rain gardens. A dark background will set off the flowers nicely. It thrives at the edges of water gardens and in bogs and will naturalize when conditions are right. It definitely takes a bit of coddling, but the cardinal red color in late summer and the hummingbirds it attracts make it worth a little extra effort.

Wildlife attraction: Cardinal flower depends on hummingbirds, which feed on the nectar, for pollination. Butterflies also like it, but not cardinals.

Maintenance: Despite its native tendency to grow in moist areas at the edge of water, cardinal flower will survive in

Lobelia cardinalis

many landscape situations. Amend the soil with lots of organic matter before planting and mulch plants. It transplants easily but is short-lived, so add seedlings every couple of years or plan to nurse along the offsets that appear in fall. Plants have shallow root systems and will not survive drought. Winter mulch is helpful in colder areas. It will self-seed prolifically in optimum growing conditions. All parts of the plant are toxic if eaten in large quantities.

Good companions: Cardinal flower looks nice with blueflags (*Iris versicolor*, *I. virginica* var. *shrevei*), autumn sneezeweed, Culver's root, and white turtlehead. A backdrop of tall ferns will help set off the red flowers.

Other prairie species: *L. siphilitica* (great blue lobelia) is native to prairie swales and wet prairies throughout the tallgrass region. This clump-forming perennial has electric blue flowers arising from the upper leaf axils mid- to late summer. The leafy stalks typically grow 2 to 3 feet tall. It is easily grown in rich, humusy, medium to wet soils in full to part sun. It will self-seed prolifically in optimum growing conditions, forming attractive colonies, so it is best used in naturalized areas. Zones 3 to 9.

L. spicata (palespike lobelia) grows in moist prairies, clearings, and marsh edges throughout the tallgrass region. It is a biennial or short-lived perennial with pale blue flowers in elongated clusters on top of 24- to 40-inch leafless stalks in summer. It is more tolerant of dry, poor soil and grows in full to part sun. Plants will self-sow once established. Plants may flop if they get too much water or fertilizer or lack adequate support from nearby plants. Flowers attract bees and butterflies, but this species is probably best suited to prairie gardens rather than landscapes. Zones 3 to 9.

Lupinus perennis
WILD LUPINE
Fabiaceae
Zones 3 to 9

Native habitat: Sandy prairies and open woodlands, mainly in the northern half of the tallgrass region.

Mature height: 15 to 30 inches

Description: Wild lupine has very showy, pealike, blue to purple flowers in a 12-inch terminal cluster on erect, unbranched stems. The alternate leaves are palmately compounded, each with seven to eleven leaflets measuring 1 to 2 inches long. It blooms from late spring into early summer.

Site requirements: Prefers dry, slightly acidic, well-drained soil in full to part sun. Thrives in poor soils and summer drought.

Landscape use: A mass planting of wild lupine is a stunning sight. Plant groups in full sun in prairie gardens and woodland borders or clearings. It can be used in perennial borders, but plants often go into dormancy after flowering, so surround them with late-blooming plants. It is great for providing late spring color in a prairie garden.

Wildlife attraction: Wild lupine is the sole larval host for the endangered karner blue butterfly; other butterflies will also visit the flowers. Hummingbirds get nectar. Deer browse the foliage, and birds and small mammals eat the seeds.

Maintenance: Wild lupine can be a bit difficult to establish in landscape settings. Do not attempt to transplant mature plants. Start with young seedlings and include some of the soil from their mother plant with them to ensure the presence of specific nitrogen-fixing bacteria associated with the roots. Plants can also be started from seeds, which should be inoculated with the appropriate bacteria before planting. Once established, wild lupine enhances soil fertility by fixing nitrogen

Lupinus perennis

from the atmosphere. Space plants 8 to 12 inches apart in groups of five to seven. Plants will be short-lived on sites not suited to them. When happy, they will self-seed to perpetuate a population. Seeds are toxic if eaten in large quantities.

Good companions: Although wild lupine looks best in large masses in naturalized settings, individual specimens look nice with prairie phlox, spiderworts, and golden alexanders.

Monarda fistulosa
WILD BERGAMOT
Lamiaceae
Zones 3 to 9

Native habitat: Dry to mesic prairies and savannas and woodland edges throughout the tallgrass region.

Mature height: 2 to 4 feet

Description: Wild bergamot has soft lavender to pale pink, 3-inch, tubular flowers in dense, round, terminal clusters. It blooms midsummer through early fall. The foliage is rather coarse, and the stems are square, a mint-family characteristic,

Monarda fistulosa

Monarda punctata

branching frequently in the upper half. The root system consists of deep, strongly branched roots and shallow rhizomes, which typically send up multiple leafy stems in a tight cluster, giving plants a bushy appearance.

Site requirements: Prefers average to rich, well-drained soil in full to part sun.

Landscape use: Wild bergamot is a beautiful summer-blooming perennial that adapts well—sometimes too well—to landscape use. It can be used in the middle to back of large perennial borders and butterfly gardens but should be kept out of small beds.

Wildlife attraction: The flowers attract bees and butterflies as well as the ruby-throated hummingbird. The caterpillars of some moths feed on the foliage, but deer and rabbits typically ignore the minty leaves.

Maintenance: Wild bergamot tolerates varying soil fertility as long as it is well drained. If the soil is too rich, stems can become weak. Plants have a tendency to die out in the middle. Dividing plants every three to four years helps keep them vigorous and reduces their spread. Powdery mildew may be a problem in wet, humid conditions; avoid overhead watering. Plants will self-sow and may become weedy.

Good companions: The soft color and uniquely shaped flower of wild bergamot is a nice complement to the brighter, deeper colored flowers of other summer-blooming prairie plants, such as black-eyed Susan, blazing stars, and butterfly flower.

Other prairie species: *M. punctata* (spotted beebalm) is native to sandy soils, mainly in the eastern portion of the tallgrass region. It grows 1 to 3 feet tall and has very unusual but showy flowers from midsummer to early fall. The multiple whorls of cream-colored flowers have purple-spotted corollas and pink to lavender bracts. It needs full sun, mesic to dry conditions, and sandy soil. The flowers attract bees and butterflies, including the endangered karner blue butterfly, and moth caterpillars enjoy all plant parts. The oregano-scented foliage keeps deer and rabbits away. Plants are drought tolerant, but summer watering will keep plants fresh and blooming longer. Spotted beebalm can become aggressive when it is happy. This species has mildew resistance, but rust can be a problem. It is an interesting addition to the sunny perennial border, meadow, or naturalized planting. Zones 4 to 9.

Oenothera macrocarpa
BIGFRUIT EVENING PRIMROSE
Onagraceae
Zones 4 to 8

Native habitat: Dry prairies in the southern portion of the tallgrass region.

Mature height: 8 to 16 inches

Description: This sprawling perennial has very large (3 to 5 inches), upright, bright yellow flowers. Flowers last for only one day, usually opening late afternoon and remaining open until the following morning, but plants bloom for most of the summer. Flowers have a subtle scent. The alternate leaves are up to 6 inches long and 1 inch across and are rather densely crowded along the stems. The upper leaf surface is often shiny with white veins. The 1- to 4-inch flower buds are quite showy with their purple spots. The taproot keeps this plant in better check than most *Oenothera* species.

Site requirements: Full sun and dry, lean soil that is either rocky or sandy. Tolerates higher pH soils.

Landscape use: This plant is ideal for a sunny rock garden. It can also be used at the front of the border, in cottage gardens, in boulevard or parking strip plantings, or anywhere conditions are hot and dry.

Wildlife attraction: Flowers are visited by moths, hummingbirds, and bees.

Maintenance: This species does not compete well with taller plants. Plants may become dormant later in the growing season. Powdery mildew may appear in humid weather, and root rot in wet, poorly drained soils. Plants can be short-lived but will self-seed.

Good companions: Bigfruit evening primrose looks nice with any summer prairie plant, including purple poppy-mallow, prairie phlox, penstemons, fringeleaf wild petunia, butterfly milk-weed, and blazing stars.

Cultivars: 'Greencourt Lemon' has gray-green foliage and pale yellow flowers. 'Lemon Silver' has silvery leaves and lemon yellow flowers.

Oenothera macrocarpa

Other prairie species: Many *Oenothera* species are found in prairies, but most are too aggressive for traditional landscape use. Here are a few to use with caution.

O. caespitosa (tufted evening primrose) is native to dry prairies in the mixed and shortgrass regions. It grows 6 to 12 inches tall and has white to pink flowers in summer and silvery foliage. It also requires dry soil and full sun and blooms late in the day. Plants sucker but not too profusely. Zones 4 to 7.

O. fruticosa (narrowleaf evening primrose) is native mainly in the eastern portion of the tallgrass region. It grows about 2 feet tall with a sprawling growth habit and spreads to form dense clumps. Plants have cheery yellow flowers for most of the summer. Many cultivars are available. 'Sonnenwende' [Solstice] has dark leaves and flowers larger than the species. Zones 4 to 8.

O. speciosa (pinkladies) is native in the southern portion of the tallgrass region. It is a beautiful plant with large, white flowers tinged with pink and showy yellow anthers, but the abundant root suckers make it too aggressive for most landscape situations. It can be used in large prairie gardens and on tough sites. Zones 4 to 8.

Opuntia humifusa

EASTERN PRICKLYPEAR
Cactaceae
Zones 4 to 8

Native habitat: Dry, often rocky or sandy prairies, savannas, and dunes throughout the tallgrass region.

Mature height: 8 to 18 inches

Description: Eastern pricklypear has large yellow flowers 2 to 3 inches wide with or without reddish centers that bloom late spring through midsummer. They appear on the top of the stems, which are flattened, fleshy pads covered with clusters of short spines—fewer than many western species of cactus, but still formidable. Each pad can get up to 10 inches long, 7 inches across, and 1½ inches thick. A few pads may develop at the top of the original pad. A fleshy fruit develops that is spiny and turns yellow when mature. The root system is fibrous, shallow, and spreading, and plants may eventually form large colonies.

Site requirements: Well-drained, sandy soil in full sun. Tolerates average amounts of moisture and a little shade and loamy soil if it is well drained.

Landscape use: Their alien look and cultural conditions limit how pricklypears can be used in landscapes, but they are great in rock gardens, stone walls, and xeriscapes, and they can be used as groundcovers on sunny slopes. This is the easiest cactus to grow in home gardens because of its greater tolerance of moisture and humidity.

Wildlife attraction: Bees visit the flowers, and fruits and seeds are occasionally eaten by wild turkeys, skunks, and ground squirrels. Fruits and pads are sometimes eaten by rabbits, deer, and coyotes.

Maintenance: Pricklypears are difficult to weed and cultivate around. The tiny

Opuntia humifusa

spines can be irritating; wear heavy gloves when handling or working around plants. They survive winter temperatures by withdrawing most of the moisture from their pads, giving them a shriveled, unhealthy look in winter and early spring. They quickly plump up in spring, however. The clump-forming plants are easily cut back if they become too sprawling. Older stems on the ground have a tendency to become brown and woody with age. Start new plants using pads, which form new roots readily.

Good companions: Grow pricklypears with other plants that like the same hot, dry conditions such as penstemons, autumn onion, harebell, purple prairie clover, rattlesnake master, and flowering spurge.

Other prairie species: *O. fragilis* (brittle pricklypear) is native to dry, open areas farther west in the mixed prairie. It is similar to *O. humifusa*, and culture and use are the same. Zones 4 to 8.

O. macrorhiza (twistspine pricklypear) is native to dry, sandy soils generally a bit farther west than *O. humifusa*. It is very similar to eastern pricklypear but usually doesn't get quite as tall, and it has more spines. Use it the same way in the landscape, if you dare. Zones 4 to 8.

Parthenium integrifolium

Parthenium integrifolium
WILD QUININE
Asteraceae
Zones 3 to 7

Native habitat: Mesic to dry prairies, savannas, and thickets throughout most of the tallgrass region.

Mature height: 2 to 3 feet

Description: Plants form large, shrub-like clumps with toothed, aromatic leaves. Very pretty, pearl-like, white flowers appear in large, flat-topped clusters up to 10 inches across. Plants begin blooming in late spring and continue to late summer. Plants have a central taproot and spreading rhizomes.

Site requirements: Medium, well-drained soil in full sun, but will tolerate moister and drier soils and some shade.

Landscape use: This long-blooming perennial can be used in borders, cutting gardens, and cottage gardens. It is a little coarse when not in flower, so plan accordingly. Flowers can be used in fresh and dried arrangements.

Wildlife attraction: Flowers attract bees, wasps, flies, beetles, and plant bugs. Deer and rabbits avoid the sandpapery leaves.

Maintenance: Deadhead flowers to keep plants looking neater. Lower leaves may turn yellow during dry spells. Plants can cause dermatitis on sensitive individuals.

Good companions: The white color looks nice with other summer bloomers, such as prairie phlox, spiderworts, and tickseeds.

Penstemon digitalis

FOXGLOVE PENSTEMON
Scrophulariaceae
Zones 3 to 8

Native habitat: Moist to mesic prairies, savannas, open woodlands, and along streams throughout most of the tallgrass region.

Mature height: 2 to 4 feet

Description: This clump-forming perennial has white, two-lipped, tubular flowers from midspring to early summer. The flowers appear in panicles atop rigid stems that rise above rosettes of semi-evergreen basal leaves. Leaves are medium green, sometimes with reddish tints. The rhizomatous root often produces new plantlets around the base.

Site requirements: Full to part sun in medium moisture, well-drained soil. Avoid wet, poorly drained soils.

Landscape use: Foxglove penstemon adapts well to cultivation and can be used in most typical garden settings. Keep in mind its rather short bloom time and uninteresting foliage, however. It is especially nice massed in sunny borders, in cottage gardens, and in rain gardens.

Wildlife attraction: Hummingbirds, bees, butterflies, and sphinx moths visit the flowers. Caterpillars of moths and butterflies feed on the foliage of this and other penstemons. Plants are not favorites of deer or rabbits.

Maintenance: Under severe drought conditions, the leaves may turn yellow and the plant will wilt. Root rot can occur in wet, poorly drained soils. Leaf spots are occasional problems. For a neat appearance, cut bloom stalks once they've turned brown. This species spreads slowly to form dense clumps, and it does reseed but not too prolifically.

Good companions: The white flowers combine well with almost all prairie forbs, including butterfly milkweed, spiderworts, black-eyed Susan, and prairie phlox.

Cultivars: 'Husker Red' is a very popular burgundy-leaved selection that greatly extends foxglove penstemon's season of interest.

Other prairie species: *P. cobaea* (cobaea beardtongue) is native to sandy or rocky, open hillsides and limestone outcrops, mainly in the southern half of the tallgrass region. It grows 1 to 2½ feet tall and has loose panicles of flowers, ranging from white to pink to deep purple, midspring through early summer. The flowers are somewhat larger than most penstemons, almost 2 inches long, and quite showy. Use it in sunny borders and rock gardens, where it will attract hummingbirds and butterflies. Plants are short-lived but self-sow readily. Zones 5 to 9.

P. gracilis (lilac penstemon) is native in the northern part of the tallgrass and mixed prairie regions. It grows only a foot tall or so and has soft lilac flowers, giving it a delicate appearance. It is a little more difficult to grow than other species but is among the hardiest and is a good choice for northern states in boulevard or parking strip plantings, rock gardens, and borders. Zones 3 to 8.

P. grandiflorus (large beardtongue) is native to upland and sandy prairies

Penstemon digitalis

Penstemon gracilis

throughout most of the tallgrass region and into the mixed prairie region. It has beautiful flowers and foliage, making it a great choice for borders and cottage gardens, and it brings early color to prairie gardens. Unfortunately it blooms for only two to three weeks. The large flowers (up to 2 inches) are lavender or pink with bluish tints. It grows anywhere from 2 to 5 feet tall. Both basal and stem leaves are blue-gray or blue-green, glabrous, with smooth margins, and have a rather succulent appearance. It needs full sun and well-drained soil, and it will tolerate poor soil containing rocks. Spider mites can be found on the foliage, but they appear to cause little damage. Bumblebees visit the flowers for nectar. Zones 3 to 7.

P. hirsutus (hairy beardtongue) is native to dry, upland woods and savannas in the far eastern part of the tallgrass region. It grows 12 to 18 inches tall with violet to pale rose flowers in early summer. It tends to be a bit weedier than other species but is a nice addition to prairie gardens. It grows best in full to part sun on moist to dry, well-drained soil. 'Pygmaeus' is a better-behaved, 6- to 12-inch selection often used in rock gardens. Zones 3 to 8.

P. pallidus (pale beardtongue) is found on dry, often rocky, upland prairies and open woodlands in the eastern portion of the tallgrass region. It is sort of like a smaller, daintier *P. digitalis*, growing 1 to 2½ feet tall with smaller white flowers. It blooms a little earlier than other species. It is a better choice in eastern states as it can tolerate more humidity. Zones 3 to 8.

P. tubiflorus (white wand beardtongue) is native to dry to mesic prairies, mainly in the southern part of the tallgrass region. It is another white species, but the individual flowers are longer and in looser panicles. It reaches 1 to 3 feet tall and is easily grown in average, dry to medium, well-drained soil in full sun. Zones 5 to 9.

Phlox pilosa

PRAIRIE PHLOX

Polemoniaceae

Zones 3 to 9

Native habitat: Moist to mesic prairies, open forests, and savannas throughout the tallgrass region.

Mature height: 1 to 2 feet

Description: This hardy perennial has showy clusters of dainty flowers that are perfectly made for butterfly sipping. Each flower is about ½ inch across and has five lobes that flare abruptly outward from a long, narrow, tubular corolla. The flowers, which can be white, pink, or lavender, have a mild pleasant fragrance. Prairie phlox starts blooming in late spring or early summer, continuing for five weeks or more, and may repeat bloom in fall. The leaves are sparsely distributed along the stem, giving plants a fine texture. This taprooted plant occasionally tillers at the base, sending up multiple stems.

Site requirements: Full to part sun and moist to mesic soil.

Landscape use: Prairie phlox is an

Phlox pilosa

excellent long-blooming plant for the perennial border, cottage garden, rock garden, or butterfly garden.

Wildlife attraction: Phlox flowers attract bees, butterflies, and hummingbirds. Some moth caterpillars eat the flowers and leaves. All *Phlox* species tend to be favorites of rabbits, deer, and groundhogs, and it may be difficult to establish this plant where these animals are prevalent.

Maintenance: This species is not bothered by powdery mildew like fall phlox (*P. paniculata*), but the lower leaves tend to turn yellow and drop off when the plant becomes stressed. Plants can be cut back hard in spring to enhance branching. It does reseed but not obnoxiously.

Good companions: Any midheight, late spring- to summer-blooming prairie plant, including harebell, butterfly milkweed, evening primroses, flowering spurge, spiderworts, and mountainmints. It also looks nice with little bluestem and prairie Junegrass.

Other prairie species: *P. pilosa* ssp. *fulgida* (downy phlox) is a naturally occurring variety throughout the tallgrass region. It has similar flowers, but its leaves have a more lustrous appearance. Zones 3 to 9.

P. bifida (sand phlox) is native on dry soil and rocky outcrops in the central tallgrass region. The sprawling, taprooted plants grow only 2 to 6 inches tall and have stiff, needlelike leaves. The pale blue to violet flowers bloom for over a month from midspring to early summer, extending above the foliage 12 inches or more. Plants reseed and may form colonies on a favorable site, which is full to part sun and mesic to dry conditions. As its common name suggests, it will also grow on very sandy or even rocky soil. Sand phlox is an excellent spring-blooming phlox for the rock garden, perennial border, or cottage garden. Zones 4 to 8.

P. glaberrima (smooth phlox) is occasional in moist to mesic prairies and openings or areas of light shade in floodplain forests, mainly in the eastern tallgrass region. It is similar to prairie phlox but may be taller (up to 2½ feet) and bloom a little later. It is a good garden plant, growing best in fertile, moist soil in full to part sun. It does well in rain gardens. It tolerates more soil moisture than other phloxes, and it has good resistance to powdery mildew. Young plants can be killed by summer heat and drought, particularly in locations that lack adequate moisture. Plants may need support to keep them from flopping over. 'Morris Berd' has pink flowers with a white center. Zones 4 to 8.

P. maculata (wild sweet William) is native to moist woods and wet prairies in the eastern part of the tallgrass region. It grows 2 to 3 feet tall with large, conical clusters of fragrant, pink, lavender, or white flowers in summer. The lance-shaped green leaves look nice all season. Plant it in average to rich, moist but well-drained soil in full to part sun in perennial borders or prairie gardens. Divide the multi-stemmed clumps every three to four years to keep plants vigorous. It is a good substitute for the more mildew-susceptible *P. paniculata* in areas where powdery mildew thrives. Spider mites can also be a problem in hot, dry conditions. Deadheading does prolong the bloom. 'Alpha' has rose-pink flowers with darker eyes. 'Rosalinde' has deep pink flowers. Zones 3 to 8.

Physostegia virginiana
OBEDIENT PLANT
Lamiaceae
Zones 3 to 9

Native habitat: Moist to mesic prairies, woodland openings and borders, and along rivers and lakes throughout the tallgrass region.

Mature height: 2 to 4 feet

Description: This perennial has tall, vertical stems lined with narrow, jaggedly toothed leaves. The showy tubular flowers bloom for about six weeks, late summer to early fall, appearing successively up the stalk in somewhat elongated clusters of pinkish, two-lipped, inch-long, snapdragon-like flowers arranged in two rows. A flower spike can be up to 10 inches long, including the unopened buds. The root system consists of a central taproot and rhizomes, which spread aggressively.

Site requirements: Full to part sun and moist to average soil conditions. Growth is best in rich loamy soil, but it can contain some gravel or clay.

Landscape use: This species is an excellent plant for a moist or wet prairie or for naturalizing along a stream. The cultivars bring nice pastel color to the late-summer border and rain gardens. The flowers have an old-fashioned look to them and are good for cottage gardens, Victorian gardens, and cut bouquets.

Wildlife attraction: Bumblebees are the most important pollinators. Other bees and the ruby-throated hummingbird also visit the flowers, seeking nectar. It is not a favored source of food for deer and rabbits.

Maintenance: This plant is easy to grow (too easy!) if the site is not too dry. In drier conditions plants will be less aggressive, but the lower leaves may turn yellow and fall off. They may need staking, especially if grown in soils with high fertility. Plants can be pruned back in early spring to reduce their overall height. Divide every two to three years to control growth. Deadheading browned flowers helps improve the plant's appearance and may prolong bloom.

Good companions: Obedient plant's pink to white flowers are a welcome addition to late-summer borders. Plant it with New England aster, closed bottle gentian, blazing stars, Culver's root, ironweeds, Joe-pye weeds, goldenrods, and grasses.

Cultivars: It's worth seeking out cultivars of this plant for landscape use since most of them are less invasive than the species. It is also one of the few native plants where you will find variegated foliage. 'Miss Manners' has bright white flowers and grows about 2 feet tall. 'Olympus Bold' has green and golden

Physostegia virginiana 'Miss Manners'

variegated foliage and pink flowers on 2½-foot plants. 'Variegata' has pale pink flowers and leaves edged in creamy white.

'Vivid' has vibrant rose-pink flowers on 2- to 2½-foot stems.

Pulsatilla patens
PASQUE FLOWER
Ranunculaceae
Zones 2 to 9

Native habitat: Gravel prairies and barrens, mainly in the northern tallgrass region and into the mixed prairie region.

Mature height: 4 to 8 inches

Description: Pasque flower has solitary, lavender, blue, or white flowers rising above clusters of basal leaves starting in early spring and blooming for several weeks. The entire plant is covered with silky hairs that give it a silvery sheen. It blooms early enough that flowers often appear in the matted remains of the previous year's foliage. Showy, long-tailed seed heads follow the flowers, extending the ornamental value. Deeply divided basal foliage is silvery hairy. The woody taproot may send out new flower stalks, but plants never become invasive.

Site requirements: Full to part sun and moist to dry, well-drained soil. A gritty soil containing gravel or rocky material is fine.

Landscape use: Pasque flower is the earliest of the prairie wildflowers, making it a must for prairie gardens. Select a spot where it won't be overwhelmed by taller plants. It also does well in perennial borders or rock gardens. The nomenclature of this plant is confusing, and you will find it also listed as *Anemone patens*, *Pulsatilla nuttalliana*, *P. patens* var. *multifida*, or *P. hirsutissima*. Avoid planting the commonly available European species, *P. vulgaris*, which is no more ornamental and less beneficial to native insects.

Wildlife attraction: Bees and hummingbirds visit the flowers for pollen and nectar. Deer and rabbits are repelled by the foliage, which contains a blistering agent.

Pulsatilla patens

Maintenance: Pasque flower is much tougher than it looks. The early flowers can handle late-spring snows and cold snaps. It needs moisture while flowering but otherwise is quite drought tolerant. Root rot can be a problem if the soil becomes waterlogged from poor drainage. If soil is heavy, add sand and organic matter before planting. Plants may go dormant in summer.

Good companions: Combine the demure pasque flower with other small spring bloomers, such as prairie smoke, pussytoes, and prairie violets.

Pycnanthemum tenuifolium
NARROWLEAF MOUNTAINMINT
Lamiaceae
Zones 4 to 8

Native habitat: Dry prairies and upland woods, mainly in the eastern half of the tallgrass region.

Mature height: 12 to 18 inches

Description: This fine-textured, branching perennial almost looks more like a small shrub. The small, white, tubular flowers often have scattered purple dots and bloom early to midsummer for up to six weeks. Only a few are in bloom at the same time, beginning with the outer circle of flowers and ending toward the center. The slender, 3-inch leaves have a mild mint scent and somewhat stronger minty taste. The root system consists of a taproot and rhizomes, which spread to form large colonies.

Site requirements: Quite adaptable but prefers full sun and moist but not wet soils.

Landscape use: Mountainmints are a little coarse and aggressive for perennial borders, but they can be used in informal wild gardens and prairies. They do surprisingly well in rain gardens. They are excellent nectar sources, and their scent is very pleasing. Plants also offer winter interest and make good cut or dried flowers.

Wildlife attraction: The flowers attract many kinds of insects, including bees, wasps, flies, butterflies, beetles, and plant bugs, usually seeking nectar. Deer and rabbits avoid this minty-tasting plant.

Maintenance: The leaves may assume a yellowish appearance during a major drought. This stoloniferous plant can become invasive. If you want to grow it in butterfly or herb gardens, plant it in large sunken nursery containers. Plants need division every few years to keep them from overwhelming nearby plants.

Good companions: Other summer bloomers, such as purple prairie clover, blazing stars, black-eyed Susan, butterfly milkweed, prairie phlox, coneflowers, and penstemons.

Cultivars: 'Cat Springs' has larger flowers and a strong fragrance of spicy peppermint.

Other prairie species: *P. virginianum* (Virginia mountainmint) is native to sandy, moist prairies and stream edges throughout most of the tallgrass region. It is similar to narrowleaf mountainmint but grows up to 3 feet in height and has wider leaves. It also blooms a little later and has a stronger minty fragrance. Culture and use are the same. Zones 3 to 9.

Pycnanthemum virginianum

Ratibida pinnata
GRAY-HEADED PRAIRIE CONEFLOWER
Asteraceae
Zones 3 to 9

Native habitat: Moist to slightly dry prairies, thickets, and woodland borders throughout most of the tallgrass region.

Mature height: 3 to 5 feet

Description: This hardy, robust perennial is somewhat coarse-looking until it blooms, midsummer into fall. Plants have pinnately divided leaves up to 5 inches long on stiff stems. The composite flowers have a grayish brown cylindrical central disk that can get up to an inch tall with droopy, showy, yellow ray flowers attached at the bottom. The central cone turns brown and offers interest after the petals fall. The root system is rhizomatous, often forming a dense clump.

Site requirements: Average to rich, well-drained soil in full to part sun. Plants cannot tolerate wet soils, but they will grow in heavier soils than many prairie plants. It tolerates poor, dry soils, but it will wilt in summer's heat.

Landscape use: This is a great plant for bringing lemon yellow color to large perennial borders. Blooms are so abundant and plants bloom for such a long time, one plant is often all you'll need. The delicate flowers sway with each passing breeze, giving a real sense of prairie to a landscape. It does well in rain gardens.

Wildlife attraction: Many kinds of insects visit the flowers, especially bees. Other insects include wasps, flies, small butterflies, and beetles. Some butterfly and moth caterpillars feed on the foliage. Goldfinches eat the seeds.

Maintenance: Gray-headed prairie coneflower is easy to grow. Foliar disease may show up after the blooming period. There is a tendency for the flowering stems to flop around if this plant is spoiled by too much water or fertile soil. It transplants readily and seldom needs division. Plants reseed abundantly, so you'll need to pull as needed. Once plants get large, the dense root system is hard to pull. Individual plants are narrow and somewhat sparsely leafed, so they should be surrounded by other plants, which will also offer support.

Good companions: If you have the room, a large garden including gray-headed prairie coneflower and other tall prairie plants, such as queen of the prairie, blazing stars, ironweeds, and wild bergamot, is striking in late summer.

Other prairie species: *R. columnifera* (upright prairie coneflower) is native to dry-soil prairies throughout the United States and Canada. It has the same softer lemon yellow ray petals, but the center disk is twice as tall, up to 2 inches. It stays under 2 feet tall and has nice stiff flower stems that never require staking. The finely cut grayish green foliage is attractive even when the plant is not in flower. It is not nearly as prolific a seeder as its taller cousin, and since it tends to be short-lived you'll want to find a few seedlings. If you're lucky, you'll find a few seedlings with showy splotches of red on the ray petals, a common occurrence in wild populations. Upright prairie coneflower is probably a better choice than its taller cousin in most landscape situations but is best grown

Ratibida pinnata

Ratibida columnifera

in small groupings rather than as individual plants. It is a nice companion for other medium-sized, summer-blooming prairie plants, such as butterfly milkweed, purple prairie clover, fringeleaf wild petunia, and little bluestem. It must have well-drained soil, however; wet feet will be its death. Its small size and long bloom also make it suitable for container culture. Bees, butterflies, insects, and birds, as well as deer, will find this plant attractive. The rays of the less common but very showy *R. columnifera* var. *pulcherrima* are brownish purple. 'Red Midget' grows 15 to 18 inches tall and has very showy mahogany red ray petals that have a narrow edging of golden yellow. Zones 3 to 9.

Rosa carolina

CAROLINA ROSE

Rosaceae

Zones 4 to 9

Native habitat: Dry to mesic prairies, openings in woodlands, and oak savannas throughout most of the tallgrass region.

Mature height: 2 to 3 feet

Description: The woody stems have slender, straight prickles. Solitary pink flowers are 2 to 3 inches across with five pink, sometimes white, petals. There is a typical rose fragrance. The blooming period occurs during early summer and lasts about a month. Flowers turn into bright red hips. Plants spread from shallow rhizomes to form colonies.

Site requirements: Average to dry soil in full to part sun.

Landscape use: Native roses are among the few shrubs found in prairies. Most species grow erect, but taller plants sometimes sprawl. Although their flowers are beautiful, this species and other native wild roses need to be used with care in the landscape, as they will spread to form large colonies. They are great for holding the soil on tough sites. With a little root pruning in spring, you can keep most of them sufficiently in check in a large mixed border.

Wildlife attraction: The flowers attract bees. Caterpillars of many species of moths feed on wild roses. Birds and small mammals eat the rose hips and use plants for nesting habitat and cover. Deer will eat plants, prickles and all.

Maintenance: Compared to most cultivated roses, native prairie species are trouble-free. They are very drought tolerant, and they rarely have any foliar disease problems. They do benefit from a light application of fertilizer in spring and a hard pruning in winter to encourage more blooms. Powdery mildew may show up when plants are grown in irrigated gardens.

Good companions: Soft-colored summer plants, such as leadplant, little bluestem, and New Jersey tea.

Other prairie species: *R. arkansana* (prairie rose) is native throughout the tallgrass region. It stays under 2 feet in height and spreads up to 8 feet, making

Rosa carolina

Rosa setigera

it a good groundcover on tough sites. Zones 4 to 8.

R. *blanda* (smooth rose) is native in the northern half of the tallgrass region. It grows 2 to 6 feet tall. Zones 3 to 7.

R. *setigera* (climbing prairie rose) is native in the central portion of the tallgrass region. It has canes up to 8 feet in length and can be trained to climb a trellis or fence. Zones 4 to 9.

R. *woodsii* (Woods' rose) is native in the western portion of the tallgrass region and into the mixed prairie region. It grows 2 to 4 feet tall and spreads to form large thickets. Zones 4 to 7.

Rudbeckia hirta

BLACK-EYED SUSAN
Asteraceae
Zones 3 to 9

Native habitat: Dry to mesic prairies, savannas, and upland forests throughout most of the United States and Canada.

Mature height: 1 to 3 feet

Description: Black-eyed Susan may well be the most recognizable native flower. It is a short-lived perennial with golden yellow rays surrounding a conical cluster of rich brown disc florets. It blooms for a long time, starting in midsummer and continuing well into fall. The lance-shaped leaves are grayish green and covered with small stiff hairs, providing them with a rough texture. It blooms the first year from seed planted in early spring and is often grown as an annual. The root system consists of a central taproot and is without rhizomes.

Site requirements: Prefers moist, average, well-drained soil in full sun but tolerates part sun and a wide range of soil conditions. Any reasonably fertile soil will be satisfactory.

Landscape use: Black-eyed Susan brings long-lasting color to prairie gardens, cottage gardens, and mixed borders. Plants bloom the second year after seeding a prairie, offering color before most other prairie plants. The flowers provide winter interest if left standing. It is one of the few native flowers that adapts well to container culture, especially the cultivars.

Wildlife attraction: The composite flowers appeal to a wide range of insects, particularly bees and flies, as well as some wasps, butterflies, and beetles. Caterpillars of silvery checkerspot feed on the leaves. The seeds are occasionally eaten by goldfinches. Deer and rabbits usually avoid the coarse leaves, but slugs and snails (remember, they are bird food!) may eat seedlings.

Maintenance: Sow seeds two years in a row for yearly blooming. Once a planting is established plants will self-seed to keep the color coming year after year. Rich soils tend to produce weak-stemmed plants. Populations are easy to increase by transplanting seedlings, which are easy to move before plants flower. The foliage of *Rudbeckia* species is susceptible to several diseases, including botrytis and powdery mildew. To help keep diseases in check, space plants properly and avoid over-

Rudbeckia hirta

head watering. Deadhead spent flowers to encourage additional bloom and/or to prevent any unwanted seedlings. Plants reproduce entirely by seed, so they never become aggressive vegetatively.

Good companions: Almost anything, but especially blazing stars, obedient plant, asters, butterfly milkweed, flowering spurge, wild bergamot, little bluestem, and prairie dropseed.

Cultivars: Showy tetraploid hybrids called gloriosa daisies are derived from *R. hirta*. They are annuals or short-lived perennials with 5- to 6-inch, yellow, orange, red, or multicolored flowers on 2- to 3-foot plants. They bloom all summer and are good for cutting. There are many cultivars available, with more being introduced every year. 'Becky' is a dwarf selection staying at about 8 inches in height. 'Cherokee Sunset' is a mix of fully double flowers in shades of yellow, orange, bronze, and russet. 'Indian Summer' is a popular tetraploid form with larger flowers on compact plants. 'Prairie Sun' has 5-inch flowers with golden petals tipped in primrose yellow surrounding a light green cone. Most are grown as annuals, and they make good containers plants.

Other prairie species: *R. fulgida* (orange coneflower) is native to dry and moist soils in open woods, glades, and thickets, mainly in the eastern part of the tallgrass region. It is similar in appearance but usually blooms later and is rhizomatous. It typically grows 3 feet tall and will form colonies. It's rare to find the species offered by nurseries; they mainly sell the very popular 'Goldsturm', which is a selection of the more compact var.

sullivantii. This cultivar appears to be more susceptible to bacterial angular leaf spot, in which brown or black angular spots on the leaves can expand to blacken the whole leaf. It self-sows and produces abundant offsets. Zones 3 to 9.

R. missouriensis (Missouri orange coneflower) has a more limited native range, primarily Missouri and Arkansas. The flower are similar to *R. hirta*, but plants have narrower leaves. It tolerates hot and humid summers and drought but is not as cold hardy. Plants spread to form large colonies. Zones 5 to 8.

R. subtomentosa (sweet coneflower) is native to mesic to wet prairies in most of the tallgrass region. It grows taller than most other species, 3 to 5 feet, and is a little more sunflower-like in appearance with its dark brown-purple center disks and yellow rays. Its gray-green, sweet-scented leaves form large bushy clumps, but it is not rhizomatous. It likes full sun but consistent moisture levels. Pinch plants back lightly in spring to reduce their height and lankiness. 'Henry Eilers' has yellow rays that are rolled instead of flat, giving the flower a quilled effect. Zones 3 to 9.

R. triloba (brown-eyed Susan) is native to moist prairies and open woodlands and along streams throughout most of the tallgrass region. It can get up to 5 feet in height. The buttonlike flowers are smaller than other species but very abundant, and they have dark brown centers. It does not tolerate drought well but will reseed prolifically when it is happy, in moist soils. Deadhead spent flowers to encourage additional bloom and/or to prevent any unwanted seedlings. Zones 3 to 9.

Ruellia humilis

FRINGELEAF WILD PETUNIA

Acanthaceae

Zones 4 to 9

Native habitat: Mesic to dry prairies, gravelly hill prairies, and dry open woodlands, mainly in the eastern portion of the tallgrass region.

Mature height: 1 to 2 feet

Description: This charming perennial has tubular, bell-shaped flowers up to 3 inches in diameter that are a lovely lavender or light purple color. It blooms for a long time, beginning in early summer and continuing sporadically to frost. The olive green leaves and the stems are hairy. The

Ruellia humilis

root system is fibrous, and plants spread to become bushy clumps.

Site requirements: Quite adaptable, tolerating full to part sun, moist to dry conditions, and practically any kind of soil.

Landscape use: Fringeleaf wild petunia is a great plant for dry, rocky, shallow soils such as in rock gardens, but it can also be grown in well-drained garden loam in perennial borders. Keep it at the front of perennial borders, so larger plants don't overwhelm it. The lovely flowers bring the rare blue-purple color to summer prairie gardens.

Wildlife attraction: Long-tongued bees are the most important pollinators of the flowers. Leafcutting bees cut the petals to use in nests. Other bees and flies visit the flowers, but they are not effective pollinators. Hummingbirds gather nectar from the flowers. This species is a favorite choice of deer.

Maintenance: Fringeleaf wild petunia is easily grown in gardens if the soil is well drained. Add sand and organic matter to heavier soils. Plants grow from fibrous-rooted crowns to form clumps. Deadhead flowers if you don't want an overabundance of seedlings.

Good companions: Plant this species with other small plants that won't hide its showy flowers. Good choices include prairie smoke, autumn onion, pussytoes, prairie phlox, little bluestem, and butterfly milkweed.

Silene regia
ROYAL CATCHFLY
Caryophyllaceae
Zones 4 to 9

Native habitat: Dry to mesic prairies, oak savannas, and openings in upland forests in the south-central part of the tallgrass region.

Mature height: 2 to 5 feet

Description: This unbranched perennial has clusters of showy red or scarlet flowers at the top of the plants. The star-shaped flowers can be up to an inch across and have five petals. They start blooming midsummer and are showy for about a month. The blue-green leaves are up to 4 inches long and 2 inches wide. The root system consists of a central taproot and short rhizomes, which enable this plant to spread vegetatively to form small colonies.

Site requirements: Full to part sun in moist to slightly dry soil. It prefers a sandy or gravelly soil but will grow on heavier clay soils as long as drainage is good.

Landscape use: Other than cardinal flower, which is more difficult to grow in garden settings, this is the only prairie plant to give red color to the summer garden. So even though it isn't all that attractive when not in flower, it's worth making a place for it in the perennial border or cottage garden. It's a must for butterfly and hummingbird plantings.

Wildlife attraction: Since many insects are insensitive to the color red, it is an uncommon color among prairie plants. Some butterflies, including black swallow-

Silene regia

tails, perceive red, and royal catchfly flowers are tailor-made for them. The long narrow tube formed by the calyx is ideal for their proboscis, and the flared petals provide a colorful landing platform. It is also a favorite of the ruby-throated hummingbird.

Maintenance: Royal catchfly is fairly easy to grow but is somewhat slower to develop than other plants and resents excessive shading. During drought, the lower leaves may turn yellow and fall off. Plant lower-growing companions around

it to help hide lower foliage. Plants begin to bloom while small in size, but it takes several years to reach their full potential. Taller plants may need some support. Most sources listed it as hardy to zone 4, but it may not survive every winter in colder regions.

Good companions: The red color provides a great contrast to the numerous yellow and gold flowers blooming at the same time. Plant it near smooth oxeye, black-eyed Susan, prairie coneflowers, and Culver's root for a striking show.

Silphium integrifolium
WHOLELEAF ROSINWEED
Asteraceae
Zones 3 to 9

Native habitat: Mesic to dry prairies and rocky or dry open woods throughout the tallgrass region.

Mature height: 3 to 4 feet

Description: There is nothing small about plants in this genus, but at least wholeleaf rosinweed is within the realm of being able to be used in traditional landscapes. It may get up to 6 feet tall but usually stays closer to 3. The lemon yellow, sunflower-like flowers, 2 to 3 inches in diameter, first appear in mid-summer and last up to two months. It has rough, medium green leaves that can be quite variable in shape and up to 6 inches long. The root system consists of a tap-root and short rhizomes, which enable this plant to form clumps. This perennial derives its common name from the

gummy, resinous sap exuded by broken or cut plant stems.

Site requirements: Full sun and mesic to dry soil.

Landscape use: Wholeleaf rosinweed can be used in large perennial borders and cottage gardens, where it brings nice height to the rear of the border. It is much less aggressive than *Helianthus* species and is a better choice if you want the look of sunflowers in your garden. The rest of the silphiums are best suited to prairie gardens, where they make interesting accent plants.

Wildlife attraction: The pollen and nectar of the flowers of all *Silphium* species attract bees. Gall wasp larvae may feed within the stems, forming galls that are invisible from the outside. Some butterflies visit the flowers, including sulfurs and painted ladies. The large seeds are eaten by goldfinches and other birds. Rabbits rarely eat the coarse foliage of

Silphium integrifolium

these tall plants, but deer find it palatable (and within reach).

Maintenance: Silphiums tend to be slow to establish and may not flower until the second or third year, but wholeleaf ros-

Silphium laciniatum

inweed matures quicker than most other species. Mature plants are easy to maintain, resist drought, and can handle competition from other plants. It is a sturdy plant that usually doesn't require staking. Downy mildew, leaf spots, and rust may occur. Plants of all species will self-sow. If you don't want the seedlings, weed them out while they are still young and easy to pull.

Good companions: Other tall prairie flowers such as rattlesnake master, blazing stars, Culver's root, New England aster, Joe-Pye weeds, big bluestem, and Indiangrass.

Other prairie species: *S. laciniatum* (compass plant) is native to mesic and dry prairies in the tallgrass region. It grows 3 to 8 feet tall and has lemon yellow, sunflower-like flowers up to 5 inches across at the ends of branched, hairy, sticky stems, starting in midsummer and lasting for about five weeks. The 12- to 18-inch, showy, cut-leaf blades orient themselves horizontally in a north-south direction to avoid the intense rays of midday sun. The taproot can extend 15 feet deep, and plants are said to live up to a hundred years. It likes full sun and a moist to slightly dry, deep, loamy soil. Several insects are specialist feeders of compass plant, including the uncommon prairie cicada, whose grubs feed on the large taproot. Compass plant needs plenty of room, so space plants 3 to 4 feet apart. Established clumps are difficult to divide or move, so choose a site carefully. Young plants may need protection from deer. The foliage turns brown after flowering, so you need to plant something in

Silphium terebinthinaceum

front of it in a landscape setting. Zones 3 to 9.

S. perfoliatum (cup plant) is native to moister sites in wet prairies, along streams, and the edges of woodlands. It grows 3 to 8 feet tall with leaves that encircle tall stems and form cups that collect dew and become a drinking fountain for birds, including hummingbirds. The 3-inch yellow flowers bloom in branched clusters just above the leaves in mid- to late summer. It takes a little more shade than other species and can be used at the edge of woodland gardens. Aphids can be a problem during hot, dry periods, and plants may drop some lower leaves in response to drought. A rainstorm with strong winds can topple blooming plants. Various birds, especially goldfinches, are very fond of the seeds. The dense colonies provide good cover for birds, which often lurk among the leaves during the heat of the day, searching for insects or pausing to rest. Zones 3 to 9.

S. terebinthinaceum (prairie rosinweed) is native to moist to dry prairies, mainly in the eastern part of the tallgrass region. It grows 4 to 8 feet tall and is noteworthy for its large paddlelike leaves, which have a tropical look. A tall, naked flowering stalk emerges from this leafy rosette and sports a panicle of yellow flowers, each up to 3 inches across. The bloom period is late summer to early fall for about a month, a bit later than other *Silphium* species. The stout taproot can go down 12 feet and may form offsets a short distance away from the mother plant. It takes full sun and moist to dry soil; rocky or gravelly soil is okay. Drought tolerance is very good. It is similar to other species in landscape use and wildlife attraction. Zones 3 to 9.

Sisyrinchium angustifolium
NARROWLEAF BLUE-EYED GRASS
Iridaceae
Zones 3 to 9

Native habitat: Moist to mesic prairies as well as floodplain forests, thickets, woodland borders and openings, moist oak savannas, and the slopes of rivers, mainly in the eastern portion of the tall-grass region.

Mature height: 10 to 20 inches

Description: This very pretty iris relative has charming flowers and neat foliage. It has blue to violet-blue flowers with yellow centers, making the common name something of a misnomer. Individual flowers up to ½ inch in diameter form loose clusters on top of the grasslike leaves, blooming for about a month, from late spring to early summer. The fibrous root system often sends out offshoots.

Site requirements: Prefers a moist, average, well-drained soil in full sun but tolerates part sun.

Landscape use: Narrowleaf blue-eyed grass should be planted in groups where it can be seen in the morning when the flowers are open. Use it in rock gardens or at the edges of perennial borders or

Sisyrinchium montanum

cottage gardens. The fine, grasslike foliage has great garden value when plants are not in flower, and it can be used as a groundcover.

Wildlife attraction: Bees and flies visit the flowers for pollen and nectar. Seeds and other plant parts are eaten by greater prairie chickens and wild turkeys.

Maintenance: Narrowleaf blue-eyed grass is easy to grow, eventually forming large clumps by spreading and by self-sown seedlings. Divide plants every other year for the best bloom. Plants may repeat bloom. Cut back plants lightly after flowering to prevent seed formation and to tidy up appearances.

Good companions: Other delicate spring bloomers such as prairie smoke, prairie violets, golden alexanders, and pussytoes.

Cultivars: 'Lucerne' has larger blue-purple flowers and is supposedly less aggressive. Zones 3 to 9.

Other prairie species: Several other *Sisyrinchium* species are native to the tallgrass region; all are very similar to *S. angustifolium* in character and use.

S. campestre (prairie blue-eyed grass) is found in sandy to mesic prairies and savannas throughout the tallgrass region. Flowers are white, light blue, or blue-violet. It is more drought tolerant and does best in full sun and mesic to dry conditions. Zones 3 to 9.

S. montanum (strict blue-eyed grass) is native to prairies, savannas, and open woods, mainly in the northern portions of the tallgrass and mixed prairie regions. It grows a little taller, to 2 feet, with violet flowers. It takes full to part sun. Zones 3 to 9.

Solidago speciosa
SHOWY GOLDENROD
Asteraceae
Zones 4 to 9

Native habitat: Mesic to dry prairies and savannas throughout the tallgrass region.

Mature height: 2 to 5 feet

Description: As the common and scientific names imply, this plant is very conspicuous while in bloom from late summer through fall. The showy inflorescence is up to 1 foot long, consisting of an erect panicle of small, bright yellow, compound flowers. The flowering stems are held erect or curve upward, unlike most goldenrod flowers, which flop down. The plant is rather coarse when not in bloom, with alternate leaves up to 6 inches long and 1½ inches wide. The root system is fibrous and rhizomatous, occasionally forming offsets. Goldenrods have been wrongly accused of causing hay fever, which is actually an allergic reaction to wind-borne pollen from ragweed (*Ambrosia*) and other plants.

Site requirements: The preference is full to part sun and slightly moist to slightly dry conditions. The soil can contain significant amounts of loam, sand, or rocky material.

Landscape use: While goldenrods are a staple of prairie gardens, most are much too aggressive for landscape use.

A few (this species is one) adapt well to sunny perennial borders, providing good color and contrast in late summer. The flowers work well in fresh and dried arrangements.

Wildlife attraction: Showy goldenrod flowers attract honeybees, bumblebees, ants, beetles, and an occasional moth or butterfly. Caterpillars of many moths feed on various parts of plants. Other insect feeders include various leafhoppers, lace bugs, and plant bugs. Seeds are eaten by the eastern goldfinch, juncos, sparrows, and the greater prairie chicken. Grouse eat the leaves. Deer and rabbits occasionally eat the leaves, stems, and flowers.

Maintenance: Cut back hard after flowering if reseeding is a problem. Rust and other foliar diseases can be a problem but are not usually serious if plants are in full sun. Plan to divide plants every two to three years to control growth. Plants may topple over if they are given excessive moisture or fertilizer.

Good companions: Other late-summer bloomers such as asters, Joe-pye weeds, white doll's daisy, blazing stars, and gentians.

Other prairie species: *S. nemoralis* (gray goldenrod) is native to dry prairies, especially in sandy and rocky soils, throughout the tallgrass region. It is more compact, growing only 1 to 2 feet tall, and has attractive gray-green foliage. The narrow, wandlike inflorescence has a tendency to nod. It blooms a little later than showy goldenrod and lasts about a month. It is somewhat shade and drought tolerant and does well in poor soils where little else does well. The rhizomatous root system will eventually form colonies. Zones 3 to 9.

S. rigida (stiff goldenrod) is native to moist to dry prairies throughout most of the tallgrass region. It grows anywhere from 2 to 5 feet tall, depending on the variety. The attractive flattened flower panicles are in contrast to most goldenrod flowers. It has nice gray-green, downy leaves that turn dusty rose in fall. It can be used in large perennial gardens, rain gardens, and cottage gardens, where it will self-sow but is usually not too invasive. Zones 3 to 9.

Solidago speciosa

Symphyotrichum novae-angliae

NEW ENGLAND ASTER
Asteraceae
Zones 3 to 8

Native habitat: Wet to mesic soils in prairies, meadows, open woods, and along water features in all but the far southern parts of the tallgrass region.

Mature height: 3 to 6 feet

Description: New England aster is a tall plant with 5-inch leaves clasping hairy stems. Mature plants have woody, fibrous root systems and form thick clumps after a few years. The showy daisylike flowers have petals ranging from violet to pink to white surrounding yellow centers and can be up to 2 inches wide. The flowers cluster at the ends of branches from late summer through fall. *Aster* species have been reclassified; most North American species are now in *Symphyotrichum*.

Site requirements: Moist, average soil in full to part sun. Avoid soils that dry out completely.

Landscape use: The species can be a bit coarse for formal landscape use, but the many cultivars are excellent garden plants, bringing late-season color to mixed borders, cottage gardens, and even large rock gardens.

Wildlife attraction: Asters are important as late-season nectar sources for butterflies, hummingbirds, and bees. The larvae of many moths and butterflies, including crescent and checkerspot butterflies, feed on plants, and birds eat the seeds.

Maintenance: The tall stems of the species can become top-heavy when in bloom and usually need some type of support.

Cut back plants to about a foot in spring to promote bushier plants. Divide plants in spring every third year to promote vigorous growth. Avoid too much nitrogen, which can result in abundant foliage and floppy plants. Plants are susceptible to leaf spots, rusts, and mildew, which can leave lower leaves in bad shape by flowering time but usually do no permanent harm. Plants can be cut to the ground after flowering if they look too unsightly.

Good companions: Plant asters with other late-season prairie plants such as goldenrods, grasses, smooth oxeye, obedient plant, closed bottle gentian, and white doll's daisy for an outstanding fall show. Lower-growing plants, especially grasses, will help hide the browned leaves and stems on lower parts of the plant.

Cultivars: Dozens of cultivars of New England aster have been selected, mainly for more compact growth habit, better lower leaf retention, and earlier and longer bloom time than the species. Here are a few of the more commonly available selections to consider for traditional landscape use: 'Andenken an Alma Pötschke' is covered in bright rose-pink flowers on 3- to 4-foot plants. 'Harrington's Pink' has unique light salmon-pink flowers but can grow up to 5 feet tall. 'Hella Lacy' grows 3 to 4 feet tall with violet-blue flowers. 'Honeysong Pink' grows about 3½ feet tall and has pink petals with bright yellow disks. 'Purple Dome' is a naturally dense dwarf cultivar (18 to 24 inches) with semi-double, deep purple flowers. 'Roter Stern' [Red Star] stays about 15 inches tall and has red flowers. 'September Ruby' has deep ruby red flowers on floppy, 3- to

5-foot plants. 'Wedding Lace' grows 4 feet tall with whitish flowers.

Other prairie species: *S. ericoides* (white heath aster) is native to dry to mesic soils in prairies, dunes, and savannas. It has hundreds of small, white or pale blue flowers on 1- to 3-foot, stiffly branched plants. Plant it in average to rich, dry to moist, slightly acidic soil in full sun. 'Blue Star' has sky blue flowers. 'Esther' has pale pink flowers on 2- to 3-foot plants. 'Pink Star' has light pink flowers in late summer. 'Snow Flurry', a selection of f. *prostratus*, grows only 6 to 8 inches tall (good for rock gardens) and has white flowers. Zones 3 to 8.

S. laeve (smooth blue aster) is native to mesic to dry prairies, savannas, and woodland edges. It has loose panicles of light blue flowers on 2- to 3-foot plants that have lovely waxy blue-gray leaves. It starts blooming in late summer and is one of the last asters to bloom in autumn. It is a very nice landscape plant. Plant it in average to rich, moist but well-drained soil in full to part sun. It is not as floppy as New

Symphyotrichum novae-angliae

England aster, but it may need staking in shadier sites. Seedlings will appear, but this beautiful plant is worth a little effort. 'Blue Bird' is a compact selection with deep sky blue flowers. Zones 3 to 8.

S. lateriflorum (calico aster) is native to open woods in poor or sandy soils. This 2- to 4-foot bushy plant has especially attractive bronzy green foliage in addition to bearing hundreds of small white flowers. It forms clumps but is never invasive. The stiff stems are slightly arching. Grow it in average to rich, well-drained soil in full to part sun. 'Lady in Black' and 'Prince' were both selected for their deep plum-purple foliage that really sets off the white flowers. They both grow 2 to 3 feet tall. Zones 3 to 7.

S. oblongifolium (aromatic aster) is native on upland and hill prairies. It has blue-purple flowers similar to New England aster but blooms a little later on 2- to 3-foot plants that are slightly fragrant when brushed against. It is also more drought tolerant. 'October Skies' is shorter and bushier at about 18 inches and can be considered for groundcover use. 'Raydon's Favorite' has large lavender flowers on 3-foot plants. Zones 4 to 7.

S. oolentangiense (skyblue aster) is native to mesic to dry prairies, savannas, and open woodlands. Its light blue flowers are smaller and more open than smooth blue aster, and it grows 2 to 5 feet tall. Zones 3 to 9.

S. sericeum (western silver aster) is native to dry, gravel, and sandy prairies and savannas, often associated with limestone or calcium-rich soils. It has lavender or pale blue flowers with yellow centers in loose clusters on many-branched, 12- to 24-inch stems that often sprawl. The silvery, silky leaves have smooth margins. Plant it in average soil in full to part sun. It competes well with prairie grasses once established. Zones 3 to 9.

S. turbinellum (smooth violet prairie aster) is native to moderately dry prairies and open woods. It grows 2 to 4 feet tall and has violet flowers with yellow-green centers. Plants often flop with the weight of the blooms and may need staking. Grow it in full to part sun in moist to dry soil. Zones 3 to 9.

Symphyotrichum laeve

Thalictrum dasycarpum

PURPLE MEADOW-RUE

Ranunculaceae

Zones 3 to 9

Native habitat: Wet prairies, low areas in mesic prairies, wetland margins, and floodplains throughout most of the tallgrass region.

Mature height: 4 to 6 feet

Description: This upright perennial has stems that often have purple coloring and three-lobed, finely textured leaves. It is dioecious (male and female flowers on separate plants), with the male flowers being far showier than their female counterparts. The creamy white male flowers occur in

Thalictrum dasycarpum

loose, delicate, drooping clusters from late spring through midsummer.

Site requirements: Prefers moist, fertile soil in full to part sun but will tolerate drier conditions.

Landscape use: This is a good background plant in cottage gardens or large perennial borders, where it provides an area of calm among showy flowers. It is a nice addition to cut-flower bouquets.

Wildlife attraction: Flowers appeal to butterflies and hummingbirds. It is a larval host plant for the swallowtail butterfly.

Maintenance: New plants should be watered well. A summer mulch will be beneficial in dry soils.

Good companions: Other moist-soil plants such as obedient plant, gentians, Michigan lily, and spotted Joe-pye weed.

Tradescantia ohiensis
BLUEJACKET
Commelinaceae
Zones 3 to 9

Native habitat: Dry to mesic prairies and savannas in all but the northwestern part of the tallgrass region.

Mature height: 2 to 3 feet

Description: This perennial has gray- or blue-green, straplike leaves up to 15 inches long and 1 inch wide, tending to bend downward toward the middle— think daylilies when not in bloom. The light violet to blue-violet flowers occur in a small cluster at the top of the plant. Each flower is about an inch across with three rounded petals. Flowers open in the morning and close by afternoon in sunny weather, remaining open longer on cloudy days. Plants can bloom from late spring right into fall, with only a few flowers in bloom at the same time. The root system is thick, fleshy, and fibrous, sending off occasional offshoots nearby.

Site requirements: Full to part sun and moist to slightly dry conditions, but plants are very adaptable.

Landscape use: Perennial borders and cottage gardens. Can be a bit aggressive for formal gardens, but the intense blue color and long bloom time are worth a little effort. Plants may go dormant after flowering, so try to place them where they will be masked by other plants. Their drought and heat tolerance make them good choices for xeriscaping.

Wildlife attraction: Bees pollinate the flowers, and deer and rabbits may eat the foliage.

Maintenance: Plants will reseed, and the seedlings can be difficult to pull. Plants can be cut back to 6 to 12 inches in midsummer to keep them neater and reduce unwanted seedlings. Divide clumps when they become overcrowded. Leaves may develop brown blotches or turn yellow in harsh weather, when in competition from other plants, or with age.

Good companions: This species and all spiderworts look nice with any summer prairie plants, including prairie phlox, tickseeds, wild quinine, and butterfly milkweed.

Other prairie species: Several other

Tradescantia sp.

species are found in various parts of the tallgrass region. They are all very similar to bluejacket, with flowers ranging in color from white to rose, to lavender to deep purple, and can be used the same way in the landscape.

T. bracteata (longbract spiderwort) is native mainly in the northern half of the tallgrass region. Zones 3 to 8.

T. occidentalis (prairie spiderwort) is native farther west in the tallgrass region and into the mixed prairie region. It is more drought tolerant than other species. Zones 3 to 9.

T. virginiana (Virginia spiderwort) is native farther east in the tallgrass region. This species is commonly crossed with other species, resulting in *T. ×andersoniana* hybrids, which are popular nursery plants. Zones 3 to 9.

Verbena stricta

HOARY VERBENA
Verbenaceae
Zones 3 to 9

Native habitat: Dry to mesic prairies throughout the tallgrass region.

Mature height: 2 to 3 feet

Description: This long-blooming, showy perennial has stems and leaves covered with fine white hairs. Beautiful intensely colored lavender flowers appear in spikes, blooming from the bottom up from mid- to late summer for about six weeks. The taproot may send up a few tillers from the base, and plants can become almost shrublike.

Site requirements: The preference is full sun and average to dry conditions.

Landscape use: The blue-purple flowers are easily combined with gold and yellow late-summer bloomers in perennial borders and cottage gardens, where they add a soft vertical accent. Plants are coarse and somewhat unsightly when not in flower, so surround them with neater-growing neighbors. Verbenas make good cut flowers.

Wildlife attraction: Many kinds of insects are attracted to the flowers, including bees, wasps, flies, and butterflies. Caterpillars of some moths feed on the foliage. Seeds are eaten by various songbirds, including cardinals, juncos, and sparrows. Hummingbirds seek its nectar. Deer and rabbits stay away from the bitter foliage.

Maintenance: Self-sown seedlings occur but are rarely a nuisance. Remove the spent flowering spikes before seeds mature to prevent any unwanted self-seeding. Individual stems may flop over if plants don't have some sort of support. Lower leaves may turn yellow and shrivel in drought conditions.

Good companions: Hoary verbena looks great with any summer prairie flower, including butterfly milkweed, black-eyed Susan, prairie phlox, and coneflowers. A clump of little bluestem nearby will keep plants upright and help hide the coarse foliage.

Other prairie species: *V. hastata* (swamp verbena) is native to wet prairies, shores, marshes, and stream banks throughout the tallgrass region. The 3- to

Verbena stricta

5-foot erect branches hold strongly vertical candelabra-like spikes of small, dark blue flowers in summer and early fall. The leaves are long and narrow-toothed. The blue flowers combine nicely with gold and yellow late-summer bloomers and grasses in perennial borders and cottage gardens, where they add a strong vertical accent.

It can also be grown in bog gardens and alongside streams and ponds. It prefers rich, evenly moist to wet soil in full to part sun. The slow-spreading rhizomes will eventually form colonies, and plants will reseed in optimum growing conditions. Zones 3 to 9.

Vernonia fasciculata

PRAIRIE IRONWEED
Asteraceae
Zones 3 to 9

Native habitat: Wet to moist prairies and marshes throughout most of the tallgrass region.

Mature height: 3 to 5 feet

Description: This butterfly-attracting, but somewhat coarse, perennial has long, narrow leaves along the thick stems. The central stem terminates in a flat-topped cluster of magenta flowers, which bloom for about a month from late summer to early fall. The root system is spreading and fibrous.

Site requirements: The preference is full sun, moist conditions, and fertile soil, but part sun and slightly moister or drier conditions are tolerated. This plant can withstand occasional flooding for short periods of time.

Landscape use: Prairie ironweed is not for every landscape, but it can be used toward the back of large perennial borders, where it offers a strong vertical presence. It is also good for screening, and the flowers are good for cutting.

Wildlife attraction: The flowers attract bees and butterflies, and caterpillars feed on plants. Deer stay away from the bitter foliage.

Maintenance: Although native to moist soils, this perennial adapts well to garden settings as long as it is not drought stressed. Soil a little on the drier side will help keep plants from getting too aggressive. Pinch back stems in late spring to keep plants more compact. Unpinched plants may need staking or support of some kind.

Good companions: Plant prairie ironweed with other late-summer bloomers such as goldenrods, smooth oxeye, Joe-pye weeds, and white doll's daisy as well as tall prairie grasses.

Other prairie species: There are several other similar species; most tolerate drier conditions.

V. arkansana (Arkansas ironweed), native mainly in the south-central part of the tallgrass region, has narrower leaves and more disk florets in each flower head, making the flowers wider. Zones 4 to 9.

V. baldwinii (Baldwin's ironweed)

Vernonia fasciculata

is native to dry prairies throughout most of the tallgrass region. It is more drought-resistant and blooms a littler earlier than other species. Zones 3 to 9.

V. gigantea (giant ironweed) is native mainly in the southern part of the tallgrass region. Zones 5 to 9.

V. missurica (Missouri ironweed) is native to moist to mesic prairies, mainly in the southern half of the tallgrass region. Zones 5 to 9.

Veronicastrum virginicum
CULVER'S ROOT
Scrophulariaceae
Zones 3 to 9

Native habitat: Moist to mesic prairies, open savannas, and moist swales throughout the tallgrass region.

Mature height: 3 to 6 feet

Description: This perennial is upright and unbranched, except near the inflorescence. The dark green, whorled leaves give the plant a horizontal effect that contrasts with the strongly vertical spires of white or pale lavender, candelabra-like flowers. Culver's root starts blooming in midsummer and continues for about a month. The root system consists of a central taproot and some rhizomes.

Site requirements: The preference is full to part sun and moist to average conditions. Growth is best in rich loamy soil, although some sand or clay is tolerated. Appreciates some afternoon shade in southern gardens.

Landscape use: This durable plant can be used in the middle or back of a perennial bed or cottage garden, where it offers a strong vertical accent. It tolerates wet soil and is great along ponds and streams. The pretty white flowers are good for cutting; unfortunately, they rapidly turn brown.

Wildlife attraction: Bees, wasps, butterflies, moths, and flies visit the flowers. Deer and rabbits usually leave it alone.

Maintenance: Culver's root likes a richer, moister soil than most tallgrass prairie plants. Add generous amounts of organic matter to the soil before planting. Mulch plants and give them an annual application of compost. Culver's root forms clumps as it ages but is not overly aggressive. Water plants during dry spells. Plants don't usually need staking, unless they are grown in too much shade. Divide every three to five years to keep good bloom. Plants usually take several years to establish in a garden. The leaves may turn yellowish green in bright sunlight or during a drought; otherwise, they normally appear healthy and are not often bothered by disease.

Good companions: The white color, long bloom time, and tall stature of Culver's root make it a good backdrop for many flowering plants, including blazing stars, lilies, smooth oxeye, wild bergamots, milkweeds, rattlesnake master, goldenrods, and asters.

Cultivars: The species is an excellent landscape plant, but if you want flower

Veronicastrum virginicum

colors besides white, there are several cultivars to consider. 'Apollo' has lavender flowers. 'Erica' has red buds and pale pink flowers. 'Lavendelturm' [Lavender Towers] has pale purple flowers. 'Roseum' has pale rose-pink flowers.

Viola pedata

BIRD'S-FOOT VIOLET
Violaceae
Zones 3 to 9

Native habitat: Acidic prairies and oak savannas in all but the far northwestern area of the tallgrass region.

Mature height: 3 to 5 inches

Description: Bird's-foot violet is a stemless perennial with deeply divided leaves. Flowers are variable, the most common color forms being bicolor with dark purple upper petals and light blue lower ones, and uniform light blue with conspicuous golden yellow stamens. Each flower rests above the foliage atop its own leafless stalk and blooms midspring and occasionally again in fall. Plants may be rhizomatous and form vegetative offsets.

Site requirements: Best grown in sandy or gravelly, dry to medium moisture, well-drained soils in full sun but tolerates part sun. Sandy or rocky soil will help reduce competition from other plants. A slightly acidic pH is preferred.

Landscape use: Unlike most woodland violets, prairie violets are usually very well behaved in the landscape. Plant them along pathways, in the front of borders, or in rock gardens. They adapt well to containers and are pretty in trough gardens.

Wildlife attraction: Flowers attract bees and small butterflies. Caterpillars of various fritillary butterflies feed on the foliage and flowers, and the caterpillars of regal fritillary may prefer this violet species. Ants are attracted to the sugary gel on the seeds and help to distribute them. Birds eat the seeds. Deer often avoid plants because they are so low to the ground.

Maintenance: Prairie species are more difficult to grow than woodland violets. Good soil drainage is key; crown rot may develop if the soil is poorly drained. Foliage may die back in summer if conditions are dry. One of their biggest threats is

Viola pedatifida

nearby plants that can crowd out the delicate violets. Plants may self-seed in optimum conditions, but the seedlings are usually a welcome sight, ensuring the population.

Good companions: Plant bird's-foot violet with other delicate early bloomers such as pasque flower, prairie smoke, blue-eyed grasses, and bluets. It really stands out against the brown grasses when it blooms in prairie gardens in spring.

Other prairie species: *V. pedatifida* (prairie violet) is native to mesic to dry prairies in all but the far southern portions of the tallgrass region. It is similar in appearance to *V. pedata*, but it has a hairy white beard at the throat of its flowers, which also tend to be a little smaller. The attractive divided leaves resemble delphinium foliage, leading to its other common name, larkspur violet. Zones 3 to 9.

Yucca glauca
SOAPWEED YUCCA
Agavaceae
Zones 4 to 10

Native habitat: Dry prairies in the western portion of the tallgrass region and into the mixed prairie region.

Mature height: 1 to 3 feet

Description: Soapweed yucca is a long-lived, taprooted perennial that eventually spreads to form colonies. The foliage is the main attraction, since the greenish white flowers bloom only for a short time, from late spring to early summer. The stiff, narrow, blue-green leaves are covered in spines.

Site requirements: Dry, well-drained soil in full sun.

Landscape use: Soapweed yucca makes an interesting accent plant in borders or rock gardens. It is a perfect plant for xeriscaping. Be sure to place it away from walkways and paths.

Wildlife attraction: The yucca moth uses the plant as a nectar and egg-laying site. Flowers also attract butterflies.

Yucca glauca

Maintenance: Choose a site carefully for this long-lived, difficult-to-transplant perennial. Water only during establishment; after that, plants are very drought tolerant.

Good companions: In borders, soften the bold texture by surrounding soapweed yucca with summer bloomers such as prairie phlox, upright prairie coneflower, flowering spurge, and evening primroses.

Zizia aurea

GOLDEN ALEXANDERS

Apiaceae

Zones 4 to 8

Native habitat: Moist to wet prairies throughout the tallgrass region.

Mature height: 1 to 3 feet

Description: Golden alexanders has bright yellow, 3-inch umbels for about a month in late spring to early summer. The shiny compound leaves are trifoliate, with leaflets up to 3 inches long. The root system is a dense cluster of coarse fibrous roots.

Site requirements: The preference is moist to wet soil in full sun, although part sun and dry soil are tolerated.

Landscape use: The flattened heads of yellow flowers are a cheery accent in a spring garden, and the delicate foliage looks nice as well. Use it in perennial borders and butterfly gardens, where it will weave its way through other plants.

Wildlife attraction: *Zizia* flowers are attractive to many kinds of insects seeking pollen or nectar, including bees, wasps, flies, and beetles. Small butterflies and plant bugs also visit the flowers. Black swallowtail caterpillars eat the leaves and flowers.

Maintenance: Once established, alexanders are carefree plants that tolerate summer dryness. Individual plants may be short-lived, but they will self-sow to maintain the population. Foliage usually declines as the summer progresses.

Good companions: The yellow flowers combine nicely with prairie smoke, prairie phlox, large beardtongue, and wild lupine.

Other prairie species: *Z. aptera* (heart-leaved alexanders) has smaller flowers but more attractive foliage, which consists of rosettes of leathery basal leaves. Compared to golden alexanders it stays a little shorter, is not as invasive, and tolerates drier sites, making it a good choice for borders, rock gardens, and other areas of the landscape. Zones 3 to 8.

Zizia aurea

GRASSES AND SEDGES

Native grasses should be a part of any prairie garden, and many are ornamental enough to be used in other areas of the landscape as well. They are easy to grow and care for, and they wave in the slightest breeze, bringing a sense of movement to a landscape. They have multi-season interest, but most are especially valuable in fall and winter, when they combine beautifully with late-blooming prairie flowers as well as evergreens and fruiting shrubs. Taller types can be used like shrubs, as background plants, as specimens, or even as a hedge. Smaller types work well with annuals and perennials in herbaceous borders.

Grasses have a pure, abstract quality that blends well with modern architecture and current naturalistic design aesthetics, and their shapes, colors, and textures contrast nicely with wood, stone, and other

The clumping, upright forms of many prairie grasses are a nice contrast to looser-growing flowering plants.

hard structural surfaces. Some people choose to create entire gardens of grasses. Beyond their landscape value, most are valuable sources of food and cover for birds, and the mature seed heads are prized for dried arrangements.

Most prairie grasses and sedges are long-lived perennials. Grasses all belong to Poaceae (sometimes still called Gramineae). Grasslike sedges are members of Cyperaceae; they can be distinguished from true grasses by their solid, three-angled flower stems and the structure of their flowers. All grasses are herbaceous, with leaves that are generally narrow with parallel veins. Stems are round and hollow except at the nodes, the point where the leaf joins the stem. They have extensive branching root systems, never a taproot. Most sedges form dense, compact clumps of bright green foliage; many species were found on prairies, but only *Carex pensylvanica* is well-adapted to typical landscape use.

There are about 150 species of grasses in tallgrass prairies, but only about a dozen achieve any dominance; the main two are the bluestems, big and little, followed by Indiangrass, American sloughgrass (*Beckmannia syzigachne*), switchgrass, prairie dropseed, sideoats grama, Canada wild rye (*Elymus canadensis*), prairie Junegrass, porcupine grass (*Hesperostipa spartea*), slender wheatgrass (*Elymus trachycaulus*), and needle and thread (*Hesperostipa comata*).

Being wind-pollinated, grasses don't need brightly colored flowers to attract insects. They release their pollen into the air to float from flower head to flower head on gentle breezes. The lack of brightly colored flowers doesn't mean these prairie grasses aren't showy. The inconspicuous flowers are arranged in tight, vertical clusters called spikes, or branched clusters called panicles. Most grasses flower from midsummer into fall, but some flower earlier. A dark fence or background of evergreens will make it easier to see the flowers. In late summer their seed heads turn a multitude of subtle but rich shades ranging from bronze to gold to crimson, and many have colorful fall foliage as well.

Grasses are classified as mounded, upright, arching, open, irregular, and combinations of these forms. Most grow from clumps and are easy to use in the landscape, but some spread by creeping rhizomes (underground stems) or stolons (horizontal stems that creep just above or just below ground and root at nodes). These spreading types are best used in prairie gardens, for erosion control, or groundcover. Bunchgrasses are shorter than other grasses and grow in clumps; they prefer the drier climates of the shortgrass prairie and the drier areas of tallgrass prairies, where little bluestem is the dominant bunchgrass. Sod grasses, such as big bluestem and Indiangrass, dominate tallgrass prairies; they spread horizontally via rhizomes or stolons.

There are both cool- and warm-season prairie grasses. Their distribution is strongly determined by latitude. As their name implies, cool-season grasses start growing much earlier than warm-season grasses. Cool-season prairie grasses include prairie Junegrass, Canada wild rye, and tufted hairgrass. These grasses usually start greening up in mid- to late spring and produce seed heads by early summer. Be sure to include some cool-season grasses in your prairie garden or landscape, to provide early season interest.

Warm-season grasses start growing later in spring and really don't look like much until midsummer, producing seed in late summer and fall. The bluestems, Indiangrass, switchgrass, and prairie dropseed are warm-season grasses. Warm-season grasses bring much grace and beauty to the late summer, fall, and winter landscape, but they don't have much to offer early on. Plant spring and early summer grasses and forbs nearby to distract from the brown clumps.

Andropogon gerardii
BIG BLUESTEM
Poaceae
Zones 3 to 8

Native habitat: A dominant species of mesic tallgrass prairies but found in all prairie types.

Mature height: 4 to 8 feet

Description: This upright, clump-forming, warm-season grass is sturdy and long-lived. The blue-green leaves are 1 to 2 feet long and softly hairy near the base. Foliage turns bronzy red-orange in late fall, often picking up deep burgundy tints with the onset of frost. Silvery white flowers appear in midsummer and are held close to the axis of the two- to three-times branched inflorescence, which resembles an upside-down turkey foot (hence another common name, turkeyfoot grass). Drooping seed heads follow in late summer.

Site requirements: Moist to dry soils in full to part sun.

Landscape use: Although attractive, big bluestem's large size limits its landscape use. It is effective singly in a large border or in a mass planting for screening and

Andropogon gerardii

naturalizing and in rain gardens. Flowers and seed heads are good for drying. Use it sparingly in a prairie garden.

Wildlife attraction: Larval host of Delaware skipper and dusted skipper butterflies. Many insects feed on the leaves. Songbirds enjoy the seeds. Birds and mammals use it for nesting and winter cover.

Maintenance: Big bluestem is long-lived and difficult to transplant, so choose a site carefully. Water as needed the first year; plants are drought tolerant once established. Mow or cut back hard in early spring. Plants may become lax if soil is too fertile or it is too shady and may lodge under the weight of winter snows.

Good companions: Tall prairie plants such as New England aster, goldenrods, Joe-pye weeds, and Indiangrass, or as a backdrop for butterfly milkweed, coneflowers, and blazing stars.

Cultivars: Most of the several available selections of big bluestem don't seem to differ all that much from the species. 'Silver Sunrise', a hybrid with *A. hallii*, grows 5 to 6 feet tall and has silvery blue foliage.

Other prairie species: *A. hallii* (sand bluestem) is native farther west on mixed prairies. The foliage is more glaucous, and it rarely grows over 6 feet tall. It is more rhizomatous and too aggressive for traditional landscape use but can be naturalized on hot, dry sites. It often hybridizes naturally with big bluestem. It is very drought tolerant and requires a well-drained soil in full sun. Zones 3 to 9.

A. virginicus (broomsedge bluestem) is native to dry prairies, mainly in the southern half of the tallgrass region. It is a clumping grass growing 2 to 3 feet tall with beautiful golden copper fall color. Its smaller size makes it worth considering for landscape use, especially on hot, dry sites. In some western states it has become a pest, so it should be used only in its native range. Zones 4 to 10.

Bouteloua curtipendula

SIDEOATS GRAMA
Poaceae
Zones 3 to 10

Native habitat: Mesic to dry prairies throughout the tallgrass, mixed, and shortgrass prairie regions.

Mature height: 2 to 3 feet

Description: This warm-season, clumping grass has erect, wiry stems and spreads slowly from rhizomes. Its distinguishing feature is the orange and purple, oatlike flower spikelets that dangle uniformly from one side of the stem, rising above the gray-green foliage. It begins blooming earlier than most warm-season grasses and often flowers until late summer. The seed heads turn tan in fall, a nice contrast to the foliage, which often turns shades of purple, orange, and red.

Site requirements: Prefers full sun in dry soils but will grow in part sun.

Landscape use: The smaller size of this grass enables it to be used in a variety of ways, either singly or in broad, dramatic drifts in gardens or landscapes. It does

Bouteloua curtipendula

well with most forbs but can be overtaken by more aggressive grasses. It is good for use between trees in an orchard. Flowers can be used in dried arrangements.

Wildlife attraction: Larval host of green skipper and dotted skipper butterflies. Leafhoppers, grasshoppers, and other insects eat the leaves. Birds eat ripe seeds and use plants for cover and nesting material. Not attractive to deer.

Maintenance: Cut back plants in late winter. Plants spread relatively slowly, but plant it in a buried nursery container if you need to restrict root growth in richer soils.

Good companions: Other low-growing, dry-soil prairie plants such as little bluestem, upright prairie coneflower, butterfly milkweed, and fringeleaf wild petunia.

Other prairie species: *B. dactyloides*

Bouteloua gracilis

(buffalograss) is native to dry soils in all types of prairies, but especially short-grass and mixed-grass prairies. It is a warm-season, rhizomatous grass growing 2 to 6 inches tall in small tufts. It has fine-textured, gray-green leaves that green up midspring. Leaves take on a purple tinge in fall and turn tan in winter. In extreme drought conditions it turns brown and goes dormant. Use it as a low-maintenance, drought-tolerant turf-grass or groundcover on hot, dry sites in full sun. It can be mowed to a height of 1 to 1½ inches every two to four weeks. Do not fertilize after plants are growing well, and water only during very dry conditions. Plants may be divided and replanted in spring to help fill in bare areas. Several cultivars have been selected; most green up earlier than the species, making them worth considering. 'Legacy' and 'Prestige' were selected specifically for lawn use. Both have a nice green color and are quicker to establish. Zones 4 to 8.

B. gracilis (blue grama), a dominant grass of shortgrass prairies, is also found in the mixed and tallgrass regions. It is a clumping grass growing 8 to 15 inches tall. The unique flowers are suspended horizontally like tiny combs at the tips of the flowering stems. They have a red tinge at first, turning tan as they dry. Give it full sun in a well-drained, dry or gravelly soil. It is not aggressive and is very effective for boulevard or parking strips and in xeriscaping. It can be planted densely to create a low or no-mow groundcover, tolerating a fair amount of foot traffic. Zones 3 to 10.

B. hirsuta (hairy grama) is native to upland sand prairies and dry hill prairies and savannas throughout the tallgrass region. It grows 10 to 16 inches tall. The seeds are borne in a curved seed head with a pointed tip and have a long "hair" hanging from the flower, distinguishing it from blue grama. It prefers full sun but tolerates part sun and dry, sandy, or rocky soils. Zones 3 to 10.

Carex pensylvanica
PENNSYLVANIA SEDGE
Cyperaceae
Zones 3 to 8

Native habitat: Oak savannas and openings and upland woods and some prairies, mainly in the eastern half of the tallgrass region.

Mature height: 6 to 10 inches

Description: This grasslike plant is abundant in part sun to full-shade areas in nearby savannas and abutting wood-lands and does make its way into prairies. It spreads by stolons, forming large colonies of loose tufts of fine-textured bright green leaves that arch over. Brownish flower spikes appear in mid- to late spring.

Site requirements: Prefers an acidic, well-drained, average to dry soil in part sun to full shade, but will tolerate a wide range of conditions, including full sun if grown in moister soil.

Landscape use: Pennsylvania sedge makes a beautiful soft-textured ground-

Carex pensylvanica

cover in part sun to full shade. It greens up very early in spring, providing a nice backdrop to spring wildflowers. It tolerates dry shade under large trees. Use it in place of traditional turfgrasses in shady areas where you don't need a tightly mown lawn. It withstands light foot traffic and periodic mowing.

Wildlife attraction: Food for several insects including leafhoppers, grasshoppers, and butterfly caterpillars. Birds eat the seeds. Deer avoid this plant.

Maintenance: Very easy to grow once established. Plants spread slowly; if you want a solid groundcover, place clumps as close together as you can afford to. Plants can be divided anytime during the growing season to increase your numbers.

Pennsylvania sedge can be mown two or three times during the growing season if desired.

Good companions: Plant among spring ephemerals to fill in after they go dormant, or use alone as a large-scale groundcover.

Other prairie species: Among the hundreds of *Carex* species found in North America, relatively few are found in the tallgrass region, and those that are are typically found in habitats too wet or too shady for prairie grasses to thrive. Some of those native to the tallgrass region worth considering for specialized landscape use include *C. bicknellii* (Bicknell's sedge), *C. lupulina* (hop sedge), and *C. vulpinoidea* (fox sedge).

Deschampsia cespitosa

TUFTED HAIRGRASS

Poaceae

Zones 2 to 7

Native habitat: Wet to mesic prairies in the northern half of the tallgrass region.

Mature height: 3 to 4 feet

Description: This cool-season clumping grass forms tight basal tufts that grow about 1 foot tall and eventually spread about 2 feet wide. During summer it produces large, open panicles of glistening silver-tinted flower heads that reach about 3 feet in height. The panicles turn yellowish tan as the seed ripens and remain attractive through much of the winter.

Site requirements: Prefers evenly moist soil in full to part sun but grows well in

most garden soils. Avoid sunny, droughty conditions.

Landscape use: This is a wonderful native grass for cooler climates, but it is not as well suited to southern areas. Use it in perennial borders, grass gardens, or for massing, where it offers the beauty of an ornamental grass long before any of the warm-season prairies grasses are showy. The fine-textured flowers and seed heads are especially effective when backlit or set off by a dark background. A tolerance for wet soils makes this plant useful for planting near water. Tufted hairgrass is one of the few native grasses that can also be used in containers.

Wildlife attraction: Larval host plant for some butterflies. Birds eat the seeds.

Maintenance: Cut back plants in late

Deschampsia cespitosa

fall or very early spring. Plants may self-sow in optimum conditions but rarely become a nuisance.

Good companions: Usually used as a single accent plant or small grouping; makes a nice backdrop for moisture-loving flowers such as cardinal flower, spotted Joe-pye weed, and obedient plant.

Cultivars: Several cultivars are available in the nursery trade, but their parentage is questionable, and some or all may have European species in them. In any case, they don't really have any redeeming qualities that make them a better choice than the species.

Koeleria macrantha
PRAIRIE JUNEGRASS
Poaceae
Zones 3 to 9

Native habitat: Dry sand prairies, hill prairies, and sandy savannas throughout the tallgrass region.

Mature height: 1 to 2 feet

Description: This cool-season perennial bunchgrass rarely forms pure stands, but rather grows in scattered clumps. Leaves are yellow green. It blooms earlier than most prairie grasses—you guessed it, in June. The flattened, gray-green spikelets grow 4 to 6 inches long and open to showy greenish white plumes, turning tan by midsummer.

Site requirements: Well-drained soil in full sun.

Landscape use: Most references don't think prairie Junegrass is ornamental enough for garden and landscape use, but I like it for the spring and early summer interest it brings. It also provides a nice vertical accent to the looser-growing, early summer prairie plants. You need to be prepared for the seed heads to turn brown in midsummer, a trait some people will find objectionable.

Koeleria macrantha

It can tolerate some foot traffic and occasional mowing.

Wildlife attraction: Deer will feed on it when it is green.

Maintenance: Cut back in fall or very early spring. Plants may go into a sort of dormancy in midsummer, but they often green up again in fall. They will self-sow.

Panicum virgatum
SWITCHGRASS
Poaceae
Zones 3 to 9

Native habitat: Mesic to dry tallgrass and mixed prairies throughout North America.

Mature height: 4 to 8 feet

Description: This warm-season clumping grass grows from a dense crown of congested rhizomes. The 1- to 2-foot-long green, blue-green, or silver leaves are sometimes tinged with red toward the tapering tip. Fall color is golden yellow to deep burgundy. The seeds are produced in open, billowy panicles in late summer. There is a lot of natural variation in switchgrass, which has helped lead to the large number of cultivars selected.

Site requirements: Very adaptable, from moist to dry soil in full sun.

Landscape use: Switchgrass cultivars are among the best native grasses for landscape use. They can be used in mixed borders, in rain gardens, as a screen, or in natural gardens. The open flower panicles look best when viewed against a dark background. The dense foliage stands up well in winter, offering welcome interest in that season. It is a good substitute for the nonnative, overused *Miscanthus* species. Dried flowers look good in arrangements.

Wildlife attraction: Insect feeders include leafhoppers and caterpillars of skippers and moths. Seeds are eaten by a variety of birds. Muskrats enjoy pondside plants. The upright foliage provides cover for birds and small mammals in winter. Spring-nesting birds use it for cover. It is usually ignored by deer.

Maintenance: Allow 2 to 3 feet between plants, as clumps become large. Plants are fairly slow to spread, but division will be needed every four years or so to keep plants under control in gardens. Most cultivars do not produce a lot of seeds, but the species will self-sow on open, moist soils. Switchgrass tolerates poor conditions, including poor drainage and occasional flooding.

Good companions: Plant switchgrass with other late-summer prairie plants such as asters, goldenrods, coneflowers, and white doll's daisy. It looks nice with an evergreen background in winter.

Cultivars: The many available selections of switchgrass are usually better choices

Good companions: A nice backdrop for early-blooming plants such as prairie smoke, prairie violets, and pasque flower. Plant showy late-summer forbs such as butterfly milkweed and fringeleaf wild petunia nearby to distract from the brown flower spikes.

Panicum virgatum

for landscape use since they tend to reseed and spread at a much lower rate than the species. Choose a cultivar based on its fall color, the degree of blue in its foliage, its height, or its ability to resist lodging and stay upright. 'Amber Wave' stays less than 4 feet in height. 'Dallas Blues' has broad steel blue to gray-green foliage and huge purple flower panicles. 'Heavy Metal' has metallic blue foliage that turns yellow in fall. 'Northwind' is very sturdy and upright. 'Rotstrahlbusch' has good red fall color. 'Shenandoah' has reddish purple foliage color by midsummer and a distinct reddish cast to the 3-inch flower heads.

Schizachyrium scoparium

LITTLE BLUESTEM

Poaceae

Zones 3 to 9

Native habitat: Mesic to dry-soil prairies throughout most of North America.

Mature height: 2 to 4 feet

Description: This attractive bunchgrass has light green to blue foliage in summer, turning golden to reddish brown in fall and remaining very showy all through winter. Flowering begins in late summer, but the thin flower heads really aren't noticeable until they turn to attractive silvery white seed heads. The fluffy seed heads and crimson-colored foliage are extremely showy in the fall landscape. It is sometimes sold as *Andropogon scoparius*, an outdated name.

Site requirements: Prefers well-drained sand or loam in full sun, but will grow in rocky soils and part sun. Not recommended for heavy clay or damp soils.

Landscape use: Little bluestem is among the best native grasses for fall color, and its small size makes it easy to use in most landscapes. Plant it in mixed borders, along walkways, and in foundation plantings, where it won't overwhelm nearby forbs. It is also wonderful massed as a groundcover and can even be used in rain gardens. Remember, however, being a warm-season grass, it won't green up until late spring.

Wildlife attraction: Larval host of several skipper butterflies and food for many other insects. Provides cover, nesting material, and seed for birds and small mammals. Highly resistant to deer feeding.

Maintenance: Little bluestem is slow to emerge in spring. Cut back clumps in late winter. Full sun is best for upright growth. Shade, high fertility, and abundant moisture contribute to lax, floppy growth. It will reseed.

Good companions: The blue-green foliage provides a great backdrop for summer prairie flowers such as prairie phlox, black-eyed Susan, coneflowers, wild bergamot, blazing stars, asters, and white doll's daisy.

Cultivars: The species is quite attractive and well behaved, but there are some cultivars to consider. 'The Blues' is the most popular, selected for its good blue-green foliage color.

Schizachyrium scoparium

Sorghastrum nutans

Sorghastrum nutans

INDIANGRASS

Poaceae

Zones 3 to 9

Native habitat: A dominant species of moist to dry prairies throughout the tall-grass region.

Mature height: 3 to 5 feet

Description: This warm-season grass develops from a loose clump of thick rhizomes. It produces showy copper-colored flowers in late summer that have large, dangling yellow-orange anthers. Its fall foliage color is golden yellow to dark orange, contrasting nicely with the golden brown silky tassels of the seeds.

Site requirements: Prefers a slightly moist to well-drained soil in full sun but will tolerate part sun.

Landscape use: When its large size can be accommodated, Indiangrass makes a nice addition to perennial borders and rain gardens, where it provides a strong vertical accent. It provides a nice backdrop for lower-growing forbs. It is effective on slopes for erosion control since it grows well on disturbed sites. Seed heads dry well and can be used in arrangements.

Wildlife attraction: Larval host of pepper and salt skipper butterfly. Finches and sparrows feast on seeds all winter. It also provides excellent nesting sites and cover for pheasants, quail, mourning doves, and prairie chickens. Highly resistant to deer feeding.

Maintenance: Cut back plants in late winter. Plants tolerate drought once mature. Plants may open up or flop in moist, rich soils. Indiangrass is not overly aggressive.

Good companions: Late-summer and fall prairie plants such as asters, white doll's daisy, smooth oxeye, rudbeckias, Joe-pye weeds, and wild bergamot. It looks nice planted against a backdrop of evergreens, to set off the flowers.

Cultivars: Several cultivars have been selected, most for their bluer foliage and upright growth habit. 'Sioux Blue' is the best known and most widely available.

Sporobolus heterolepis

PRAIRIE DROPSEED

Poaceae

Zones 3 to 9

Native habitat: Mesic to dry prairies in all but the far southern part of the tall-grass region.

Mature height: 2 to 3 feet

Description: Prairie dropseed is a warm-season, clump-forming grass that slowly expands to form a fountain-like mound about 18 inches in diameter. It has narrow individual blades that are bright green in summer, turning yellow and orange in fall. It blooms in late summer, producing many upright flower stalks topped with pale pink panicles. These flowers have a luscious scent reminiscent of fresh popcorn.

Site requirements: Prefers a well-drained soil with moderate moisture levels and full sun, but will tolerate drier conditions. Avoid constantly wet soils.

Landscape use: Prairie dropseed has an

elegant, refined look that makes it easy to use in many areas of the landscape. Include it in perennial borders and foundation plantings. A mass planting is stunning. Plants usually stay upright all winter.

Wildlife attraction: Foliage is eaten by grasshoppers and leafhoppers. Seeds are an important fall and winter food source for ground-feeding birds.

Maintenance: Prairie dropseed is slow to grow from seeds; start with plants if possible. Once established it is long-lived. Cut back in early spring before new foliage emerges. Dig and divide clumps in spring as needed. Give plants plenty of room to fully arch. Plants do not spread, but they do set some seed.

Good companions: Plant fine-textured prairie dropseed with butterfly milkweed, tickseeds, asters, coneflowers, and blazing stars, or use alone as a large-scale groundcover.

Sporobolus heterolepis

Tallgrass Prairie Plants for Gardens and Landscapes

The following plants are native to the tallgrass prairie and are available through several retail sources. Any of the plants in these four lists (flowers, grasses and sedges, shrubs and small trees, and trees) can be considered for use in large prairie gardens, but some may be too coarse or aggressive for smaller gardens and traditional landscape use. Flowers, grasses, and sedges that are described in the Plant Profiles section are listed in boldface. These lists are based on "Vascular Plants of Midwestern Tallgrass Prairies" by Douglas Ladd, included as an appendix to *The Tallgrass Restoration Handbook* (Packard and Mutel 2005).

FLOWERS
Achillea millefolium (common yarrow)
Acorus calamus (calamus)
Allium canadense (meadow garlic)
Allium cernuum (nodding onion)
Allium stellatum (autumn onion)
Amorpha canescens (leadplant)
Amorpha fruticosa (desert false indigo)
Amorpha nana (dwarf false indigo)
Anemone canadensis (Canadian anemone)

Anemone caroliniana (Carolina anemone)
Anemone cylindrica (candle anemone)
Anemone multifida (Pacific anemone)
Anemone quinquefolia (wood anemone)
Anemone virginiana (tall thimbleweed)
Angelica atropurpurea (purplestem angelica)
Antennaria neglecta (field pussytoes)
Antennaria parlinii (Parlin's pussytoes)
Antennaria parvifolia (small-leaf pussytoes)
Antennaria plantaginifolia (plantain pussytoes)
Antennaria rosea (rosy pussytoes)
Arnoglossum atriplicifolium (pale Indian plantain)
Artemisia frigida (prairie sagewort)
Artemisia ludoviciana (white sagebrush)
Asclepias hirtella (green milkweed)
Asclepias incarnata (swamp milkweed)
Asclepias purpurascens (purple milkweed)
Asclepias speciosa (showy milkweed)
Asclepias sullivantii (prairie milkweed)
Asclepias syriaca (common milkweed)
Asclepias tuberosa (butterfly milkweed)
Asclepias verticillata (whorled milkweed)

Asclepias viridiflora (green comet
  milkweed)
Asclepias viridis (green antelopehorn
  milkweed)
Astragalus canadensis (Canadian
  milkvetch)
Astragalus crassicarpus (groundplum
  milkvetch)
Baptisia alba var. **macrophylla** (largeleaf
  wild indigo)
Baptisia australis var. **minor** (blue wild
  indigo)
Baptisia bracteata var. **leucophaea** (long-
  bract wild indigo)
Baptisia tinctoria (horseflyweed)
Blephilia ciliata (downy pagoda-plant)
Boltonia asteroides (white doll's daisy)
Callirhoe alcaeoides (light poppymallow)
Callirhoe bushii (Bush's poppymallow)
Callirhoe digitata (winecup)
Callirhoe involucrata (purple
  poppymallow)
Callirhoe triangulata (clustered
  poppymallow)
Calopogon tuberosus (tuberous
  grasspink)
Caltha palustris (yellow marsh marigold)
Calylophus serrulatus (yellow sundrops)
Camassia angusta (prairie camas)
Camassia scilloides (Atlantic camas)
Campanula rotundifolia (harebell)
Castilleja coccinea (scarlet Indian
  paintbrush)
Castilleja sessiliflora (downy paintedcup)
Ceanothus americanus (New Jersey tea)
Ceanothus herbaceus (Jersey tea)
Chamaecrista fasciculata (partridge pea)
Chelone glabra (white turtlehead)
Claytonia virginica (Virginia spring
  beauty)

Cleome serrulata (Rocky Mountain
  beeplant)
Coreopsis grandiflora (largeflower
  tickseed)
Coreopsis lanceolata (lanceleaf tickseed)
Coreopsis palmata (stiff tickseed)
Coreopsis tripteris (tall tickseed)
Cypripedium parviflorum (lesser yellow
  lady's slipper)
Cypripedium parviflorum ssp. **pubescens**
  (greater yellow lady's slipper)
Cypripedium reginae (showy lady's
  slipper)
Dalea candida (white prairie clover)
Dalea purpurea (purple prairie clover)
Delphinium carolinianum (Carolina
  larkspur)
Desmanthus illinoensis (Illinois
  bundleflower)
Desmodium canadense (showy ticktrefoil)
Desmodium illinoense (Illinois ticktrefoil)
Dodecatheon meadia (prairie shooting
  star)
Doellingeria umbellata (parasol whitetop)
Echinacea angustifolia (blacksamson
  echinacea)
Echinacea pallida (pale purple
  coneflower)
Echinacea paradoxa (Bush's purple
  coneflower)
Echinacea purpurea (eastern purple
  coneflower)
Eryngium yuccifolium (rattlesnake
  master)
Eupatoriadelphus maculatus (spotted
  Joe-pye weed)
Eupatorium altissimum (tall
  thoroughwort)
Eupatorium perfoliatum (common
  boneset)

Euphorbia corollata (flowering spurge)

Euphorbia marginata (snow on the mountain)

Filipendula rubra (queen of the prairie)

Fragaria virginiana (Virginia strawberry)

Gaillardia aristata (common gaillardia)

Gaillardia pulchella (firewheel)

Galium boreale (northern bedstraw)

Gaura biennis (biennial beeblossom)

Gaura coccinea (scarlet beeblossom)

Gentiana alba (plain gentian)

Gentiana andrewsii (closed bottle gentian)

Gentiana puberulenta (downy gentian)

Gentiana saponaria (harvestbells)

Gentianella quinquefolia (agueweed)

Gentianopsis crinita (greater fringed gentian)

Geum triflorum (prairie smoke)

Helenium autumnale (autumn sneezeweed)

Helenium flexuosum (purplehead sneezeweed)

Helianthus annuus (common sunflower)

Helianthus decapetalus (thinleaf sunflower)

Helianthus divaricatus (woodland sunflower)

Helianthus giganteus (giant sunflower)

Helianthus grosseserratus (sawtooth sunflower)

Helianthus hirsutus (hairy sunflower)

Helianthus maximiliani (Maximilian sunflower)

Helianthus mollis (ashy sunflower)

Helianthus occidentalis (fewleaf sunflower)

Helianthus pauciflorus (stiff sunflower)

Helianthus salicifolius (willowleaf sunflower)

Helianthus strumosus (paleleaf woodland sunflower)

Helianthus tuberosus (Jerusalem artichoke)

Heliopsis helianthoides (smooth oxeye)

Heterotheca villosa (hairy false goldenaster)

Heuchera americana (American alumroot)

Heuchera richardsonii (prairie alumroot)

Houstonia caerulea (azure bluet)

Houstonia longifolia (longleaf summer bluet)

Hypoxis hirsuta (common goldstar)

Iris virginica var. *shrevei* (Shreve's iris)

Lespedeza capitata (roundhead lespedeza)

Liatris aspera (tall blazing star)

Liatris cylindracea (Ontario blazing star)

Liatris ligulistylis (northern plains blazing star)

Liatris mucronata (cusp blazing star)

Liatris punctata (dotted blazing star)

Liatris pycnostachya (prairie blazing star)

Liatris spicata (dense blazing star)

Liatris squarrosa (scaly blazing star)

Lilium michiganense (Michigan lily)

Lilium philadelphicum (wood lily)

Lobelia cardinalis (cardinal flower)

Lobelia siphilitica (great blue lobelia)

Lobelia spicata (palespike lobelia)

Lupinus perennis (wild lupine)

Lysimachia ciliata (fringed loosestrife)

Lythrum alatum (winged lythrum)

Maianthemum stellata (starry false lily of the valley)

Monarda citriodora (lemon beebalm)

Monarda fistulosa (wild bergamot)

Monarda punctata (spotted beebalm)

Oenothera biennis (common evening primrose)

Oenothera caespitosa (tufted evening primrose)

Oenothera fruticosa (narrowleaf evening primrose)

Oenothera macrocarpa (bigfruit evening primrose)

Oenothera pilosella (meadow evening primrose)

Oenothera speciosa (pinkladies)

Oenothera triloba (stemless evening primrose)

Oligoneuron album (prairie goldenrod)

Oligoneuron riddellii (Riddell's goldenrod)

Onosmodium bejariense (soft-hair marbleseed)

Opuntia fragilis (brittle pricklypear)

Opuntia humifusa (eastern pricklypear)

Opuntia macrorhiza (twistspine pricklypear)

Oxalis violacea (violet woodsorrel)

Packera aurea (golden ragwort)

Packera plattensis (prairie groundsel)

Parthenium integrifolium (wild quinine)

Pedicularis canadensis (Canadian lousewort)

Pedicularis lanceolata (swamp lousewort)

Penstemon cobaea (cobaea beardtongue)

Penstemon digitalis (foxglove penstemon)

Penstemon gracilis (lilac penstemon)

Penstemon grandiflorus (large beardtongue)

Penstemon hirsutus (hairy beardtongue)

Penstemon pallidus (pale beardtongue)

Penstemon tubiflorus (white wand beardtongue)

Phlox bifida (sand phlox)

Phlox glaberrima (smooth phlox)

Phlox maculata (wild sweet William)

Phlox pilosa (prairie phlox)

Phlox pilosa ssp. *fulgida* (downy phlox)

Physostegia angustifolia (narrowleaf false dragonhead)

Physostegia virginiana (obedient plant)

Platanthera ciliaris (yellow fringed orchid)

Polygonatum biflorum var. *commutatum* (smooth Solomon's seal)

Polytaenia nuttallii (Nuttall's prairie parsley)

Potentilla arguta (tall cinquefoil)

Prenanthes racemosa (purple rattle-snakeroot)

Prunella vulgaris (common selfheal)

Pulsatilla patens (pasque flower)

Pycnanthemum tenuifolium (narrowleaf mountainmint)

Pycnanthemum virginianum (Virginia mountainmint)

Ratibida columnifera (upright prairie coneflower)

Ratibida pinnata (gray-headed prairie coneflower)

Rosa arkansana (prairie rose)

Rosa blanda (smooth rose)

Rosa carolina (Carolina rose)

Rosa foliolosa (white prairie rose)

Rosa setigera (climbing prairie rose)

Rosa woodsii (Woods' rose)

Rudbeckia fulgida (orange coneflower)

Rudbeckia hirta (black-eyed Susan)

Rudbeckia missouriensis (Missouri orange coneflower)

Rudbeckia subtomentosa (sweet coneflower)

Rudbeckia triloba (brown-eyed Susan)

Ruellia humilis (fringeleaf wild petunia)

Salvia azurea var. *grandiflora* (pitcher sage)

Sanguisorba canadensis (Canadian burnet)

Senna marilandica (Maryland senna)

Silene regia (royal catchfly)

Silene stellata (widowsfrill)

Silphium integrifolium (wholeleaf rosinweed)
Silphium laciniatum (compass plant)
Silphium perfoliatum (cup plant)
Silphium terebinthinaceum (prairie rosinweed)
Sisyrinchium albidum (white blue-eyed grass)
Sisyrinchium angustifolium (narrowleaf blue-eyed grass)
Sisyrinchium campestre (prairie blue-eyed grass)
Sisyrinchium montanum (strict blue-eyed grass)
Solidago gigantea (giant goldenrod)
Solidago juncea (early goldenrod)
Solidago missouriensis (Missouri goldenrod)
Solidago nemoralis (gray goldenrod)
Solidago ohioensis (Ohio goldenrod)
Solidago rigida (stiff goldenrod)
Solidago rugosa (wrinkleleaf goldenrod)
Solidago speciosa (showy goldenrod)
Spiranthes cernua (nodding lady's tresses)
Symphyotrichum dumosum (rice button aster)
Symphyotrichum ericoides (white heath aster)
Symphyotrichum laeve (smooth blue aster)
Symphyotrichum lateriflorum (calico aster)
Symphyotrichum novae-angliae (New England aster)
Symphyotrichum oblongifolium (aromatic aster)
Symphyotrichum oolentangiense (skyblue aster)
Symphyotrichum pilosum (hairy white oldfield aster)
Symphyotrichum praealtum (willowleaf aster)

Symphyotrichum puniceum (purplestem aster)
Symphyotrichum sericeum (western silver aster)
Symphyotrichum turbinellum (smooth violet prairie aster)
Taenidia integerrima (yellow pimpernel)
Tephrosia virginiana (Virginia tephrosia)
Teucrium canadense (Canada germander)
Thalictrum dasycarpum (purple meadow-rue)
Tradescantia bracteata (longbract spiderwort)
Tradescantia occidentalis (prairie spiderwort)
Tradescantia ohiensis (bluejacket)
Tradescantia virginiana (Virginia spiderwort)
Verbena hastata (swamp verbena)
Verbena stricta (hoary verbena)
Vernonia arkansana (Arkansas ironweed)
Vernonia baldwinii (Baldwin's ironweed)
Vernonia fasciculata (prairie ironweed)
Vernonia gigantea (giant ironweed)
Vernonia missurica (Missouri ironweed)
Veronicastrum virginicum (Culver's root)
Viola pedata (bird's-foot violet)
Viola pedatifida (prairie violet)
Viola sagittata (arrowleaf violet)
Viola sororia (common blue violet)
Yucca glauca (soapweed yucca)
Zigadenus elegans (mountain deathcamas)
Zizia aptera (heart-leaved alexanders)
Zizia aurea (golden alexanders)

GRASSES AND SEDGES
Andropogon gerardii (big bluestem)
Andropogon glomeratus (bushy bluestem)
Andropogon hallii (sand bluestem)

Andropogon virginicus (broomsedge bluestem)

Bouteloua curtipendula (sideoats grama)

Bouteloua dactyloides (buffalograss)

Bouteloua gracilis (blue grama)

Bouteloua hirsuta (hairy grama)

Bromus ciliatus (fringed brome)

Bromus kalmii (arctic brome)

Bromus latiglumis (earlyleaf brome)

Calamagrostis canadensis (bluejoint)

Carex bebbii (Bebb's sedge)

Carex bicknellii (Bicknell's sedge)

Carex brevior (shortbeak sedge)

Carex comosa (longhair sedge)

Carex cristatella (crested sedge)

Carex lacustris (hairy sedge)

Carex lupulina (hop sedge)

Carex pensylvanica (Pennsylvania sedge)

Carex vulpinoidea (fox sedge)

Deschampsia cespitosa (tufted hairgrass)

Elymus canadensis (Canada wild rye)

Elymus trachycaulus (slender wheatgrass)

Elymus villosus (hairy wild rye)

Elymus virginicus (Virginia wild rye)

Eragrostis spectabilis (purple lovegrass)

Eragrostis trichodes (sand lovegrass)

Hesperostipa comata (needle and thread)

Hesperostipa spartea (porcupine grass)

Hierochloe odorata (sweet grass)

Koeleria macrantha (prairie Junegrass)

Panicum virgatum (switchgrass)

Schizachyrium scoparium (little bluestem)

Schoenoplectus acutus (hardstem bulrush)

Scirpus atrovirens (green bulrush)

Scirpus cyperinus (wool grass)

Sorghastrum nutans (Indiangrass)

Spartina pectinata (prairie cordgrass)

Sporobolus cryptandrus (sand dropseed)

Sporobolus heterolepis (prairie dropseed)

Tridens flavus (purpletop tridens)

SHRUBS AND SMALL TREES

Cephalanthus occidentalis (common buttonbush)

Comptonia peregrina (sweet fern)

Cornus amomum (silky dogwood)

Cornus drummondii (roughleaf dogwood)

Cornus racemosa (gray dogwood)

Cornus sericea (redosier dogwood)

Dasiphora fruticosa ssp. *floribunda* (shrubby cinquefoil)

Hypericum kalmianum (Kalm's St. Johnswort)

Prunus angustifolia (Chickasaw plum)

Prunus virginiana (chokecherry)

Ptelea trifoliata (common hoptree)

Rhus aromatica (fragrant sumac)

Rhus copallinum (winged sumac)

Rhus glabra (smooth sumac)

Salix discolor (pussy willow)

Salix humilis (prairie willow)

Salix interior (sandbar willow)

Spiraea alba (white meadowsweet)

Spiraea tomentosa (steeplebush)

Symphoricarpos occidentalis (western snowberry)

Symphoricarpos orbiculatus (coralberry)

TREES

Diospyros virginiana (common persimmon)

Juniperus virginiana (eastern redcedar)

Malus ioensis (prairie crab apple)

Populus tremuloides (quaking aspen)

Prunus americana (American plum)

Quercus imbricaria (shingle oak)

Quercus macrocarpa (bur oak)

Quercus prinoides (dwarf chinkapin oak)

Quercus stellata (post oak)

Sassafras albidum (sassafras)

Ulmus americana (American elm)

Ulmus rubra (slippery elm)

Resources

PLACES TO BUY PRAIRIE PLANTS

Stick with sources as close to home as possible, especially if you are planting a large habitat garden. The following are mail-order sources of plants.

Beeches Nursery, Ashdon, Essex, United Kingdom
www.beechesnursery.co.uk

Doyle Farm Nursery, Delta, Pennsylvania
www.doylefarm.com

Earth First Native Plant Nursery, Egg Harbor, New Jersey
www.earthfirstnatives.com

Envirotech Consultants, Inc., Somerset, Ohio
www.envirotechcon.com

Fragrant Path, Fort Calhoun, Nebraska
www.fragrantpathseeds.com

Great Basin Natives, Holden, Utah
www.greatbasinnatives.com

Grow Wild Native Plant Nursery, Claremont, Ontario
www.grow-wild.com

Holland Wildflower Farm, Elkins, Arkansas
www.hwildflower.com

Ion Exchange Native Seed, Harpers Ferry, Iowa
www.ionxchange.com

J. F. New and Associates, Walkerton, Indiana
www.jfnew.com

Kaw River Restoration Nurseries, Lawrence, Kansas
www.appliedeco.com/krrn

Kinnickinnic Native Plants, River Falls, Wisconsin
www.kinninatives.com

Knoll Gardens, Wimborne, Dorset, United Kingdom
www.knollgardens.co.uk

Morning Sky Greenery, Morris, Minnesota
www.morningskygreenery.com

Native American Seed, Junction, Texas
www.seedsource.com

Naturally Native Nursery, Bowling Green, Ohio
www.naturallynative.net

Naturescape, Langar, Notts., United Kingdom
www.naturescape.co.uk

Oak Prairie Farm, Pardeeville, Wisconsin
www.oakprairiefarm.com

Ohio Prairie Nursery, Hiram, Ohio
www.ohioprairienursery.com

Prairie and Wetland Center, Belton,
Missouri
www.critsite.com

Prairie Flower, Spencer, Iowa
www.theprairieflower.com

Prairie Frontier, Waukesha, Wisconsin
www.prairiefrontier.com

Prairie Moon Nursery, Winona,
Minnesota
www.prairiemoon.com

Prairie Nursery, Westfield, Wisconsin
www.prairienursery.com

Prairie Restorations, Inc., Princeton,
Minnesota
www.prairieresto.com

Prairie Seed Source, North Lake,
Wisconsin
www.prairiebob.com

Prairie Wild, Cottonwood, Minnesota
www.prairiewild.com

Spring Lake Restoration Nurseries, Prior
Lake, Minnesota
www.appliedeco.com/slrn

Stock Seed Farms, Murdock, Nebraska
www.stockseed.com

Sunscapes, Pueblo, Colorado
www.sunscapes.net

Taylor Creek Restoration Nurseries,
Brodhead, Wisconsin
www.appliedeco.com/tcrn

Western Native Seed, Coaldale, Colorado
www.westernnativeseed.com

Wildflower Farm, Coldwater, Ontario
www.wildflowerfarm.com

Wind River Seed, Manderson, Wyoming
www.windriverseed.com

Yellow Springs Farm, Chester Springs,
Pennsylvania
www.yellowspringsfarm.com

PLACES TO SEE PRAIRIE PLANTS

Badlands National Park, Cedar Pass,
South Dakota
www.nps.gov/badl/index.htm

Chicago Botanic Garden, Illinois
www.chicago-botanic.org

Cofrin Memorial Arboretum, Green Bay,
Wisconsin
www.uwgb.edu/biodiversity/arboretum/
index.htm

Dyck Arboretum of the Plains, Hesston,
Kansas
www.dyckarboretum.org

Goose Lake Prairie State Natural Area,
Morris, Illinois
dnr.state.il.us/LANDS/Landmgt/PARKS/
I&M/EAST/GOOSE/HOME.HTM

Grasslands National Park of Canada, Val
Marie, Saskatchewan
www.pc.gc.ca/eng/pn-np/sk/grasslands/
index.aspx

Houston Arboretum and Nature Center,
Texas
www.houstonarboretum.org

Kauffman Museum, North Newton, Kansas
www.bethelks.edu/kauffman/index.html

Konza Prairie Biological Station, Manhattan, Kansas
kpbs.konza.ksu.edu

Lady Bird Johnson Wildflower Center, Austin, Texas
www.wildflower.org

Minnesota Landscape Arboretum, Chaska, Minnesota
www.arboretum.umn.edu

Missouri Botanical Garden, St. Louis, Missouri
www.mobot.org

Morton Arboretum, Lisle, Illinois
www.mortonarb.org

Nachusa Grasslands, Franklin Grove, Illinois
www.nachusagrasslands.org

National Grasslands, various states
www.fs.fed.us/grasslands

Neal Smith National Wildlife Refuge, Prairie City, Iowa
www.tallgrass.org

Nichols Arboretum, Ann Arbor, Michigan
www.lsa.umich.edu/mbg/default.asp

Overland Park Arboretum and Botanical Gardens, Overland Park, Kansas
www.artsandrec-op.org/arboretum

Pipestone National Monument, Pipestone, Minnesota
www.nps.gov/pipe/index.htm

Prairie State Park, Mindenmines, Missouri
www.mostateparks.com/prairie.htm

Royal Saskatchewan Museum Native Plant Garden, Regina, Saskatchewan
www.royalsaskmuseum.ca/index.shtml

Shaw Nature Reserve, Gray Summit, Missouri
www.shawnature.org

Tallgrass Prairie National Preserve, Strong City, Kansas
www.nps.gov/tapr/index.htm

Tallgrass Prairie Preserve, Pawhuska, Oklahoma
www.nature.org/wherewework/
northamerica/states/oklahoma/
preserves/tallgrass.html

University of Wisconsin-Madison Arboretum, Madison, Wisconsin
www.uwarboretum.org

Plant Hardiness Zones

AVERAGE ANNUAL MINIMUM TEMPERATURE

ZONE	TEMPERATURE (°F)			TEMPERATURE (°C)		
1		below −50		−45.6	and below	
2a	−45	to	−50	−42.8	to	−45.5
2b	−40	to	−45	−40.0	to	−42.7
3a	−35	to	−40	−37.3	to	−40.0
3b	−30	to	−35	−34.5	to	−37.2
4a	−25	to	−30	−31.7	to	−34.4
4b	−20	to	−25	−28.9	to	−31.6
5a	−15	to	−20	−26.2	to	−28.8
5b	−10	to	−15	−23.4	to	−26.1
6a	−5	to	−10	−20.6	to	−23.3
6b	0	to	−5	−17.8	to	−20.5
7a	5	to	0	−15.0	to	−17.7
7b	10	to	5	−12.3	to	−15.0
8a	15	to	10	−9.5	to	−12.2
8b	20	to	15	−6.7	to	−9.4
9a	25	to	20	−3.9	to	−6.6
9b	30	to	25	−1.2	to	−3.8
10a	35	to	30	1.6	to	−1.1
10b	40	to	35	4.4	to	1.7
11	40	and above		4.5	and above	

$$°C = 5/9 \times (°F - 32)$$
$$°F = (9/5 \times °C) + 32$$

Further Reading

Armitage, Allan M. 2006. *Armitage's Native Plants for North American Gardens*. Portland, Oregon: Timber Press.

Brown, Lauren. 1985. *Grasslands*. Audubon Society Nature Guides. New York: Alfred A. Knopf.

Burghardt, Karin T., Douglas W. Tallamy, and W. Gregory Shriver. 2009. Impact of native plants on bird and butterfly biodiversity in suburban landscapes. *Conservation Biology* 23: 219–224.

Cullina, William. 2000. *The New England Wild Flower Society Guide to Growing and Propagating Wildflowers of the United States and Canada*. New York: Houghton Mifflin.

——. 2002. *Native Trees, Shrubs, and Vines: A Guide to Using, Growing, and Propagating North American Woody Plants*. New York: Houghton Mifflin.

——. 2008. *Native Ferns, Moss, and Grasses*. New York: Houghton Mifflin.

Darke, Rick. 2007. *The Encyclopedia of Grasses for Livable Landscapes*. Portland, Oregon: Timber Press.

DiSabato-Aust, Tracy. 2006. *The Well-Tended Perennial Garden*. Expanded ed. Portland, Oregon: Timber Press.

Henderson, Richard. 1995. Oak savanna communities. In *Wisconsin's Biodiversity as a Management Issue*. Wisconsin Department of Natural Resources Bulletin, Madison.

Jones, Stephen R., and Ruth Carol Cushman. 2004. *A Field Guide to the North American Prairie*. Peterson Field Guides. New York: Houghton Mifflin.

Kilde, Rebecca. 2000. *Going Native: A Prairie Restoration Handbook for Minnesota Landowners*. Minnesota: Department of Natural Resources.

Ladd, Doug, and Frank Oberle. 2005. *Tallgrass Prairie Wildflowers: A Field Guide to Common Wildflowers and Plants*. Falcon Guides Wildflowers. Guilford, Connecticut: Globe Pequot Press.

Leopold, Donald J. 2005. *Native Plants of the Northeast*. Portland, Oregon: Timber Press.

Madson, John. 2004. *Where the Sky Began: Land of the Tallgrass Prairie*. Rev. ed. Iowa City: University of Iowa Press.

Nowak, Mariette. 2007. *Birdscaping in the Midwest: A Guide to Gardening with Native Plants to Attract Birds*. Blue Mounds, Wisconsin: Itchy Cat Press.

Packard, Stephen, and Cornelia F. Mutel, eds. 2005. *The Tallgrass Restoration Handbook: For Prairies, Savannas, and*

Woodlands. Rev. ed. Washington, D.C.: Island Press.

Royer, France, and Richard Dickinson. 1999. *Weeds of the Northern U.S. and Canada*. Edmonton: University of Alberta Press.

Shirley, Shirley. 1994. *Restoring the Tallgrass Prairie*. Iowa City: University of Iowa Press.

Steiner, Lynn M. 2005. *Landscaping with Native Plants of Minnesota*. Minneapolis: Voyageur Press.

———. 2007. *Landscaping with Native Plants of Wisconsin*. Minneapolis: Voyageur Press.

Tallamy, Douglas W. 2007. *Bringing Nature Home*. Portland, Oregon: Timber Press.

Wasowski, Sally. 2002. *Gardening with Prairie Plants: How to Create Beautiful Native Landscapes*. Minneapolis: University of Minnesota Press.

Index

white wand. See *Penstemon tubiflorus*

Beckmannia syzigachne 260

bedstraw, northern. See *Galium boreale*

beeblossom
biennial. See *Gaura biennis*
scarlet. See *Gaura coccinea*

beebalm
lemon. See *Monarda citriodora*
spotted. See *Monarda punctata*

beeplant, Rocky Mountain. See *Cleome serrulata*

bellwort
largeflower. See *Uvularia grandiflora*
sessileleaf. See *Uvularia sessilifolia*

Berberis species 101

bergamot, wild. See *Monarda fistulosa*

Betula pendula 127

Betula nigra 99, 127

birch
European white. See *Betula pendula*
river. See *Betula nigra*

bird's-foot trefoil. See *Lotus corniculatus*

bittersweet
American. See *Celastrus scandens*
Oriental. See *Celastrus orbiculatus*

black cherry. See *Prunus serotina*

black-eyed Susan. See *Rudbeckia hirta*
sweet. See *Rudbeckia subtomentosa*

blackfoot daisy. See *Melampodium* species

blacksamson echinacea. See *Echinacea angustifolia*

blazing star
cusp. See *Liatris mucronata*

cylindric. See *Liatris cylindracea*
dense. See *Liatris spicata*
dotted. See *Liatris punctata*
northern plains. See *Liatris ligulistylis*
Ontario. See *Liatris cylindracea*
prairie. See *Liatris pycnostachya*
Rocky Mountain. See *Liatris ligulistylis*
rough. See *Liatris aspera*
scaly. See *Liatris squarrosa*
tall. See *Liatris aspera*

Blephilia ciliata 278

bloodroot. See *Sanguinaria canadensis*

bluebell bellflower. See *Campanula rotundifolia*

blue-eyed grass
mountain. See *Sisyrinchium montanum*
narrowleaf. See *Sisyrinchium angustifolium*
prairie. See *Sisyrinchium campestre*
strict. See *Sisyrinchium montanum*
white. See *Sisyrinchium albidum*

blue flax. See *Linum perenne*

blueflag
harlequin. See *Iris versicolor*
southern. See *Iris virginica* var. *shrevei*

bluejacket. See *Tradescantia ohiensis*

bluejoint. See *Calamagrostis canadensis*

bluestem
big. See *Andropogon gerardii*
broomsedge. See *Andropogon virginicus*

bushy. See *Andropogon glomeratus*
little. See *Schizachyrium scoparium*
sand. See *Andropogon hallii*

bluet
azure. See *Houstonia caerulea*
longleaf summer. See *Houstonia longifolia*

Boltonia asteroides 52, 62, 88, 106, 111, 120, 129, 151–153, 278

boneset
common. See *Eupatorium perfoliatum*
upland. See *Eupatorium altissimum*

bouncing bet. See *Saponaria officinalis*

Bouteloua curtipendula 18, 19, 24, 260, 262–264, 282

Bouteloua dactyloides 18, 98, 264–265, 282

Bouteloua gracilis 18, 19, 20, 264, 265, 282

Bouteloua hirsuta 265, 282

Bouteloua species 49, 62, 86, 97, 103, 111, 129

brome
arctic. See *Bromus kalmii*
earlyleaf. See *Bromus latiglumis*
fringed. See *Bromus ciliatus*
Kalm's. See *Bromus kalmii*

Bromus ciliatus 282

Bromus kalmii 282

Bromus latiglumis 282

broom snakeweed. See *Gutierrezia sarothrae*

brown-eyed Susan. See *Rudbeckia triloba*

Buchloe dactyloides. See *Bouteloua dactyloides*

buffalograss. See *Bouteloua dactyloides*

bulrush
    green. See *Scirpus atrovirens*
    hardstem. See *Schoenoplectus acutus*
bundleflower, Illinois. See *Desmanthus illinoensis*
burnet
    American. See *Sanguisorba canadensis*
    Canadian. See *Sanguisorba canadensis*
burningbush. See *Euonymus alatus*
bush clover, round-headed. See *Lespedeza capitata*
butterfly weed. See *Asclepias tuberosa*
button eryngo. See *Eryngium yuccifolium*
buttonbush, common. See *Cephalanthus occidentalis*

Cacalia atriplicifolia. See *Arnoglossum atriplicifolium*
Calamagrostis canadensis 25, 282
Calamagrostis stricta ssp. *inexpansa* 25
Calamovilfa longifolia 19
calamus. See *Acorus calamus*
Callirhoe alcaeoides 154, 278
Callirhoe bushii 154, 278
Callirhoe digitata 154, 278
Callirhoe involucrata 121, 153–154, 278
Callirhoe triangulata 154, 278
Callirhoe species 62, 103, 111
Calochortus nuttallii 18
Calopogon tuberosus 278
Caltha palustris 278
Calylophus serrulatus 278
camas
    Atlantic. See *Camassia scilloides*

prairie. See *Camassia angusta*
    white. See *Zigadenus elegans*
Camassia angusta 155, 278
Camassia esculenta. See *C. scilloides*
Camassia scilloides 73, 106, 154–155, 278
Camassia species 62
Campanula rotundifolia 48, 49, 65, 103, 111, 156–157, 278
campion, starry. See *Silene stellata*
Campsis radicans 101
Canada mayflower. See *Maianthemum canadense*
Canada thistle. See *Cirsium arvense*
Canadian wildginger. See *Asarum canadense*
Caragana arborescens 101
cardinal flower. See *Lobelia cardinalis*
Carpinus caroliniana 99
Carex bebbii 282
Carex bicknellii 267, 282
Carex brevior 282
Carex comosa 282
Carex cristatella 282
Carex filifolia 19
Carex lacustris 282
Carex lupulina 267, 282
Carex pensylvanica 24, 49, 52, 62, 87, 97, 108, 109, 129, 133, 260, 265–267, 282
Carex vulpinoidea 267, 282
Carex species 25, 106
Carya species 21, 24
Cassia fasciculata. See *Chamaecrista fasciculata*
Cassia marilandica. See *Senna marilandica*
Castilleja coccinea 18, 278

Castilleja sessiliflora 278
Castilleja species 54
catchfly, royal. See *Silene regia*
Ceanothus americanus 22, 62, 65, 103, 137, 157–158, 278
Ceanothus herbaceus 278
Ceanothus obovatus. See *C. herbaceus*
Celastrus orbiculatus 101
Celastrus scandens 101
Cephalanthus occidentalis 282
Chamaecrista fasciculata 278
Chamerion angustifolium 153
Chelone glabra 43, 52, 54, 62, 65, 106, 108, 129, 159–160, 278
Chicorium intybus 66
chicory. See *Chicorium intybus*
chokeberries. See *Photinia* species
chokecherry. See *Prunus virginiana*
Chrysopsis villosa. See *Heterotheca villosa*
cinquefoil, shrubby. See *Dasiphora fruticosa* ssp. *floribunda*
cinquefoil, tall. See *Potentilla arguta*
Cirsium arvense 115
Claytonia virginica 52, 73, 97, 108, 160–161, 278
Cleome serrulata 278
columbine, Canada. See *Aquilegia canadensis*
columbines. See *Aquilegia* species
compass plant. See *Silphium laciniatum*
Comptonia peregrina 282
coneflower
    gray-headed prairie. See *Ratibida pinnata*

rosinweed
  prairie. See *Silphium tere-binthinaceum*
  wholeleaf. See *Silphium integrifolium*
Rubus species 59
Rudbeckia fulgida 230, 280
Rudbeckia fulgida var. *missouriensis*. See *R. missouriensis*
Rudbeckia fulgida var. *sullivantii* 125, 230
Rudbeckia hirta 14, 20, 28, 29, 73, 88, 103, 127, 137, 228–230, 280
Rudbeckia missouriensis 230, 280
Rudbeckia subtomentosa 106, 120, 230, 280
Rudbeckia triloba 43, 106, 230, 280
Rudbeckia species 62, 64, 111, 124, 129, 138
Ruellia humilis 28, 65, 77, 103, 111, 231–232, 280
Russian olive. See *Elaeagnus angustifolia*

sage
  pitcher. See *Salvia azurea* var. *grandiflora*
  prairie. See *Artemisia ludoviciana*
  wood. See *Teucrium canadense*
sagebrush, white. See *Artemisia ludoviciana*
sagewort, prairie. See *Artemisia frigida*
Salix discolor 59, 282
Salix humilis 59, 282
Salix interior 59, 282
Salvia azurea var. *grandiflora* 280
Sanguinaria canadensis 22, 107, 108
Sanguisorba canadensis 280

Saponaria officinalis 66
Sassafras albidum 282
sassafras. See *Sassafras albidum*
Schizachyrium scoparium 18, 24, 25, 52, 62, 80, 81, 85, 86, 87, 88, 97, 103, 106, 111, 129, 260, 261, 272–273, 282
Schoenoplectus acutus 282
Scirpus acutus. See *Schoenoplectus acutus*
Scirpus atrovirens 282
Scirpus cyperinus 282
Securigera varia 282
sedge
  Bebb's. See *Carex bebbii*
  Bicknell's. See *Carex bicknellii*
  bottlebrush. See *Carex comosa*
  crested. See *Carex cristatella*
  fox. See *Carex vulpinoidea*
  hairy. See *Carex lacustris*
  hop. See *Carex lupulina*
  lake. See *Carex lacustris*
  longhair. See *Carex comosa*
  Pennsylvania. See *Carex pensylvanica*
  shortbeak. See *Carex brevior*
  threadleaf. See *Carex filifolia*
selfheal, common. See *Prunella vulgaris*
Senecio aureus. See *Packera aurea*
Senecio plattensis. See *Packera plattensis*
Senna fasciculata. See *Chamaecrista fasciculata*
Senna marilandica 280
senna, Maryland. See *Senna marilandica*
serviceberries. See *Amelanchier* species

shooting star, prairie. See *Dodecatheon meadia*
Siberian peashrub. See *Caragana arborescens*
Silene regia 62, 65, 111, 232–234, 280
Silene stellata 280
Silphium integrifolium 37, 234–236, 281
Silphium laciniatum 30, 73, 87, 106, 236, 281
Silphium perfoliatum 64, 65, 80, 106, 238, 281
Silphium terebinthinaceum 31, 37, 52, 87, 237, 238, 281
Silphium species 22, 54, 62, 69, 70, 121, 133, 138, 234–238
silvergrass. See *Miscanthus* species
Sisyrinchium albidum 281
Sisyrinchium angustifolium 238, 240, 281
Sisyrinchium campestre 240, 281
Sisyrinchium montanum 239, 240, 281
Sisyrinchium species 49, 52, 103, 111
Smilacina stellata. See *Maianthemum stellata*
sneezeweed
  autumn. See *Helenium autumnale*
  common. See *Helenium autumnale*
  purplehead. See *Helenium flexuosum*
snow on the mountain. See *Euphorbia marginata*
snowberry, western. See *Symphoricarpos occidentalis*
soap plant. See *Yucca glauca*
soapwort. See *Saponaria officinalis*
Solidago flexicaulis 22